Curing World Poverty

The New Role of Property

Curing World Poverty

The New Role of Property

John H. Miller, C.S.C., S.T.D., Editor

Michael D. Greaney, Associate Editor
Dawn K. Brohawn, Editorial Advisor

Published by
Social Justice Review

In collaboration with the
Center for Economic and Social Justice

Social Justice Review
Saint Louis, Missouri
1994

ISBN 0-9626257-5-2

Printed by
Saint Martin de Porres Press
New Hope, Kentucky 40052

Cover, layout and diagrams by Rowland L. Brohawn

Contents

Preface

This book takes its origin from a seminar which several representatives of the ecumenical Center for Economic and Social Justice
(CESJ) gave in Rome in November of 1991 for members of religious
communities having missionaries in the Third World. The reactions
of those who attended our seminar are exemplified by a beautiful letter sent to our President, Norman Kurland, by the Rev. Harry Reusch,
C.P. In it, among other things, Fr. Reusch remarks: "I found your
CESJ seminar to be one of the most meaningful and thought-provok-
ing of any I have recently attended."

Much of Fr. Reusch's time is spent traveling through the mission
fields of the Passionist Fathers, and he sees all too clearly that, "while
there is much economic and social injustice in the U.S. and other First
World nations, the problem is compounded beyond belief in our Third
World nations. With Communism on the downgrade, some people
may be tempted to believe that Capitalism has been thoroughly justi-
fied and should now move ahead with full vigor. You and I know that
is wrong. Some center road between Communism and Capitalism
must be found. And this is what I believe you are trying very val-
iantly to do."

We in CESJ find capital necessary, but so do the communists,
socialists and laissez-faire capitalists. What a difference, however,
there is among our understanding and uses of it. In communism,
capital is used, but it is *owned* entirely by the State. Socialism indeed requires capital, but it is completely *controlled* by the State.
Laissez-faire capitalism uses capital solely for the personal profit of a
few. Even "democratic capitalism" is a well-intentioned but unworkable attempt to harmonize political democracy with economic plutocracy.

In CESJ's proposal of expanded ownership of the means of production, we also retain the use of capital. Yet we insist that every
worker—that is, everyone who works—has the God-given natural right
to have the opportunity to own the most technologically advanced
forms of capital, the means of production, exercise his right in deciding how that capital is to be used, and earn profits from what that
capital produces.

After our seminar in Rome, I insisted that we must not lose what we had just done, not stop there. We simply had to go forward and complete what we had started and publish in book form CESJ's "center road" solutions to world poverty. It was thus that I was gently asked to "put my money where my mouth is," to edit and publish the book. All too gladly I acquiesced. This proposal, as a Catholic priest, I believe to be the solution to what the Vicars of Christ have been pleading for society to do: extend ownership to the worker. For me, their pleadings have the ring of the Good News of the Gospel Applied. This Gospel of social and economic justice for all would not add another bureaucracy to the already top-heavy nation-states of the world, but would sound a clarion call to entrepreneurs, bankers, labor leaders and workers in the United States and other countries to apply in practical ways the Church's doctrine that the goods of the earth are destined for all to possess and enjoy.

As editor I am especially privileged to call attention to a work promoting what has been, for over a century, an intimate part of Papal social doctrine, namely, the wider distribution of private ownership of property.

The very title of this work—*Curing World Poverty: The New Role of Property*—is itself intriguing. Our approaches to caring for the world's poor and needy have been, so far, merely temporary and superficial reactions. The in-depth causes of poverty—apart from unwillingness to work and certain unavoidable personal tragedies—are clearly the concentration of the world's wealth in the hands of so few and the exclusion of the less well-off from the means, particularly productive credit, by which they can acquire property and proportionately augment their material and social well-being.

To think of ownership of the means of production itself as the cure for poverty seems, at first, almost novel. And yet, besides making eminently good sense, the idea was first proposed a century ago by the illustrious world spiritual leader, Pope Leo XIII, in his 1891 encyclical *Rerum Novarum*. Subsequently, the concrete proposal was developed in the 1950s by Louis O. Kelso and Mortimer J. Adler in their monumental contribution to economics, published under the possibly misleading title of *The Capitalist Manifesto* (1958). This book promotes, not ownership in common (through the State or collective), but ownership by each person as a sacred and inalienable natural right. It insists that, as members of the human family, each one of us is entitled to equal access to institutions, laws, and other "social goods" that will empower everyone directly to acquire and share in the productive wealth of society.

Starting in 1965 when CESJ's president Norman Kurland joined Louis Kelso as his Washington counsel and political strategist, Kelso's ideas began to take root in Washington. Then in late 1973, these two soldiers of justice found a powerful champion in Senator Russell Long, who single-handedly orchestrated the first of over 20 laws in America encouraging one of Kelso's innovations— the employee stock ownership plan (ESOP). Today, United Airlines, AVIS, and Weirton Steel are among the most celebrated of the 10,000 U.S. companies with ESOPs covering over 10 million workers. This new "social technology"—a mere first step in the re-humanization of the world's major economic institutions and laws envisioned in Kelso's radical breakthrough in economic theory—is catching on today in over twenty countries.

So, there is nothing new about either the idea or the working out of a specific implementation. The tragic fact, however, is that both Kelso's overall solution to world poverty and his practical ways of implementing it have been only superficially studied, grossly misunderstood, but mainly ignored by economists and policy-makers wedded to traditional schools of economic thought.

There is no need for me to go into the reasons why so simple an idea and such realistic programs, so much in accord with consistent Catholic social teaching, have been ignored. For what is the use of perhaps giving offense? What is important, indeed necessary, is to show mankind that widespread poverty is unnecessary. There is a workable means of effectively combatting poverty, and this is not through a redistribution of past wealth accumulations, but through the expansion of future ownership and profit sharing opportunities among working people, and their educated participation in management and shareholder decisions.

No one claims, least of all I, that this solution will offset the manufacture of a non-marketable or even harmful product, or will prevent a poorly-managed enterprise from failing, or will bring some form of utopia to the workplaces of the world. But the new solution honors well the dignity of the working man and woman. It gives them added impetus to contribute worthily to any enterprise, and indeed challenges them to rise above a given status and job. And it is a way of providing workers with a supplemental and independent income from profits, beyond wages alone.

Additionally, this new approach to economic development would provide a genuine preferential option for the poor, based on the principle of equality of opportunity, not equality of results. Through programs which equalize access among all persons to the means for becoming capital owners—including access to such uniquely "social goods" as monetary credit—these ideas and applications would systematically lift unjust historic barriers between those at the top of the social ladder and those most affected by the lack of equal opportunities, privilege, status and personal sovereignty. Distributive justice would then follow naturally from full and equal justice in participation.

We believe there is room for the State in our proposal, but it must always remain a strictly limited one: limited by the principle of subsidiarity. Despite what certain parties say, we are among the few economic and political proponents of the *requirement* of reduced government. Chief among our reasons is that the more the State interferes in the lives of its citizens, the bigger it gets and the more wasteful it becomes. It must, even in theory, be restricted by the very dignity of the human beings who compose its citizenry. Let human beings resolve their own problems. Let us stop worshipping the Golden Calf of the State's infallible omniscience. It is almost self-evident to most informed people that their rights are NOT granted by the State.

Yes, we do look to government for some help, but only the minimum required to protect fundamental human rights and to correct unjust imbalances, particularly in the distribution of opportunities to share in the ownership and profits from newly created assets. Yes, we do need the State to reform its monetary machinery to provide universal access to bank credit for workers at low, non-subsidized interest rates (so long as the funds are prudently invested in the private sector for *productive* purposes only) and to encourage private insurance to spread the risk of bad bank loans. And yes, we also look to the State to correct an unjust imbalance that is already in place; that is, the crushing impact of excessive taxes taken from the wage earner and taxes on businesses which, in the name of redistribution, make the rich richer and the poor poorer, as we explain later in this book.

While willingly taking the blame for asking you to read this volume, I gladly and cheerfully extend a friendly challenge to other religious bodies to provide society with their response to the problems of economic and social injustice. Humbly I acknowledge that they may well come forward with differently nuanced principles, but rather immodestly I truly believe they will embrace something rather close to this application of the Papal requests for expanded ownership.

To all men and women of good will—I address a heartfelt entreaty to give a fair hearing to a more equitable extension of private property, a serious analysis of the proposals contained in this book, and earnest consideration of their relevance toward curing world poverty.

So many good and thoughtful people, when confronted by "the system," have thrown up their hands in despair. They have given up hope that what Pope John Paul II calls "structures of sin" can be transformed into "structures of justice." Such hopelessness is a festering sore on our moral order. It is a debilitating point-of-view that starts when people become dissatisfied with the dissolution of moral order in society and cannot see how universal principles can help guide them in dealing with everyday realities of life. They somehow do not appreciate that social structures are human artifacts. As such, these structures can be re-designed only by people inspired by what is right and willing to work together with others to bring about change for the common good.

This book aims to restore hope and inspire good people to take the future in their own hands, to help them pose new questions, new possibilities and new visions to today's leaders and to defenders of the status quo. In the final analysis, this book is offered to challenge good people who are troubled by the decline in moral standards and the economic aspects of that decline. Some look at the world as it is and merely ask, "Why?" Each reader who finds the vision of this book compelling and wonders what he can do, can take the first step by challenging others with the question, "Why not?"

John H. Miller, C.S.C., S.T.D.

Acknowledgements

I must begin by thanking all the authors who have contributed to this volume. Obviously, without their generous cooperation and the support of all those who participate in the activities of our ecumenical Center for Economic and Social Justice (CESJ), we would have no book to offer.

Profoundest gratitude must also be expressed to the president of CESJ, Norman G. Kurland. With the passing of Louis O. Kelso, he is respected, along with Patricia Hetter Kelso and Robert Ashford, as one of the foremost world authorities on the Kelsonian theory of economics. He is an inspired master teacher of the Kelso-Adler theory of economic justice, and has been a boundless source of enlightenment and encouragement for all of us who worked on this book.

Nor can I omit expressing warm thanks to my assistant editor, Michael D. Greaney, who contributed to the overall organization of the book and drafted the section introductions, coordinated multitudinous details and kept the project on schedule. In addition to all this, he even found the time to contribute an article. A debt of gratitude is owed to our graphic designer, Rowland Brohawn, who gave so generously of his sparkling talent and time. The cover, illustrations and overall appearance of the book are due almost solely to his professional hand and eye. Also due great thanks is our ingenious editorial advisor, Dawn Kurland Brohawn. She not only greatly assisted the task of organizing and editing the text, but made certain that the book maintained its conceptual integrity and clarity. And this was in addition to contributing a pivotal article on Value-Based Management. Thanks are also due to the Rev. Cassian Yuhaus, C.P., who graciously arranged for the CESJ seminar in Rome which began this whole book project.

On purpose I waited till last to mention His Eminence Achille Cardinal Silvestrini, prefect of the Vatican's Congregation for the Oriental Churches, precisely to draw special attention to his strong leadership. Without him our seminar in Rome would not have taken place. He hosted it and opened its sessions with a beautiful speech on Papal social doctrine, and encouraged us all along the way. Our grateful esteem for him knows no bounds. Only God can reward him as we would wish.

John H. Miller, C.S.C.
Editor and Publisher

— Introduction —

Papal Tradition on Distribution of Ownership

by Rev. Matthew Habiger, O.S.B., Ph.D.
Executive Director, Human Life International

Ownership has always been important for a stable society. It is inherent in the very nature of men and women that they have some claim to material goods for a sense of security for themselves and for all their dependents. We see this all throughout recorded history. The fact that private property has been abused does not invalidate the importance of this institution for a just society. Karl Marx analyzed the social evils of his day and concluded that the main culprit was private property. If that could be abolished, then everyone would receive from society according to his needs and contribute to society according to his abilities. History has proven this to be both utopian and cruel to millions of people forced to live under Marxist ideology.

Distribution of ownership among workers and their families is the issue here. In the United States 10% of American households own 72% of all wealth, and 1% own more than 58% of all individually owned corporate stock (Joint Economic Committee of Congress, "The Concentration of Wealth in the United States: Trends in the Distribution of Wealth among American Families," 1986). On April 20, 1992, the Federal Reserve and the Internal Revenue Service reported that total private wealth grew in the decade, and people at many income levels owned more assets at the peak of the boom in 1989 than they had six years earlier. But the richest 1% of American households accounted for 37% of net worth in 1989, up from 31% in 1983. By 1989, the top 1%—834,000 households with about $5.7 trillion of net worth—was worth more than the bottom 90% of Americans—84 million households, with about $4.8 trillion in net worth (*The New York Times*, April 21, 1992, A1).

In broad terms the present distribution of corporate ownership in the United States is illustrated in the first part of the figure below. The second part shows how that distribution would be changed under a national policy favoring universal access to the ownership of newly-added capital assets.

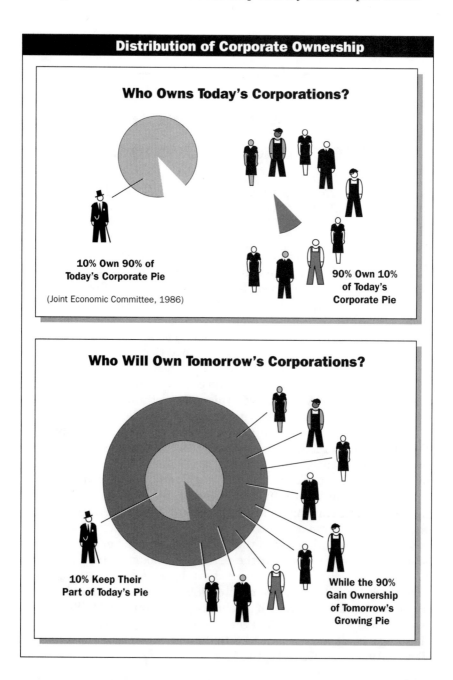

Distribution of Corporate Ownership

Who Owns Today's Corporations?

10% Own 90% of Today's Corporate Pie

(Joint Economic Committee, 1986)

90% Own 10% of Today's Corporate Pie

Who Will Own Tomorrow's Corporations?

10% Keep Their Part of Today's Pie

While the 90% Gain Ownership of Tomorrow's Growing Pie

In this book, *Curing World Poverty: The New Role of Property*, ownership takes center stage. We begin with a chapter on Papal religious traditions dealing with the distribution of ownership.

There are two ways I could go in laying out a Catholic understanding of ownership. I could appeal directly to major social encyclicals of this century and extract pertinent teachings. (The interested reader may consult my *Papal Teaching on Private Property: 1891—1981* [University Press of America, Maryland: 1990].) Or I could appeal to a recent restatement of the Vatican's position on ownership as found in its Intervention at the Rio de Janeiro Earth Summit on June 4, 1992. Since this Intervention addresses many current controversies and issues regarding property and ownership, I have chosen this option. In part two of this chapter, I will give some commentary.

Statement of
Archbishop Renato R. Martino,
Apostolic Nuncio, Head of the Holy See Delegation to the United Nation Conference on Environment and Development
Rio de Janeiro, 4 June 1992

The people of the whole world look with keen interest and great expectations to this United Nations Conference on Environment and Development. The challenge facing the international community is how to reconcile the imperative duty of the protection of the environment with the basic right of all people to development.

The Centrality of the Human Person

The Catholic Church approaches both the care and protection of the environment and all questions regarding development from the point of view of *the human person*. It is the conviction of the Holy See, therefore, that all ecological programs and all developmental initiatives must respect the *full dignity and freedom* of whomever might be affected by such programs. They must be seen in relation to the needs of actual men and women, their families, their values, their unique social and cultural heritage, their responsibility toward future generations. For the ultimate purpose of environmental and developmental programs is to enhance the quality of life, to *place creation in the fullest way possible at the service of the human family*.

The ultimate determining factor is the human person. It is not simply science and technology, nor the increasing means of economic and material development, but the human person, and especially groups of persons, communities and nations, *freely choosing* to face the problems together, who will, under God, determine the future.[1]

The word *environment* itself means "that which surrounds." This very definition postulates the existence of a center around which the environment exists. That center is the human being, the only creature in this world who, is not only capable of being conscious of itself and of its surrounding, but is gifted with intelligence to explore, the sagacity to utilize, and is ultimately responsible for its choices and the consequences of those choices. The praiseworthy heightened awareness of the present generation for all components of the environment, and the consequent efforts at preserving and protecting them, rather than weakening the central position of the human being, accentuate its role and responsibilities.

Likewise, it cannot be forgotten that the true purpose of every economic, social and political system and of every model of *development* is the integral advancement of the human person. Development is clearly something much more extensive than merely economic progress measured in terms of gross national product. True development takes as its criterion the human person with all the needs, just expectations and fundamental rights that are his or hers.[2]

Complementing respect for the human person and human life is the responsibility to respect all creation. God is creator and planner of the entire universe. The universe and life in all its forms are a testimony to God's creative power, His love, His enduring presence. All creation reminds us of the mystery and love of God. As the Book of Genesis tells us: "And God saw everything that He had made, and behold, it was very good" (Gn 1:31).

The Moral Dimension

In the very early stages that led to the convening of this Conference, the General Assembly emphasized that "in view of the global character of major environmental problems, there is a common interest of all countries in pursuing policies aimed at achieving a sustainable and environmentally sound development within a sound ecological balance."[3]

The Holy See has been and continues to be keenly interested in the issues which this Conference is addressing. During the laborious preparatory phases, the Holy See delegation has carefully and respectfully examined the many proposals of technological, scientific and political nature put forth and appreciates contributions made by so many participants in the process. Faithful to its nature and its mission, the Holy See has continued to emphasize the rights and the duties, the well-being and the responsibilities of individuals and of societies. For the Holy See, the problems of environment and development are, at their root, *issues of a moral, ethical nature* from which derive two obligations: the urgent imperative to find solutions and the inescapable demand that every proposed solution meet the criteria of truth and justice.

"Theology, philosophy and science all speak of a harmonious universe, of a 'cosmos' endowed with its own integrity, its own internal, dynamic balance. *This order must be respected.* The human race is called to explore this order, to examine it with due care and to make use of it while safeguarding its integrity."[4] The Creator has placed human beings at the center of creation, making them the responsible stewards, not the exploiting despots, of the world around them. "On the other hand, the earth is ultimately *a common heritage, the fruits of which are for the benefits of all.* This has direct consequences for the problem at hand. It is manifestly unjust that a privileged few should continue to accumulate excess goods, squandering available resources, while masses of people are living in conditions of misery at the very lowest level of subsistence. Today, the dramatic threat of ecological breakdown is teaching us the extent to which greed and selfishness both individual and collective are contrary to the order of creation, an order which is characterized by mutual interdependence."[5]

The Resulting Obligations: *Stewardship* and *Solidarity*

The concepts of an ordered universe and a common heritage both point to the necessity of developing in the heart of every individual and in the activities of every society a true sense of *stewardship* and *solidarity*.

It is the obligation of a responsible steward to be one who cares for the goods entrusted to him and not one who plunders, to be one who conserves and enhances and not one who destroys and dissipates. Humility, and not arrogance, must be the proper attitude of humankind vis-à-vis the environment. The exciting scientific discoveries of our century have enabled the human mind to pierce with equal success into the infinitesimally small as well as into the immeasurably large. The results have been ambivalent, for we have witnessed that, without ethics, science and technology can be employed to kill as well as to save lives, to manipulate as well as to nurture, to destroy as well as to build.

Responsible stewardship demands a consideration for the common good: no one person, no one group of people in isolation are allowed to determine their relationship with the universe. The universal common good transcends all private interests, all national boundaries, and reaches, beyond the present moment, to the future generations.

Hence *solidarity* becomes an urgent moral imperative. We are all part of God's creation. We live as a human family. The whole of creation is everyone's heritage. All equally created by God, called to share the goods and the beauty of the one world, human beings are called to enter into a solidarity of universal dimensions, "a cosmic fraternity" animated by the very love that flows from God. Education to solidarity is an urgent necessity of our day. We must learn again to live in harmony, not only with God and with one another, but with creation itself. The *"Canticle of Creatures"* of Francis of Assisi could well become the anthem of a new generation that loves and respects in one embrace the Creator and all God's creatures.

Responsible *stewardship* and genuine *solidarity* are not only directed to the protection of the environment, but, equally so, to the inalienable right and duty of all peoples to development. The earth's resources and the means to their access and use must be wisely monitored and justly shared. The demands for the care and protection of the environment cannot be used to obstruct the right to development, nor can development be invoked in thwarting the environment. The task of achieving a just balance is today's challenge.

The scandalous patterns of consumption and waste of all kinds of resources by a few must be corrected, in order to ensure justice and sustainable development to all, everywhere in the world. Pope John Paul II has reminded that: "Simplicity, moderation and discipline, as well as a spirit of sacrifice, must become part of everyday life, lest all suffer the negative consequences of the careless habits of a few."[6] The developing countries, in their legitimate ambition to improve their status and emulate existing patterns of development, will realize and counteract the danger that can derive to their people and to the world by the adoption of highly wasteful growth strategies hitherto widely employed, that have led humanity into the present situation.

New resources, the discovery of substitute new materials, determined efforts at conservation and recycling programs have assisted in the protection of known reserves; the development of new technologies has the promise of using resources more efficiently. For developing nations, at times rich in natural resources, the acquisition and use of new technologies is a clear necessity. Only an equitable global sharing of technology will make possible the process of sustainable development.

When considering the problems of environment and development one must also pay due attention to the complex issue of population. The position of the Holy See regarding procreation is frequently misinterpreted. The Catholic Church does not propose procreation at any cost. It keeps on insisting that the transmission of, and the caring for human life must be exercised with an utmost sense of responsibility. It restates its constant position that human life is sacred; that the aim of public policy is to enhance the welfare of families; that it is the right of the spouses to decide on the size of the family and spacing of births, without pressures from governments or organizations. This decision must fully respect the moral order established by God, taking into account the couple's responsibilities toward each other, the children they already have and the society to which they belong.[7] What the Church opposes is the imposition of demographic policies and the promotion of methods for limiting births which are contrary to the objective moral order and to the liberty, dignity and conscience of the human being. At the same time, the Holy See does not consider people as mere numbers, or only on economic terms.[8] It emphatically states its concern that the poor not be singled out as if, by their very existence, they were the cause, rather than the victims, of the lack of development and of environmental degradation.

Serious as the problem of interrelation among environment, development and population is, it cannot be solved in an over-simplistic manner and many of the most alarming predictions have proven false and have been discredited by a number of recent studies. "People are born not only with mouths that need to be fed, but also with hands than can produce, and minds that can create and innovate."[9] As for the environment, just to mention one instance, countries with as few as 5% of the world population are responsible for more than one quarter of the principal greenhouse gas, while countries with up to a quarter of the world population contribute as little as 5% of the same greenhouse gas.

A serious and concerted effort aimed at protecting the environment and at promoting development will not be possible without *directly addressing the structural forms of poverty* that exist throughout the world. Environment is devastated and development thwarted by the outbreak of wars, when internal conflicts destroy homes, fields and factories, when intolerable circumstances force millions of people desperately to seek refuge away from their lands, when minorities are oppressed, when the rights of the most vulnerable women, children, the aged and the infirm are neglected or abused.

"The poor, to whom the earth is entrusted no less than to others, must be enabled to find a way out of their poverty. This will require a courageous reform of structures, as well as new ways of relating among people and States."[10]

Finally, the Holy See invites the international community to discover and affirm that there is a *spiritual* dimension to the issues at hand. Human beings have the need for and right to more than clean air and water, to more than economic and technological progress. Human beings are also fragile and an alarm must be sounded against the poisoning of minds and the corruption of the hearts, both in the developed and developing worlds. The dissemination of hatred, of falsehood and vice, the traffic and use of narcotic drugs, the ruthless self-centeredness which disregards the rights of others—even the right to life—are all phenomena that cannot be gauged by technical instruments, but whose chain-effects destroy individuals and societies. Let us strive to give every man, woman and child a safe and healthy physical environment, let us join forces in providing them with real opportunities for development, but in the process, let us not allow them to be robbed of their souls. On a closely related level, the *aesthetic* value of the environment must also be considered and protected, thus adding beauty and inspiring artistic expression to the developmental activities.

The Holy See regards this Conference as a major challenge and a unique opportunity that the people of the world are presenting to the international community. The problems facing today's world are serious indeed and even threatening. Nonetheless, the opportunity is at hand. Avoiding confrontation, and engaging in honest dialogue and sincere solidarity, all forces must be joined in a positive adventure of unprecedented magnitude and cooperation that will restore hope to the human family and renew the face of the earth.

Commentary

A few brief remarks now to clarify the connection between this Intervention and the distribution of ownership. Although this intervention is focused on environment and development, it draws heavily upon Catholic Social Teaching with its concept of private property and ownership.

In today's world there is a growing population, diminishing labor-intensive economies and increasing capital-intensive economies. More provision must be made for the material security of the ordinary worker. Trends for the next 100 years indicate shorter working weeks, a greater use of robots, and more sophisticated technology. Unless provisions are made for the worker to have ownership in the wealth producing instruments of the future, his economic position will be very precarious. Discussions on "just wage" or a "family wage" must give way to access to ownership of wealth producing instruments, The New Role of Property.

Every just social order can be judged according to the services it provides for the people who live under it. Since the economic order affects everyone, we are all interested in it. The presumption is that the good Earth has great resources and can easily provide for a population many times the present size. The fact that today there is starvation, underdevelopment, substandard medical care, education, housing, etc., cannot be attributed to the inadequacy of the Earth and its Creator, but to the mismanagement, greed and corruption of people who manage these resources. All these problems are man-made, and admit of man-made solutions.

The Intervention lists human ills which cannot be gauged by technical instruments and must be fought against: hatreds, deceptions, vice, drugs and "ruthless self-centeredness which disregards the rights of others—even the right to life." Clean air and water, economic and technological progress are insufficient to advance the common good.

God created the universe we live in and commanded us to "be fruitful, multiply and fill the earth." The Earth will not be found wanting in its natural resources. But we must use intelligence, planning, effort and discipline to make the Earth yield the material goods needed for a decent standard of living for every man, woman and child.

The *full dignity and freedom of the human person* figures greatly here. Since mankind is the apex of God's material creation, everything exists for the service and benefit of human persons. The environment was made for man, not vice versa. So also the economic order and the political order. In our planning, we are to so arrange the economic order that the material needs of all people may be fulfilled. Human intelligence, ingenuity, and the social virtues come into play here. "True development takes as its criterion the human person with all the needs, just expectations and fundamental rights that are his or hers."

There is a *moral dimension* to all of this. This means that the Creator has a plan not only for His physical universe, but most especially for His human universe. Only human persons are moral agents. In secular terms we speak about justice and fairness, hoping that everyone understands the values these terms refer to, and that these will guide our dealings with one another. But there are greater human needs and hungers than mere material ones. Morality is much more than economic justice. A true sense of the common good, even a universal common good, includes the development of individuals and societies in all the features which go into their perfection as unique human persons. The need for economic justice for all arises from the sacred dignity, the liberty and the sovereignty of the person. Our individual dignity, in turn, is derived from the fact that God made us to His own image and likeness. That is why our dignity is inalienable.

Since much of our time and energy is devoted to providing a livelihood, a just moral order must deal with economics. "The earth is ultimately a common heritage, the fruits of which are for the benefits of all." This means that if an elite of the world are over-consumers, while millions are destitute, something is terribly wrong. The Center for Economic and Social Justice argues, correctly in my judgment, that the solution is not merely redistribution of present wealth, but providing new ownership to workers in an ever expanding economy. The created goods of the earth, e.g., food, fuel, wood, metal, fibers, etc., were meant for the use of everyone. Whether or not this destination is realized depends upon our planning, our convictions and resourcefulness.

The fact that there is a moral order in the world which can be known and implemented, and that all created goods are the common heritage of the human race have concrete implications. The Intervention summarizes these as *stewardship* and *solidarity*. Responsible stewardship refers to how we manage the resources we own, our private property. Since property has both a private dimension (benefiting the owner) and a social one (benefiting the broader society), a good steward will make his or her property as productive as possible. Property (any means for generating new wealth) is a gift temporarily entrusted to our care. It is to be used wisely for the common good which "transcends all private interests, all national boundaries, and reaches beyond the present moment to the future generations."

Solidarity refers to the fact that we are all part of the human family, all part of God's creation. We are in solidarity with each other. Furthermore, since God created the whole universe for mankind, we are called to share the goods and beauty of the one world. We must learn to live in harmony with one another, and with creation itself. One concrete expression of human solidarity is the right and duty of all peoples to development. For the developed nations this means that simplicity, moderation, and discipline as well as a spirit of sacrifice must become part of their life-styles. The curse of war is to be reserved as a last resort for protection against an unjust aggressor. Foreign debts owed by poor countries must be reduced or absolved. For the developing nations it means making every effort to take advantage of present opportunities, and to adopt strategies of development which avoid waste and ostentation (e.g. sophisticated military hardware).

Immediately germane to the distribution of ownership is the sharing of new technology. If developed nations keep this to themselves, then they deprive developing nations of the benefits which could also be theirs. The process of sustained development depends upon responsible stewardship and a spirit of solidarity. The authors of this book are very interested in the advantages to be had from new technology. Technology is the most important form of new wealth, and since it is a new form of wealth, it could easily be shared with the poor and the wage-earner. Because it creates new wealth, and a new form of property, we need not think in terms of taking property away from its present owners. If developed nations can devise methods for sharing ownership in new technology with their unpropertied compatriots, then the same dynamic can be devised for developing nations. The alternative to this is a growing world debt, which is terribly destabilizing for world peace.

We see the same dynamics at work in the issue of population. Most of the world is underpopulated. These countries should welcome immigrants from those highly concentrated centers of human living. Everyone stands to gain.

The late Rev. William Ferree, a noted scholar on the topic of social justice and a cofounder of the Center for Economic and Social Justice, developed the following figure, "The Development Curve," to illustrate how the growth of the earth's population relates to new discoveries and technological development. From less than one-half billion people throughout most of history, the human population has grown to over 5.5 billion today as we approach the Third Millennium. It confirms that new technology can be life-sustaining.

One great treasure we all share in is our human fertility. The wanton destruction of nascent human life through abortion, abortifacient forms of contraception, IUDs, and sterilization are beneath our human dignity, and a direct affront to the Author of the moral order. There are morally good ways to plan one's family, which are very effective, e.g., natural family planning. It is a mistake to consider the poor and their babies to be the cause, rather than the victims of the lack of development and of environmental degradation.

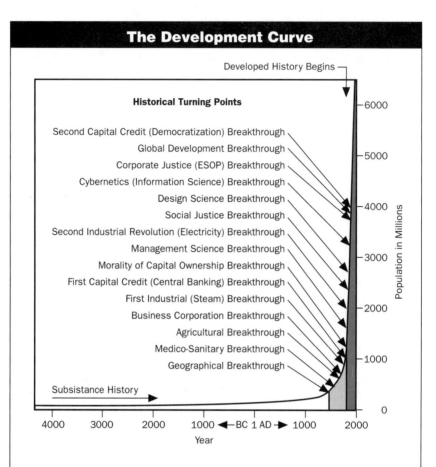

The Development Curve

Developed History Begins

Historical Turning Points

Second Capital Credit (Democratization) Breakthrough
Global Development Breakthrough
Corporate Justice (ESOP) Breakthrough
Cybernetics (Information Science) Breakthrough
Design Science Breakthrough
Social Justice Breakthrough
Second Industrial Revolution (Electricity) Breakthrough
Management Science Breakthrough
Morality of Capital Ownership Breakthrough
First Capital Credit (Central Banking) Breakthrough
First Industrial (Steam) Breakthrough
Business Corporation Breakthrough
Agricultural Breakthrough
Medico-Sanitary Breakthrough
Geographical Breakthrough

Subsistance History

6000
5000
4000
3000
2000
1000
0

Population in Millions

4000   3000   2000   1000 ◄—BC 1 AD—► 1000   2000
Year

This graph traces the growth of population through all recorded history, and projects it into the future to the year 2000 A.D. However, the same sort of curve — a near right angle slightly rounded at the corner — is of quite general application, and would be followed fairly closely by almost any significant factor of modern civilization. The reason why one curve fits so many and such varied factors of modern life is that what it really measures is the passage of the human race from one kind of history to another: from subsistence to what is now called development. This passage and its implications constitute the single most important clue to an understanding of our civilization — and of all history before it.

If the political divisions of the world at this moment were distributed according to their degree of development, they would be strung out along the same curve, with the United States at the top of the curve, the western and westernized countries below it on the "vertical" leg, the more "advanced" Communist countries on the rounded corner, and most Communist and all "developing" countries along the bottom.

"The poor, to whom the earth is entrusted no less than to others, must be enabled to find a way out of their poverty. This will require a courageous reform of structures, as well as new ways of relating among people and States." This summarizes everything we have tried to say. Expanded ownership of productive property, e.g., ESOPs, are one such reform of economic structures which merit consideration.

A Friendly Challenge

The author of this article is a Catholic moral theologian who knows the Catholic tradition. However, it would be valuable to have articulations from scholars in other major world religions on the distribution of ownership, e.g., Jewish, Islamic, Buddhist, etc. These could serve as a stimulus for the business community sharing those religious traditions to make modern applications. If such terms as human dignity, the common good, and the universal destination of all created goods, etc., mean the same for all major religions, then there is common ground in finding the cure for world poverty. Hopefully major thinkers in other faiths will publish a book similar to this one in the near future.

Notes

[1] Cf. Address of Pope John Paul II to the United Nations Centre for the Environment, Nairobi, 18 August 1985.

[2] Cf. Address of Pope John Paul II to the 21st Session of the Conference of the Food and Agricultural Organization. The Vatican, 13 November 1981.

[3] Resolution 43/196 of the General Assembly, 20 December 1988.

[4] Message of Pope John Paul II for the 1990 World Day of Peace on the theme "Peace with God the Creator, Peace with All of Creation" (8 December 1989) 8.

[5] Ibid.

[6] Ibid. 13.

[7] Cf. Message of His Eminence Cardinal Maurice Roy, President of the Pontifical Commission "Justice and Peace" to H.E. U Thant, Secretary-General of the United Nations, on the occasion of the launching of the Second Development Decade. The Vatican, 19 November 1970.

[8] Cf. Address of Pope John Paul II to Mr. Rafael Salas, Secretary-General of the 1984 International Conference on Population, and Executive Director of the United Nations Fund for Population Activities (UNFPA). The Vatican, 7 June 1984.

[9] *The Wall Street Journal*, in "Review and Outlook": Prince Malthus, Tuesday, 28 April 1992.

[10] Message for the 1990 World Day of Peace, op. cit., 11.

I

Redefining the Problem of Poverty

Redefining the Problem
of Poverty

We are told that the poor are with us always. Some then have an excuse to do nothing—if a problem won't go away, why should we waste time and resources trying to solve it? Others have seen in this dictum a surrender to conditions and a basic dismissal of the problem. In turn, people are led to dismiss the efforts of the Church as maintaining the status quo and leading us on with "pie in the sky" promises of better things to come in the next life.

Moral indignation over widespread poverty has increased as the problem has become the norm in many areas. While some attribute the rise in concern about poverty to improved communications which increase the visibility of the plight of the poor, the fact is that the condition of poverty has reached epidemic proportions. One result of the growth in moral indignation and concern has been to increase agitation that "something be done." Yet traditional methods of alleviating poverty not only appear to be completely ineffective, they actually seem to increase the magnitude of the problem.

It becomes abundantly clear that the disease of poverty has been misdiagnosed. Although the symptoms are well understood, there is a tendency to define the problem in terms of those symptoms, rather than in terms of the cause. Since the obvious trait of poverty is lack of wealth, it then follows that giving handouts will cure the disease of poverty. Although this cure does not appear to work, the diagnosticians insist that, to be effective, it is only necessary to apply greater quantities of medicine. Yet, in addition to being ineffective, the amount of medicine available is not unlimited. Wealth cannot be expended forever without replenishing it, and redistribution policies concentrate on handing out existing wealth without producing more. What is needed is a different analysis of the situation in order to develop a cure that is not only morally sound, but economically viable. People must be empowered with a moral and effective means of acquiring productive property.

The two articles that follow in this section, although written more than half a century apart, come to startlingly similar conclusions about the real causes of poverty, and the trends that give birth to those causes. By focusing on the root causes of the matter rather than merely attempting to alleviate the symptoms, Louis Kelso and Peter Grosscup point the way to an effective and lasting solution.

In "Uprooting World Poverty: A Job for Business," lawyer-economist Louis Kelso identifies the major causes of widespread, epidemic poverty: concentrated ownership of the means of production, and direct competition of the worker with improving technology. In this 1964 prize-winning article, coauthored with his wife, Patricia Hetter Kelso, Louis Kelso details both the underlying assumptions and flaws of traditional economic aid programs for developing countries, and demonstrates not only that they do not work, but that they tend to concentrate further economic power in governments or an elite. The authors do not merely point out the problem, they outline how productive credit can be channeled to businesses in ways that create new owners of corporate equity as new wealth is created. They depart from the more common view that the creation of new corporate equity must be financed in some manner by past savings, which restricts ownership of new assets to the already wealthy.[1]

In "How to Save the Corporation," Judge Peter Grosscup, speaks in 1905 from the vantage point of one who had seen the beginning of the escalating deterioration of the small propertyholder and the growth of the modern mega-corporation. He states the problem with remarkable clarity. Yet he does not see the crisis as one of poverty, but of human political and economic liberty. In the end, these are the same, but Judge Grosscup does not explain this. His diagnosis of the problem leads him to point out that the obvious solution to the dilemma of the concentrated wealth of the modern corporation coexisting with the aim of general economic independence is to expand the ownership of the corporation. Yet he does no more than say what must be done. He leaves it to others to develop the specifics of a solution.

Any cure must begin with a correct diagnosis. Rather than diagnose poverty in terms of its obvious trait—lack of wealth—the Kelsos define poverty in terms of its cause: lack of access to the means of becoming an owner of productive assets. The Kelsos and Grosscup provide a different perspective to the problem of widespread poverty, and address the basic elements of a cure, which are expanded upon in the articles in later sections of this book.

One element of a cure, briefly hinted at by Grosscup and explicitly stated by the Kelsos, is the proper understanding and use of credit. There are essentially two kinds of credit: productive credit (loaned to create capital assets) and nonproductive credit (loaned to spend on goods and services to be consumed). A manifestation of a gross misuse of credit is the world debt crisis, to which the United States of

America, with a $4 trillion Federal debt that increases at the rate of $1 billion each day, is not immune.

Much of the world's debt problem today could have been avoided if the Kelsos' 1964 article had been taken more seriously by those responsible for United States and international development policies. Nonperforming state-owned enterprises, mostly financed by Western banks and development agencies, demonstrate how credit can be and is misused. The current wave of privatizations around the world is an ill-conceived attempt to redress the mistakes of the past, but still without understanding the message of Kelso and Grosscup.

Clearly many, including governments and individuals, believe non-productive (consumer) credit to be an unmitigated and unlimited good. Yet nothing can so quickly condemn an individual or country to poverty as borrowing money at interest to spend in nonproductive ways. The borrower is then forced to repay not only the original loan—long since spent—but also an additional amount (the interest) that he either must draw from another source, or simply does not have. It is not unheard of even today for poor families to sell their children into slavery in order to repay consumer debt. Likewise, debtor nations are forced into acceding to bargain sales of the national patrimony (industries or natural resources), or even to coercive population control measures that can result in a situation that is slavery in all but name.

The Kelsos, however, advocate widespread use of productive (capital) credit. While the debt still has to be repaid—with interest—productive credit has the advantage of being used to acquire or create wealth producing assets that generate an income (i.e., profits) to repay that very debt. The key distinction is the use to which credit is put. Are the proceeds of the loan spent on goods and services to be consumed, such as an individual's food and clothing or a government's wars and social welfare programs, or on capital assets that pay for themselves, and subsequently produce income for their owners?

But what about this word "capital"? The reader will note that, in a number of the articles in this book the word "capitalism" is used to mean simply a system based on private property. Louis Kelso, referring to capital-intensive, as opposed to labor-intensive production, speaks of a capitalism "purified of its internal flaw" (i.e., concentrated ownership). Yet "capitalism" and "capitalist"—not to be confused with "capital" or "capital ownership"—are words invented by the socialists as derogatory expressions describing a system based on greed. Thus the proponents of a system based on envy—socialism—hid the defects of their own system by focusing attention on the faults of others.

While rejecting all forms of socialism as an economic system, the editors of this book would also agree with Hilaire Belloc's observations on capitalism in *The Crisis of Civilization*:

We mean by Capitalism a condition of Society under which the mass of free citizens, or at any rate a determining number of them, are not possessed of the means of production in any useful amount and therefore live upon wages doled out to them by the possessors of land and capital, men who thus exploit at a profit the dispossessed, known as the "Proletariat."

It is all-important to note that the word "Capitalism" thus used as the name for the great evil which, in its maturity, threatens the very existence of our society does *not* signify the rights of property. It signifies rather an abuse of property; property developed into an unnatural top-heavy form, under which it cannot normally function, and only threatens disaster. Capitalism no more means the affirmation of an individual, or a family's right to possess land, machinery, housing, clothing, reserves of food and the rest, than fatty degeneration of the heart means the normal function of the heart as the circulator of the blood in a healthy human body. Capitalism is an evil not because it defends the legal right to property, but because it is of its nature the use of that legal right for the defense of a privileged few against a much greater number who, though free and equal citizens, are without economic basis of their own.[2]

Clearly capitalism, when understood as the monopolization of the opportunities and means to acquire capital ownership, is not a cure for poverty, but a cause. Yet it is not the goal of this book simply to diagnose, and determine what won't work, but to find a cure. This book does not merely restate the unworkability of capitalism, socialism, or any of their various combinations. It proposes something new, a *Third Way*.

Notes:

[1]After reading the Kelsos' "Uprooting World Poverty," the reader interested in exploring further Louis Kelso's economic alternative to both socialism and plutocratic capitalism outside the confines of this book should read *The Capitalist Manifesto*, by Louis O. Kelso and Mortimer Adler (New York: Random House, 1958) and *Democracy and Economic Power: Extending the ESOP Revolution Through Binary Economics*, by Louis Kelso and Patricia Hetter Kelso, Lanham-New York-London: University Press of America, 1991).

[2]Hilaire Belloc, *The Crisis of Civilization, Being the Matter of a Course of Lectures Delivered at Fordham University, 1937* (Rockford, Illinois: TAN Books and Publishers, Inc., 1992) 139.

— 1 —

Uprooting World Poverty: A Job for Business

by Louis O. Kelso and Patricia Hetter Kelso
*(First published in **Business Horizons**,*
Graduate School of Business, Indiana University, Fall 1964)

"The overall objective of foreign aid is to help to create conditions in the world under which free societies can survive and prosper."
(Foreign Assistance Act of 1963)

"Not so very many years ago in Iran the United States was loved and respected as no other country, and without having given a penny of aid. Now, after more than $1 billion of loans and grants, America is distrusted by most people, and hated by many."
(Abol Hassan Ebtehaj, President of Iranians Bank, Iran)

"Today, we want you to assist us to develop. We need foreign capital, we need machine tools, we need machines, we need this and we need that. You might say that we heard this before, too. You are getting a bit tired of the story. But may I put it to you like this, that we are pressing against you today as friends, and if we make good I think you will in some fashion get it back, in many ways you will get it back. If we do not make good and if, heaven forbid, we go under Communism, then we shall still press against you but not as friends."
(Mohammad Ayub Khan, President of Pakistan)

For summing up the American foreign aid program to date—its aspiration, its failure, and its challenge—these three quotations outspeak a dozen monographs.

Our foreign aid program is not helping to create conditions in the world under which free societies can survive and prosper. As presently conceived and executed, it is creating conditions that are just the opposite. Instead of winning converts to Western political institutions, it is estranging the uncommitted. Instead of impeding communism, it is preparing the way for it. Instead of furthering good will between the peoples of the recipient country and our own, it is sowing the seeds of dissension and hatred even among our friends.

Most sadly, our methods have proved incapable of penetrating the vicious circles of poverty in which the poor nations are hopelessly entrapped. Far from industrializing fast enough to support their burgeoning populations, the "emerging nations" are in fact submerging deeper into that primordial misery from which our foreign aid program so grandly hoped to lift them. In most, the per capita production of wealth is declining or at best stationary.

So far, the rich nations have treated the chronic, self-perpetuating poverty of the underdeveloped countries like a baffling pathological syndrome, prescribing, in the absence of exact diagnosis, massive shots of the standard poverty antibiotic—money—on the theory that if the patient does not survive, he would have died anyhow. About $6 billion a year now goes into these capital injections, more than half supplied by the United States. As the *Wall Street Journal* editorialized: "From the standpoint of the givers, it is treading the path of least resistance; if they can't solve any basic problems, they can pretend to do so by handing out money."

Yet we know well enough what we want foreign aid to accomplish. The difficulty is that so far the results have been the reverse of our intentions. We understand that it is the causes of poverty that have to be attacked, that we cannot alleviate its proliferating symptoms with all the riches of the West, assuming our willingness to donate them. Yet through some mysterious process, we find our resources committed to the impossible, to the neglect of the things that must be done.

We also recognize our duty and our right to use foreign aid in ways that positively encourage the poor nations to develop into free societies in the full Western sense. We know that freedom in the Western sense is absolutely inseparable from a private property, free enterprise economy. But again, as if agents of a mysterious force, we find ourselves in a race with Russia to see which of us can be the first to build socialistic or communistic economies in the poor nations.

Plans that Do Not Work

All of this irony, confusion, and failure is a consequence of our blind obeisance to methods of finance that are not suitable for industrializing the developing economies. These methods have a common flaw. Unfortunately for both ourselves and the poor nations, this flaw happens to be a cornerstone of the Puritan ethos, namely, the concept of becoming wealthy through sacrificial saving. To the Puritan, saving was not only a pleasure but a duty. That God Himself approved of frugal underconsumers could be inferred from the fact that He so regularly blessed their investments. From there it was only a short step to the next article of Puritan faith, the identification of virtue with wealth; the good man was a rich man who held his riches in stewardship and was liberal in charity and good works. In this context, poverty was a God-inflicted punishment for vice and sin.

Although the edifice of Puritanism is crumbling fast, this cornerstone is as yet unchipped. Most of us with credit cards in our pockets and margin accounts at our brokers have puritan thrift in our souls— even though we know that this "virtue," taken seriously, would quickly destroy a modern industrial economy.

Our Puritan reverence for saving, in theory at least, keeps us from devising financial techniques that could industrialize the developing economies. Conventional financial methods depend exclusively on accumulated savings, that is, financial capital. Obviously, if the underdeveloped economies had savings accumulations to any significant extent, they would not be poor. What small savings they do have are owned by a microscopic portion of the population; many of these owners, not oblivious to the political instability of a poor nation in a potentially affluent world, transfer their wealth to countries that are safer.

Conventional Aid Techniques

To the poor nations, pressed by the aspirations of their impoverished masses, the West offers only three alternatives: foreign capital, as loan or investment; foreign charity, that is, so-called foreign aid; or financing through domestic capital owned by their own wealthy few. For the broad masses, as we shall see, all of these avenues end in frustration because *capital produces affluence, while labor produces only subsistence.*

This basic economic truth, which automation is now painfully teaching the West, explains why foreign investment eventually becomes intolerable to the host country. It leads to foreign ownership. It cannot provide affluence to the masses because affluence, the product of capital, it exported to the foreign owners or accumulated for foreign account. True, foreign-owned enterprise, like any other enterprise, creates some jobs and some jobs are better than none. But the mutual political objective of both the rich nations and the poor nations is to make the poor nations richer, not merely to provide some of their citizens with subsistence toil and make the business firms of the rich nations richer.

Use of domestic capital, to the extent that there is any, has exactly the same consequence as foreign ownership, with one difference.

Affluence is not necessarily exported. It concentrates in the hands of the people who already own capital—no more than *one-half of 1 per cent* of the total population in any of the developing economies. This elite cannot generally increase its already maximum consumption, nor could it solve the poverty problem by doing so. Some jobs are, of course, a by-product of this financing process, providing a negligible fraction of the masses with work opportunities. But subsistence is no substitute for affluence. As the rich grow richer and the poor poorer, an endemic process in the underdeveloped countries, the social tensions leading to political violence move inevitably toward eruption.

Government loans to private enterprise in the developing economies have the same effect as use of concentrated domestic capital. This is true because they simply further concentrate the capital ownership of the people who presently own the poor nations' productive capital.

Myth has it that all of these tired techniques are good because they create jobs. "Say a Mass, then, Father, for the success of the new sugar mill. It will provide work for your parishioners," says the American businessman to the Venezuelan priest. The fact is that the new sugar mill—a golden goose for its capital owners—will provide a *few* jobs for the priest's parishioners. And the fewer jobs it provides, the greater success it is because the logic of technology is not to make work but to save it.

Industrialization of a primitive economy in the mid-twentieth century is not analogous to the Western industrial revolution of the eighteenth and nineteenth centuries. A steel mill, power plant, or factory introduced into an underdeveloped economy is already in an advanced stage of technological sophistication; its potential for providing mass drudgery has been systematically eliminated. For example, it was a great event for America when telephone lines finally connected the Atlantic Coast with the Pacific, and people on both coasts with everyone in between. This feat required an enormous amount of the most exhausting physical labor—armies of workers chopping, digging, trenching, and blasting their way across a continent. Today all that is required is a string of relay stations, which can be put up by a handful of skilled men using helicopters and other highly productive machines.

In the age of automation, the huge unskilled labor force of a poor nation is not a resource but a liability. Unless the price of labor is artificially elevated by legislation and coercive bargaining to many times its competitive market value, even full employment merely dooms labor to subsistence toil.

Government-to-government aid, either as loan or outright gift, creates state-owned enterprise in the recipient country and has a second effect of which we are uncomfortably aware. Abol Hassan Ebtehaj, President and Chairman of the Iranians Bank, Iran, told us the truth as bluntly as we are ever likely to hear it. Speaking at a San Francisco conference in 1961, he said: "Bilateral aid poisons the relationship between nations, frustrates the donor, and causes revulsion in the recipient."

There is no reason to believe that government-owned enterprise built by multilateral aid would be less socialistic than government-owned enterprise built by bilateral aid. The most to be said in favor of the former is that it would presumably direct the hatred of the recipient country toward many nations instead of one. The choice, if there is one, is between charity dispensed in the old-fashioned basket or by modern welfare check.

The Totalitarian Approach

We may conclude that foreign aid in its present form cannot possibly contribute to stable democratic governments. Frustrated by their own ruling classes, goaded by their impatient masses, their problems only aggravated by misguided foreign help, the political leaders of the poor nations can hardly be blamed for coming to believe at last that affluence for them can only be achieved by totalitarian means and that freedom is a luxury a poor nation cannot afford.

The totalitarian approach, after all, has its advantages. By fusing ownership of land and other capital with political power, it creates a central authority strong enough to force raw materials, land, and manpower into the priorities of industrialization. Totalitarian power can enforce austerity on the affluent few and hinder them from exporting their money; it provides a deceptive ideology around which energies can mobilize, and it may convince a desperate nation that it is able to bring about industrialization faster than could insufficient or irresponsible private savings.

But these short-term advantages are bought at the price of freedom; the totalitarian approach forecloses any hope of democratic institutions. It also deliberately frustrates the acquisitive instinct—the instinct to own property rights in farms, factories, and productive assets generally. To the extent that it increases the number of jobs, it has some incentive effect, but the property-acquisition incentive, which so spectacularly powered the industrial revolution in the West, is methodically suppressed and discouraged.

While the strength of totalitarian ideology springs largely from its promise to eliminate the evils of concentrated ownership, in practice it simply replaces one form of concentration with another. And it lays the foundations of a virtually unsolvable future dilemma, the same dilemma now afflicting our own economy, in which labor is erroneously recognized as the primary factor in production, thus setting the stage for total confusion as automation eliminates the usefulness of an expanding portion of the labor force.

The Savings Method

When the developing nations look to the industrialized nations of the West for delivery from their impasse, we can only counsel the austere principle that worked for us—save now, consume later. But Puritan virtues cannot be imposed from without; besides, our ancestors, living in a world where nearly everyone was poor, were not tempted by the luxuries of their neighbors. Poverty was easier to bear before a flourishing technology offered liberation.

During our own industrial revolution, the limitations to economic growth were mainly technological. Thus we did not feel the pinch of financing new productive enterprises exclusively from slowly hoarded savings. In their rush to industrialize, the developing economies want only our latest technology. They also want—and properly suspect they can get—a sound correlation between their growing industrial power and the individual power of their peoples to consume. For them, the piggy-bank approach is much too slow; the hobbles it imposes are felt immediately and painfully.

Like the totalitarian approach, the conventional savings method is only partially incentive. It harnesses the energies of those who get new jobs, as a result of new industry, and the acquisitive instincts of those few who can save and whose savings are used to finance new capital formation. But it is disincentive for the masses for whom capital ownership is forever beyond reach.

Something else can be said for the savings method. It does create a free enterprise-private property economy—for awhile. But capital is the main producer of wealth in an industrial economy, and ownership of new capital automatically goes to the people whose money has been used to finance it. These people are, of course, the already wealthy. Although total concentration of political power is avoided, ownership of economic power necessarily is forced to concentrate in the hands of a stationary— or even shrinking—proportion of the population.

As industrialization advances, this process continues in an accelerating spiral. Consumption, which is left to chance, cannot keep up with production, which is systematically expanded. Finally, forced redistribution of income is compelled in order to restore a semblance of balance. And after a series of these operations, where principle is cut away by expediency, what remains is only the hollow shell of a private property economy. As the lawyer-economist Adolf A. Berle, Jr. has put it: "The capital is there; and so is capitalism. The waning factor is the capitalist."

Concentration of economic power is the evil specter of capitalism, which still haunts the Western economies. It is an evil inherent in the technique of financing new capital formation exclusively out of savings. It is the inner flaw that eventually destroys the private property economy it has created and with it the entire superstructure of individual liberties and rights.

Totalitarianism now, or countless more years of wretched poverty as down payment on a private property-free enterprise society that will have to be socialized later—it is a dismal choice. If we step boldly up to this dilemma and inspect its horns, we shall discover that they are the horns of a sacred cow. The savings theory, far from being an immutable absolute, is merely an old and deeply ingrained business custom, a technique for organizing the people and things that are to take part in forming the new capital.

Everyone knows that money, that is, savings, does not enter directly into the physical construction of things like new steel mills. In one sense only are savings indispensable to their creation; the physical plant and equipment are designed to produce steel; they are not used, or suitable for being used, eaten, or worn, or to immediately satisfy any other human want. And since these specialized objects are owned by someone, they become, in a physical sense, savings in the hands of the owner. Since he can sell them at will, or pledge them to secure loans, they may be regarded as the equivalent of the money they would bring if pledged or sold. Similarly, since money can readily be converted into a steel mill, or a steel mill converted into money, the distinction between financial capital and physical capital can often be disregarded.

Moreover, while the new steel mill is still in the prospectus stage, a body of experts has pronounced it economically feasible. By definition, these experts are people whose judgment is accepted by banks, suppliers of equipment, and others who stand to gain or lose by accepting the experts' judgment. What the experts means by "economically feasible" is that they expect the new steel mill, after paying its current operating costs, not only to produce wealth equivalent to its costs of capital formation but a hundred or thousand times that figure. And if the new enterprise is soundly conceived and well managed, this is generally what it does.

Now we can see the real function of savings is the building of new physical capital. Stripped of its hoary mystique, savings, or money, or financial capital, is simply insurance. The money subscribed for investment in a new enterprise merely ensures that the factory, ship, railroad, or other newly formed capital will produce income sufficient to defray the costs of its formation and that the income will be so applied.

A Plan That Would Work

Once we have torn off the blindfold of convention and seen that the use of savings in the new capital formation process is simply a form of insurance, we understand that the poor nations desperately and urgently need a second and supplementary financing technique that does not depend on *past savings*. Such a technique—by treating an insurance problem in an insurance manner—could enable the developing economies to organize new capital formation in such a way that the goods and services involved could be paid for out of the wealth produced by the newly formed capital.

Nor is there any theoretical or practical reason for not spreading the insurance risk by imposing premiums upon the new equity owners, who would be credit financed in a manner that would bring about a rapidly growing ownership base. In effect, the developing economies using this method would be able to finance much of their industrialization through future savings owned by households that previously were without capital.

Such a technique, built into a rational plan, could launch the underdeveloped economies on an industrialization breakthrough beyond the scope of imagination—Western or Communist. Even more momentous, the industrial revolutions powered by this technique would be enormously superior to our own. They would reveal capitalism purified of its internal flaw imposed by the total domination of the savings technique that compels unlimited concentration of capital ownership and economic power in the Western nations.

In other words, by severing the rigid historic linkage between new capital formation and past savings, it would at last be possible to generate capital ownership broadly throughout a population, building for political democracy its only possible economic support and, for the first time in the history of capitalism, synchronizing the industrial power to produce with the economic power to consume.

We can better understand the plan by taking inventory of our assets. The underdeveloped countries have land, trainable manpower, and natural resources, at least some. The industrial nations have technology, including talent and experience in industry, commerce, engineering, and science. They also have the machinery and equipment needed by the underdeveloped nations until their own capital goods industries are built. The owners of all these ingredients must be induced to contribute them at the proper time and in the required combinations and amounts, to build or expand productive enterprises in the developing economies while payments for these contributions, and of interest on credit, must be deferred until the enterprise is producing the income for these payments.

As these various resources are being organized into corporate structures capable of channeling their net incomes into the deferred payments, we must devise ways of getting ownership of these corporations into the hands of a growing number of families in the developing economies who previously have owned little or no capital. Through these steps, *future savings*, that is, future capital ownership, will begin to be created in the form of individually owned equity securities of the new or expanded enterprises that have paid from their operations the costs of their new capital formation.

These "paid-up" enterprises must then be required to pay out most, if not all, of their net incomes to their growing bodies of stockholders. Through this measure, the purchasing power produced by capital, as well as the purchasing power produced by labor will support the economic power of the masses to consume. Methods of financing expansion from future savings must be always available to such enterprises so that they will not have to withhold purchasing power from their stockholders for this purpose.

As for the actual techniques, we see at once that we already have them. The following procedure is only one of several that might be employed. It involves methods already widely used and well understood in other areas of finance. The possibility that the new enterprise might fail to produce its costs, or make the deferred payments, could be insured against by creating an agency similar in function to the Federal Housing Insurance Agency. With or without such an agency, capital stock equal in par or stated value to the required capital costs could be sold, on a nonrecourse basis, to new stockholders chosen from families previously incapable of acquiring capital ownership.

Under loans that might or might not be guaranteed by the corporation being financed, commercial banks could loan the new stockholders the purchase price. Medium-sized portfolios of such stock could be held in individual escrow accounts in the financing bank until their earnings defray the purchase price and interest. The loan proceeds can go directly to the corporation to pay for new capital formation. The portfolio purchased on credit would certainly be diversified. It should contain stocks selected from a number of enterprises that have been financed along similar lines.

In the hands of the banks making stock purchase loans, the loan paper should be discountable with the central bank or the development bank of the developing economy. For an insuring fee, U.S. or international financing agencies might indemnify the rediscount bank and provide currency exchange arrangements for the mutual benefit of the developing economy and U.S. or European capital goods suppliers.

Xlandia's Experience

A simplified but realistic example illustrates the technique. A developing economy—call it Xlandia—seeks to materially improve its economic condition by expanding its production of food and fiber, both for consumption and for export. A key factor in increasing its agricultural output is the construction of facilities for the production of nitrogenous fertilizers, including basic anhydrous ammonia, aqua ammonia, ammonium sulfate, and the usual liquid and dry mixes containing nitrogen, phosphorus, and sulphur compounds. Building such a chemical complex in Xlandia, supplying it with raw materials, and operating it are technically feasible.

Study shows that the largest plant that can be profitably operated at the outset would cost $10 million, complete with sufficient distribution equipment, storage facilities at the plant and at other locations in the market area, also including financing, organizational, and start-up expenses. An average annual net return of 20 per cent after depreciation and taxes would be extremely modest in many locations justifying such enterprises.

After careful study, it is determined that a fertilizer corporation, Agroboost, Inc., will be financed entirely through the issuance of shares of $100 par value capital stock, and that personal capital acquisition loans will be made to families meeting certain qualifications to enable the purchase of forty shares per family. For purely psychological reasons, a down payment of 5 per cent or $200 is imposed. At this point the details of what the qualifications should be, in addition to the 5 per cent down payment, are unimportant except that they should encourage socially desirable attributes such as education, skills, business or public service, experience, and the like, and should exclude already affluent families. The objective of such a program is not to encourage greed but to make affluence accessible to those not presently possessing it. The officers and employees of Agroboost, Inc. might well be given priority in such eligibility.

Thus 2,500 families would be able to arrange through their local commercial bank nonrecourse loans of $3,800, the proceeds of which, together with the $200 down payment, would be deposited in individual escrow accounts in the name of each new stockholder. The fiduciary handling the escrow account should be the equivalent of the trust department of a commercial bank where the trust officer, over the life of the loan, would have firsthand opportunity to explain to the new stockholder the nature and significance of stock ownership, the importance of using only the income and not the principal for consumption when the escrow account is closed and the loan paid off, and so forth. Thus the bank trust officer in such cases would become a teacher of elementary private property economics to a pupil who has a personal interest in the subject matter.

The proceeds of each stock acquisition loan, together with the down payment, would be used to purchase from Agroboost, Inc. forty shares of its capital stock. Since there presumably would be no lack of buyers for such securities under these conditions, elaborate underwriting arrangements would be unnecessary, and the stock might well be issued in installments over the construction period as funds are needed. In such a case, the financing loans need not begin to draw interest until the actual stock purchase is made. This procedure would also minimize the brief inflationary period between the loan and the commencement of production by the Agroboost, Inc. plant, marking the beginning of its anti-inflationary contribution to the economy that would continue for the life of the plant.

The shares so purchased would be deposited in each shareholder's escrow account, to be held there as security for the particular loan until it is paid off. Contractual or governmental regulations or both could require Agroboost, Inc. to pay out all or at least a very high percentage of its net earnings each year and to look to further similar personal stock acquisition loan financing for future expansion. Contractual arrangements would also determine the rate of application of dividends on the stock to repayment of the loan and bank interest, which can be assumed to be a desirably low administered rate of, say, 4 per cent.

This arrangement might apply all of the portfolio income on the interest and principal of the loan until the principal has been reduced to $3,000 and thereafter permit 25 per cent of the dividends to flow into the owner's hands and 75 per cent to be applied on the loan account. When the loan balance has been reduced to $2,000, the division might be 50 per cent to the loan account and 50 per cent to the stockholder. While such an arrangement does extend the stock acquisition financing period, it also serves the basic economic purpose of accelerating the buildup of the economic power of stockholding families to consume. It must be kept in mind that this is as important as the building of the industrial power to produce, in this case, chemical fertilizers.

Depending on the extent to which dividends on the stock of Agroboost, Inc. are permitted to be paid to the stockholder prior to full discharge of the financing loan, the principal and interest loan in this instance might be fully discharged out of dividends in a period of six to eight years. If Agroboost's net income were higher than here assumed—and it could generally be expected to be higher—the loan amortization period could be even shorter.

Ideally, the loan paper in the hands of commercial banks that made the stock acquisition loans should be discountable at a low rate with the Xlandia Central Bank. This is the essence of the technique of *monetizing new capital formation*.

Further desirable refinements may be added to the system, including the establishment of an FHA-like insuring agency (which we might call the Capital Diffusion Insurance Corporation or CDIC), which would set uniform and comprehensive feasibility testing standards to be met by corporations seeking to qualify for such financing. For a fee charged against each loan account, CDIC would insure the lending bank against loss through failure of the financed portfolio to pay its acquisition costs. If greater leverage were desired in the capital stock of Agroboost, Inc., a portion of the $10 million initial capitalization might be provided by term commercial loan, which might similarly be discountable and insurable.

In this simplified example, we have considered only the stock of a single corporation. Good financing and investment practice would lead the financing banks under this plan, and also the insuring agency if one is employed, to insist upon diversification of each financed portfolio. Each should contain a balanced selection of stocks issued by corporations seeking new capital formation that have satisfactorily met governmentally supervised feasibility tests in addition to the requirements of each particular commercial bank that makes personal capital acquisition loans. Such feasibility tests would be nothing but a reflection of good management judgment that the stocks approved would "throw off" their acquisition financing costs within an acceptable period. Figure 1 and Figure 2 illustrate the arrangement.

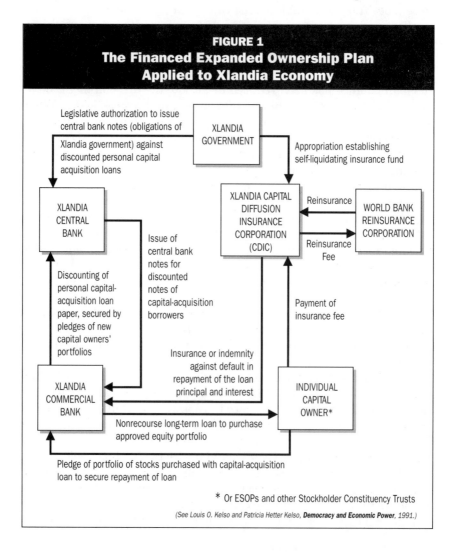

FIGURE 1
The Financed Expanded Ownership Plan
Applied to Xlandia Economy

Legislative authorization to issue central bank notes (obligations of Xlandia government) against discounted personal capital acquisition loans

XLANDIA GOVERNMENT

Appropriation establishing self-liquidating insurance fund

XLANDIA CENTRAL BANK

XLANDIA CAPITAL DIFFUSION INSURANCE CORPORATION (CDIC)

Reinsurance

WORLD BANK REINSURANCE CORPORATION

Reinsurance Fee

Issue of central bank notes for discounted notes of capital-acquisition borrowers

Discounting of personal capital-acquisition loan paper, secured by pledges of new capital owners' portfolios

Payment of insurance fee

Insurance or indemnity against default in repayment of the loan principal and interest

XLANDIA COMMERCIAL BANK

INDIVIDUAL CAPITAL OWNER*

Nonrecourse long-term loan to purchase approved equity portfolio

Pledge of portfolio of stocks purchased with capital-acquisition loan to secure repayment of loan

* Or ESOPs and other Stockholder Constituency Trusts

*(See Louis O. Kelso and Patricia Hetter Kelso, **Democracy and Economic Power**, 1991.)*

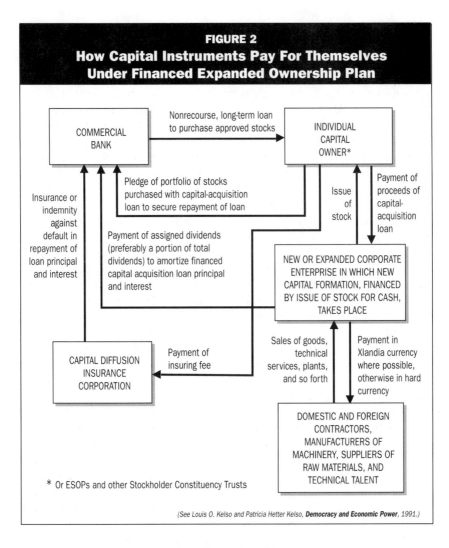

FIGURE 2
How Capital Instruments Pay For Themselves Under Financed Expanded Ownership Plan

COMMERCIAL BANK

Nonrecourse, long-term loan to purchase approved stocks

INDIVIDUAL CAPITAL OWNER*

Insurance or indemnity against default in repayment of loan principal and interest

Pledge of portfolio of stocks purchased with capital-acquisition loan to secure repayment of loan

Payment of assigned dividends (preferably a portion of total dividends) to amortize financed capital acquisition loan principal and interest

Issue of stock

Payment of proceeds of capital-acquisition loan

NEW OR EXPANDED CORPORATE ENTERPRISE IN WHICH NEW CAPITAL FORMATION, FINANCED BY ISSUE OF STOCK FOR CASH, TAKES PLACE

CAPITAL DIFFUSION INSURANCE CORPORATION

Payment of insuring fee

Sales of goods, technical services, plants, and so forth

Payment in Xlandia currency where possible, otherwise in hard currency

DOMESTIC AND FOREIGN CONTRACTORS, MANUFACTURERS OF MACHINERY, SUPPLIERS OF RAW MATERIALS, AND TECHNICAL TALENT

* Or ESOPs and other Stockholder Constituency Trusts

*(See Louis O. Kelso and Patricia Hetter Kelso, **Democracy and Economic Power**, 1991.)*

Effecting the Plan

Finally, who is to supply the organizational impetus for putting this technique to work in the poor nation? International entrepreneurial companies especially organized for the purpose could be the answer. The rich nations could easily organize such companies by the dozens if the industrialization of the developing economies were treated as a mutual undertaking for mutual profit, in other words, as a business partnership between enterprises of the developed country and those of the developing one. Each entrepreneurial company would commit itself by private or governmental contract or both to maintain its sponsored project corporations in the developing economy not in perpetuity, as foreign companies now do until they are national-ized, but for a specified length of time, for specific accomplishments, in return for a reasonable profit. The firm would arrange temporary operating contracts with experienced firms in the industrialized coun-tries and transfer technological know-how to citizens of the develop-ing economy. At the end of the booster stage, the firm would sell its equity in its project corporations through secondary reoffering of shares to local households who have little or no capital, using the insured bank-financed method of effecting purchase of the shares.

This plan is in the spirit of the Puritan ethos; in fact, it conserves and renews it by placing its chief virtue, thrift, in a new and workable context. Capital ownership is acquired by the individual through his savings—his investment in lieu of consumption. But this time, the income produced by his newly acquired equity capital is saved and applied in repayment of the credit extended to him to purchase stocks.

Aside from its main attraction, namely, that it would work, this fi-nancing method is free of all taint of charity. It does not concentrate ownership of new affluence-producing capital in the hands of a tiny class. It does not create or promote communistic or socialistic enterprise. It is efficient. It is aimed at the proper economic target: the causes of pov-erty. It creates the conditions under which free institutions can take root and grow; it provides progressively larger numbers of the broad masses with the opportunity, through capital ownership, to produce and enjoy affluence, not merely to engage in subsistence toil.

These social blessings will spring naturally from an economy that prac-tices the first principle of economic symmetry: building the economic power to consume simultaneously with the industrial power to produce.

One could marshal an army of facts and quote a legion of observers and prophets to prove that unless we apply new concepts to the prob-lems of the underdeveloped countries, and apply them soon, we are speed-ing toward disaster. But it is one thing to cry for new concepts and another to have the courage to recognize them and to try them.

It is easy to deplore the spectacle of a poor native scratching at the soil with a pointed stick and ignoring the shiny new ploughshare at this feet. But not only the technologically unsophisticated are thralls of the past. The blind spot that prefers the ancestral stick to the unknown potential of the plough is the same human blind spot that keeps us devoted to outmoded methods of finance and oblivious to the powerful new techniques we have in our hands.

We can, if we choose, lead the poor nations of the world to free-dom and affluence; or we can go on giving them the stone of foreign aid instead of teaching them how to produce their own bread.

— 2 —

How to Save the Corporation

by Peter S. Grosscup
Judge of the U.S. Circuit Court of Appeals
(First published in McClure's Magazine, February, 1905)

This article, written at a time when there is so much public discussion regarding the exact status of the great railroad corporations and trusts in this country, possesses a peculiar significance, force, and finality as coming from a federal judge so distinguished as Judge Grosscup. All of Judge Grosscup's decisions and public addresses have been marked, not only by a breadth of knowledge of the law, but by a keen sensitiveness to all the immediate problems and conditions of American life. He is more than a judge, he is a statesman. When the Rapid Transit problem in Chicago came before him, he considered not only its strict legal bearings, but made a thorough study of the whole subject of municipal transit, of its physical, financial and civic aspects. One of his earliest decisions as a federal judge was his dissenting opinion, afterward sustained by the Circuit Court of Appeals, upon the application to close the World's Columbian Exposition on Sunday; one of his latest was a decision enjoining the Beef Trust from combinations or conspiracies in restraint of trade. At the time of the Northern Securities litigation Judge Grosscup was offered a large retainer—several times his judicial salary—to become attorney for the railroad combine. He refused, with the assertion that he must continue to protect the interests committed to his care. Judge Grosscup comes of old Dutch stock. He was born, 1852, in Ashland, Ohio; educated at Wittenberg College and the Boston Law School; practised his profession at Ashland, Ohio, and in Chicago; was appointed United States Judge of the northern district of Illinois, 1892, and Judge of the United States Circuit Court of Appeals, 1899.

—The Editor, *McClure's Magazine*, 1905.

If, by national prosperity, we mean what the American people, in the mass, are achieving, in the way of increased material output, and power of productivity; if, by national prosperity, we mean that in the mass, our people are richer than in any previous period; that our territory and dominion have been pushed forward, and our influence in the councils of the nations established, as never before; if these things, relating to the people as a whole, constitute national prosperity, then, as never before, we are in a time of the very greatest prosperity. But is there not with a nation, as with an individual, apart from the mere outward life, an inner spirit or soul? *And what shall it profit our country if it gain the world,* and *lose its soul?*

Loss of Individual Hope

The soul of republican America is not in our ambition, as a people, to be great commercially and politically; nor our ambition for increased national territory, national power, or national wealth. The soul of republican America, as a civil government ordained to promote the welfare and happiness of its people, is individual opportunity—the opportunity and encouragement given to each individual to build up, by his own effort, and for himself and those dependent upon him, some measure of dominion and independence all his own. In that one phrase—measurable individual independence, and the opportunity to measurably exercise individual dominion—is comprised the civil history of the Anglo-Saxon race. Our commercial greatness as a people is not in danger of being lost; nor is our increasing national power and prosperity. *The loss that republican America now confronts is the loss of individual hope and prospect*—the suppression of the instinct that heretofore coming into the American boy's first grasp of the idea of individual career, and stimulating him ever afterwards, has made us a nation of individually independent and prosperous people. We are, I believe, in the first stage of a sweep of events, that unless turned to a purpose widely different from that now served, will carry us, eventually, to a time when the acquisition of property, by the individuals who constitute the bulk of our people, will cease to be one of the opening and controlling purposes of their lives. This means that, as a republican political institution, America will have lost the spirit which alone promises it life. *It means social and, eventually, political revolution.*

The thing at which I point is no apparition. It is an approaching fact—a fact that the people of this country have already intuitively discerned. On what theory, other than that of the existence of deep-seated popular apprehension, can be explained the widespread popular movement that brought about the Sherman Anti-Trust act; the anti-trust acts of the several states; the movements against large corporations, based on no better reason, in most instances, than that the corporations were large; the disposition manifest in every quarter, not to accept, but to combat, the rising forms of modern industrial activity? This popular apprehension does not rise solely from anxiety about prices. It grows out of the intuitive perception that, somewhere, something is wrong—that in the face of the future there is a disturbing, even sinister look. To test this intuition by the facts—to turn the feeling, so far as I can, into a correct perception of the facts—is one of the purposes of this article.

Let me preface it by saying that against corporations, as corporations, I have no enmity. Modern civilization requires that capital shall be wielded in large masses. The corporation is civilization's method of wielding capital in large masses. On that account the corporation is here to stay. The big corporation is here to stay. The only institution in sight to supplant it is state socialism; and state socialism is revolution accomplished.

"Private Property": The Foundation of Civilization

But the fundamental basis of the corporation is the institution of private property and the guaranties our government gives to private property. Now it so happens that the fundamental basis of the thing I have called measurable individual independence, and the opportunity measurably to exercise individual dominion, is also this institution of private property.

Around the institution of private property, therefore, more distinctively than anywhere else, center those changes, in our social and national life, that have been brought about by the appearance of the corporation as the great industrial, modern agent, and that the corporation is destined, I believe, to still more radically bring about. What, then, is this institution of private property, and what is the distinctive transformation it is undergoing as the result of corporate dominion?

In the beginning the Creator so conditioned mankind, that always underneath him would be the earth; always about him the air; always above him the sky. On this, as a dowry, He started us. In the earth He placed the seed, and the powers of motherhood that transform the seed into the full ear. In the bowels of the earth He stored the minerals. In the upper air He leashed the lightnings. And in the earth and air He left them all to wait—to wait for mankind to put forth *its* hands.

The seeds flowered and bore fruit; but in primitive inadequacy. In course of time mankind discovered that, by intelligence and industry, the flower could be beautified and the fruits sweetened. The minerals were alive, but with energies imprisoned. In course of time mankind found the key to the prison door; and the prisoners, liberated, have built the material structures of civilization. The lightnings glowed and zigzagged, calling out to us unceasingly, at times startling us, determined, like sentient beings, that their capacity of usefulness should not be overlooked.

In the course of time, the yoke was found that, adding these energies of the air to the forces of earth, brighten and strengthen our possession of the earth. The distance thus traveled, from primitive man to the man of today, has been a long one. But every mile was made under the spur, and governed by the rein, of private property. It was the institution of private property that, more than any other secular agency, brought us to civilization; and on this institution, as on a rock, the civilization of the world, and the world's republican institutions, must continue to rest.

The Foundation is Shifting

Now, it is just this institution of private property that is undergoing, at this time, a strain never put on it before. The weight producing the strain is the corporation. Not because the corporation, in essence, is retrogressive and unrepublican; but because, in fact, it is unrepublican, and for that reason retrogressive also. Not because the corporation is big and growing bigger; but because, in all this growth of superstructure, the base is narrowing—*the proprietorship of the private property of the country, by the bulk of the people of the country, is radically narrowing.*

A generation ago, the artisans of the country lived in the country towns. In the country towns were made the shoes we wore, the wagons and carriages, the stoves, the saddlery we used—all the appliances of life; and over the door of each shop hung the sign of the proprietor within. A generation ago, the farm work was done by men living on the farms.

All this is now changed. Nearly one-half of the population of the United States—twelve million active workers, supporting as dependents twenty four millions more—are now connected with the mechanical trades. The men who, in the time of which I have just spoken, with their own hands did the planting and cultivating and harvesting, are now in the manufacturing centers, making the machines that plant and cultivate and harvest. The artisan proprietors in the towns have been succeeded by artisan employees in the great factories. The whole scene of industrial activity has been shifted from town and country to the cities; from the numerous small dominions exercised by individuals, to colossal corporate dominions.

The extent of this shift is told in the census figures. In 1900, according to the census of that year, the whole value of all the farms, the farming utensils, horses, reapers and binders, plows and farm products on hand unsold—that which on a single day would have constituted an inventory of all the agricultural interests from Maine to California—amounted to between eighteen and nineteen billions of dollars; while the capital invested in corporations, including railroads, factories of all kinds, and their products on hand unsold, amounted to twenty-two billions of dollars. Thus corporate dominion has, within thirty years, beginning with almost nothing, outstripped agricultural ownership by more than three billions of dollars; and, barring city real estate, comprises now nearly one-half of the whole wealth of the country.

In the swing of the industrial system, the corporation has come to be the gravitating force that holds the activities in their orbits. Is it much wonder that, in the eyes of those who look upon the corporation as an interloper, it has come to be regarded as a usurper also—the usurper of what the labor of individual men has created; or, that in the eyes of those who, with clearer vision, look upon it as an indispensable phase of industrial evolution, *the way in which the corporation shall thereafter be organized, and the bounds given to its dominion, are coming to be the paramount political problems of our time?*

Banks and Bonds Starve Small Enterprises

Now the shift in dominion over private property, from the individual of a generation or so ago to the corporation of today, would have little significance comparatively, if the corporation were only this age's new way of unifying, massing, individual ownership—leaving the people of the country, generally, though under this new form, the ultimate real owners. But such, unhappily, is not the case. The effect of the corporation, under the prevailing policy of the free, go-as-you-please method of organization and management, has been to drive the bulk of our people, other than farmers, out of property ownership; and, if allowed to go on as at present, it will keep them out. When the individual proprietor of the past sells out his business to the corporation, he does not reinvest his capital in his old line of business. He puts it in the bank, or in some bond. When the workman has got together some savings, he does not become a proprietor or part proprietor. He spends it, or puts it in the bank. To men like these, no kind of active investment, practically considered, is left open. The industries are now dominated by the corporation, and proprietorship in the corporation has come to be for those only who are experienced in corporate ways, or who are willing to take a chance at the corporate wheel. And thus it happens, that just at this moment, we are in the midst of a sweep of events, that unless arrested and turned to a different account, will transform this country from a nation whose property is within the proprietorship of the people at large, to a nation whose industrial property, so far as active proprietorship goes, will be largely in the hands of a few skilled or fortunate so-called captains of industry, and their lieutenants.

Let me set out some of the proofs of the case I have thus undertaken. I might appeal, and with convincing success, too, to the memory of my readers. But I do not rest my case there. I call as witness the figures gathered from the Treasury Department of the United States, and distributed as a part of its official publications. These figures show that the deposits in the banks of the United States in 1880— national, state, and savings—amounted to a little over two billion and a quarter dollars. The same deposits, in 1904, had grown to about eleven billions. In these figures are included no redeposits. The figures represent the actual bank credits for the years named. Now bank credits, outside the sums that constitute the mere fluid working capital of the country, represent the capital that one class of people are withholding or withdrawing from other forms of investments, that another class of people may borrow and utilize it to push forward their own investments. Would we know who are the people who are withholding and withdrawing from other forms of investment the capital thus deposited, we must inquire who are the depositors; and would we know whether these people are withholding and withdrawing from other investments in a ratio greatly disproportionate to the growth of the general property, we must compare the ratio of deposits with the general growth of property.

Hoards of the Working People

Now, in the main, the depositors in our banks and savings societies are not people whom we call the rich. The deposits are gathered largely from the working people and from other people of moderate means. The bulk of the deposits are in the money centers, but their source, like the sources of a great river, are not in the volume of the river itself, nor its larger branches, but in the little springs and raindrops that, unnoticed, form the rivulets; these in turn uniting to form the branches and finally the river itself. To test this my reader need but go to the savings and other banks of his own town. I know of one county with a population of less than twenty-five thousand—an agricultural county without a millionaire in it—whose deposits are well upward of a million. I know another county with a population of perhaps fifty thousand—one-third of whom are connected with the mechanical trades—whose deposits are three and one-half millions. This means, then, that the people who are withholding or withdrawing from active proprietorship the capital thus represented by bank credits, are not the rich, but the people of ordinary means; and it brings us to the next inquiry. What is the disproportion, if any, between the growth in general wealth and this growth of bank credits?

From 1880 to 1904, the population of the country (estimated since 1900) has grown a little over fifty per cent. From 1880 to 1904 (estimated again since 1900), the general wealth of the country—farms, farm implements, city real estate, corporate ownership, bank deposits, everything of every kind and nature—has grown as much perhaps as sixty per cent. In 1900 it was estimated by the government that an equal distribution of the wealth of the United States among its people in 1880 would have yielded to each about one thousand dollars, while such distribution in 1900 would have yielded about eleven hundred dollars. The growth of wealth per capita, therefore, during these two decades, was about ten per cent.

Now mark! During this same period, the amounts invested by our wage-workers and people of ordinary means, in bank deposits—that is, the amount withheld or withdrawn by them from active proprietorship, and left with the banking institutions to loan out to those skilled in the ways of corporations—have grown over five hundred per cent.

To illustrate: suppose a community in 1880 possessed a million dollars, one hundred thousand of which was in bank credits, and the balance in other forms of property; suppose this same community is found in 1904 to have five hundred thousand dollars in bank deposits alone, or five times the former amount. One of two things is apparent: either the community's population and general wealth have grown proportionately—that is five hundred per cent—or the growth of the bank credits has been at the expense of proprietorship in other forms of active property. Now, what conclusion would be forced upon us if in that community the growth and general wealth was, not five hundred per cent, but only fifty per cent; or, taking the per capita growth as a nearer guide, only ten per cent? Could any one doubt, on such a state of affairs, what was taking place in the community? Can any one doubt, then on the figures I have named, what is taking place respecting the proprietorship of the active properties of the country by the bulk of the people in the country?

It should be borne in mind, too, that the transformation indicated is not a mere pin speck on an otherwise spotless sheet of paper. Were it so, it could perhaps, in the wider vision that makes up judgment on great questions, be safely overlooked. But it cannot be safely overlooked, for the transformation relates to the whole of property that makes up, almost entirely, the last quarter of a century's addition to our national wealth; to just that property, too, that attracts and fills most completely the public eye.

Nor, viewed purely as a question of economics, can the transformation be ignored. The industrial complaint that has greatest voice today is the danger of monopoly. Corporations owned widely by the people might, perhaps, become monopolies; though I know of no actual instance of a monopoly widely owned. *But the antidote of monopoly is competition*; and let it come about that corporations be made reasonable safe, and therefore desirable, investments—let it come about that the corporation shall no longer be regarded as a mere financial sinkhole, except for those skilled in its ways—and there will be abundance of capital at hand, as the bank deposits show, to put in the field a competitive corporation, whenever in that field monopoly seems to have established itself. Indeed, the chief reason why any monopoly can now maintain itself is, that besides having a grasp on all the physical sources of productivity within a given field, it has a large grasp, also, on all the financial resources that would otherwise go into the building up of competitors.

A Nation of Dependents

But the transformation strikes deeper than mere economic conditions, or the natural laws that govern monopoly and competition. The transformation of the ownership of a country's industrial property, from its people generally to a few of its people only, reaches the bedrock of social and moral forces on which, alone, the whole structure of republican institutions rests; for, under such conditions, instead of depending, each on himself and his own intelligence chiefly for success, the great bulk of our people, increasingly, will become dependents upon others. Those who possess investible means will come to rely solely upon the great financial institutions; and those who possess nothing but capacity for labor, upon the great organizations of labor. That is paternalism; paternalism in almost its final form; the paternalism that will eventually divide the country into two hostile camps, the camp of those who have, and the camp of those who have not; the paternalism that speedily descends into actual state socialism, or a dry-rotted citizenship as nerveless and squalid as state socialism.

Here, then, in our own day, and at this early hour of the day, is the parting of the ways. Ahead lies the road to paternalism. To the left is the open road to state socialism. They look now like distinct ways, these two roads, over bogs and precipices all their own. But a little way ahead, within the distance that any clear eye can carry, the two roads meet. For let it not be forgotten by those who preach the so-called rights of "industrial liberty," that the out and out socialists and radical labor men are not the only influences that are pushing our country to the edge of the socialistic precipice. These have allies; and the ally on which they most rely, and justifiably rely, are just those men who, regardless of all considerations other than those of money and power greed, are launching the dishonest corporate contrivances, that, under our existing corporation policy, obtain without hindrance the credit and sanction of the government's great seal.

The Safe Road to Individual Proprietorship

It is only by a turn to the right, by what may seem to some a sharp turn, that our one safe pathway forward will be found. That way lies over high ground, *Individual Opportunity—the opportunity, actual as well as in theory, to each individual to participate in the proprietorship of the country*. That ground is, in its best and highest sense, republican ground. To gain that ground, the paramount problem, is not how to stop the growth of property, and the building up of wealth, but how to manage it so that every species of property, like a healthful growing tree, will spread its roots deeply and widely in the soil of a popular proprietorship. The paramount problem is not how to crush, or hawk at, or hamper the corporation, merely because it is a corporation; but how to make this new form of property ownership a workable agent toward *repeopleizing the proprietorship of the country's industries*.

The first step in the solution of that problem is that the government obtain a full grasp of the whole subject matter; and this, in my judgment, can adequately be done only by putting aside the five-and-forty bewildering state hands, for the one great national hand.

The second step, the step for which the first is taken, is to take care upon what kind of corporate proposal the government's great seal is set—to cut out the stock-jobbing corporation; the waterlogged corporation; the mere vision of visionaries; the labyrinthian corporation whose stock and bond issues are so purposely tangled that no mind, not an expert's, can follow their sinuosities. In short, to regenerate the corporation.

The third step is to open to the wage-earner of the country the road to proprietorship. The basis of every successful enterprise is the command: go forth, increase, and multiply; and to no enterprise can rightfully be denied the fruits of that command. But capital is not the sole thing that enters into enterprise. The skill that puts the ship together, or that subsequently pilots her, is not the sole thing. The men who drive the bolts, and feed the fires, contribute; and to them, as to the capitalists, and to the captains and lieutenants of industry, should go a part of the increment; not as gratuity, but as their proper allotment out of the combined forces that have made the enterprise successful. Of course, to make such partnership between capital and labor a thing that ought to be done, is the work of the big hearts and big brains in the industrial field. But to make such partnership a thing that *can* be done, is the work of those who shall recast and regenerate the country's corporation policy.

Will Democrats or Republicans Enlist?

Whether either of the present great political parties will be found willing to undertake this work of regeneration, I do not know. The main body of the Democratic party would, I believe, enlist. But on one of its wings are the influences of semi-socialism, and on the other a band of so-called conservatives, so conservative, that a single utterance against the sanctity of the present go-as-you-please corporation license is looked upon as political profanity.

The main body of the Republican party would enlist. It was the early Republican party that, through the Homestead and Preëmption laws, peopleized the proprietorship of the public domain. But the Republican party, too, has wings: and it cannot yet be said that the wings may not, on this vital issue, hold back the main body.

But the day of regeneration will come, the day when some party of the people will cease to minimize, to compromise, to hide behind promises and looks; but, going to the root of the matter—the depeopleization of industrial ownership under present policies—it will build from that point upward. That day will come, because higher and higher within the heart of our country is rising the voice, *What shall it profit us if we gain the world, and lose our soul?*

II

Principles
for Social
Reconstruction

Principles
for Social
Reconstruction

In 1789, Jean-Paul Marat, convicted thief, quack scientist, physician-by-purchase, and a prime mover behind the French Reign of Terror stated his basic principle of social reconstruction:

> When a man is in want of everything, he has a right to take from another the superfluity in which he is wallowing: nay, more, he has a right to cut his throat and devour his palpitating flesh.[1]

While this view has achieved a wide measure of popularity in the two centuries since it was articulated, the mere fact that it is widespread does not make the principle right. A realistic program for the elimination of widespread world poverty must be based on sound moral principles. Flawed principles will inevitably result in flawed programs, even with the best intentions.

Communism and socialism, the most widely touted and widely implemented programs ever developed for eliminating poverty, embody a flawed and unrealistic conception of human nature. Both assume that man will produce and work for others out of pure altruism, and that the necessary surrender of individual sovereignty under such systems will be more than compensated for by material security. Yet ultimately, both these systems are based on the vice of envy, having as their end and means a forced equality of results, keeping everyone at the same economic level.

Capitalism, on the other hand, is cynical about man's nature (which, as it was created by a Being all-good and all-knowing, must be basically good in itself). Yet capitalism denies this, grounding itself on greed and unbridled competition—an economic Darwinism, with monopoly as the end result. The concentration of ownership and power in a small elite as embodied in capitalism is a major cause of poverty, being based on the worst in man. Not even by the wildest stretch of the imagination could capitalism be termed a cure for poverty of any kind, much less widespread world poverty.

That traditionally capitalist economies have a greater degree of affluence is because they contain, to varying degrees, certain institutional "pillars" (particularly private property, free markets, and limited power of the state), which allow for greater freedom and initiative than is allowed under socialist systems. However, even in a nearly perfect capitalist economy such as that of Japan, the great mass of people rely on wage-system jobs to derive an income, and only a microscopic elite owns productive assets. As suggested by Kanezo Ichikawa, Professor of Law at Kagawa University, Japan is rich, but the ordinary Japanese citizen can be described as relatively poor, living in cramped and stressful conditions.

Traditional solutions, whether those of capitalism or socialism, have lost whatever relevance they might have had through their demonstrable failure in the former Soviet Union, the growing disparities of wealth and income in the more traditional capitalist countries, and the impending bankruptcy of the various permutations of the welfare state. What principles, then, can be developed to guide the effort to cure widespread world poverty?

The three articles in this section, "Charity or Justice: Where is the Hope of the Poor?," "Economic Justice in the Age of the Robot" and "Reevaluating Private Enterprise," attempt to address the problem of widespread poverty by examining the underlying moral principles of a workable solution.

"Charity or Justice: Where is the Hope of the Poor?" analyzes the classical definitions of charity and justice, and contrasts them with modern misconceptions about charity and justice. While pointing out that what is called justice today is often the most rank injustice, the paper also acknowledges the inadequacy of the classical individual virtues when dealing with the complexity of today's interlocking social institutions and how man relates to those institutions. The article concludes that only the consistent applicaation of justice, firmly based on classical principles, but expanded and fulfilled by the concepts of social and participatory justice, holds any hope at all for the alleviation of the plight of the poor.

In "Economic Justice in the Age of the Robot," Norman Kurland picks up where "Charity or Justice: Where is the Hope of the Poor?" leaves off. He demonstrates that justice is the single overriding principle in any real advance in pursuing a program of effective social or economic change. After briefly recapping the meaning of justice within the classical framework, Kurland gives an in-depth analysis and logical framework for understanding social justice, economic justice and their application for the common good.

Combining the rights of private property with consistently applied, properly defined and clearly understood principles of justice leads to the formulation of the essential elements of an expanded ownership theory of economic justice, a refinement of the theory first formulated by Louis Kelso and Mortimer Adler. These three principles—the Principle of Participation, the Principle of Distribution, and the Principle of Harmony—are interdependent. If any of them is weakened or missing, the system of economic justice inevitably collapses.

Lorenzo Servitje Sendra, one of Mexico's most respected industrial statesmen and head of a 45,000-employee company, shares some of his insights on the nature of human work and the business enterprise in his paper "Reevaluating Private Enterprise." Written nearly a decade ago, this paper relates how business and the entrepreneurial spirit developed from its most primitive manifestation to the complexities of the modern corporation. Servitje demonstrates that business, while an activity concerned largely with the material aspects of existence, is integral to the development of the whole human being, both physical and spiritual. Segregating or isolating any part of the human person by concentrating business solely on the material not only results in economic difficulties, but has disastrous effects on the dignity of the person, and on society as a whole.

Since business is a human enterprise, it must take into consideration all that which makes up the human being. While there can be conflict in business between economic needs and social needs, the strictly material aspect of business must always be tempered by the demands of freedom, responsibility, solidarity and justice. Governments and the general public must be educated as to the real nature of business, and even businessmen themselves must learn to ask about some project, not only "Is it profitable?" but also "Is it socially responsible? Is it right? Is it *just*?"

Clearly, then, justice is the overriding principle that governs any realistic program of social reconstruction. Yet it cannot be something that is called justice for want of a better term, or a case where a principle is called justice as a way to whitewash gross injustice. Only the application of true justice instead of false charity will result in developing a real and effective cure for the disease of widespread world poverty.

Notes

[1]Jean-Paul Marat, as quoted in Warren H. Carroll's **The Guillotine and the Cross,** (Manassas, Virginia: Trinity Communications, 1986) 36.

— 3 —

Charity or Justice:
Where is the Hope of the Poor?

by Michael D. Greaney

Ever since Karl Marx promulgated his socialist agenda for overcoming the evils of capitalism and building a just society, the idea has gained momentum that the poor and oppressed have the right to take by force the accumulations held by the wealthy. Since many of the world's poor lack even the basic essentials of survival, more so of comfort, some argue that justice demands that anyone possessing an excess of worldly wealth have that excess confiscated and distributed among the needy.

Some even declare that anyone possessing a significant excess of worldly goods must have, *ipso facto*, obtained them by robbing the underprivileged, and therefore should be imprisoned or executed.

This attitude has become prevalent to a degree unexpected even by Marx. The assumption that anyone who possesses wealth must be forced to support those who do not is generally unquestioned, as is the assertion that "the people" have a right to the fruits of someone else's labor, simply because they are in want or need, and the wealth exists. Keeping wealth from the poor is thus seen as a violation of their "rights." Therefore, any means to confiscate wealth for redistribution among the less fortunate is seen as right and proper.

Many people in the world today lack the basic essentials of life. Multitudes of others have nothing that "makes life worth living." It is incumbent upon those who have an excess of the goods of this world to care for those who are deprived of even the bare minimum subsistence. But is it justice that makes this demand?

If justice indeed demands that the affluent care for the poor and underprivileged, it is perfectly right that any individual's excess wealth be confiscated for redistribution to the needy. Attempts to retain an excess would make an individual a criminal, subject to prosecution and appropriate punishment.

This has generally been the case in a society run along Marxist lines. "From each according to his ability, to each according to his need" justifies the draconian measures which communist governments, and, more recently, the various forms of the welfare state, have taken to redistribute wealth.

If justice demands that the wealthy care for the poor, then any duly constituted government has not only the right, but the duty, to make and enforce laws to that effect. Yet deprived of a legitimacy lent by the demands of justice, any social welfare system based on forced redistribution is inevitably unjust.

What is Justice?

According to traditional philosophy, justice is the cardinal and moral virtue by which a person, including institutional "persons," renders to everyone his due (and is rendered his due in return).[1] Justice is the virtue which observes the rights of all;[2] it is concerned with one's dealings with and actions toward others.[3]

What are the demands of justice? What acts may be required and forced? What acts may be morally required yet completely voluntary? It is difficult for contemporary people to remember that justice, while permeating all other virtues, is distinct of itself and is not merely a component of the other virtues.[4]

Justice seeks to preserve equality of proportion in all affairs of human life.[5] This "equality of proportion" is realized when each person has received his due.[6] The act of justice renders to each what he has a right to have.[7]

The key to justice is *suum cuique*, "to each his own."[8] This is the point where many of those who confuse justice with charity go astray. Some mistakenly reason that because a person is in need of something, he has a right to it.

It is true that classical philosophers such as Thomas Aquinas recognize that under certain circumstances a person may take what belongs to another and incur no moral guilt. If an individual (or those for whom he is directly responsible, such as children or spouse) is in absolute need of the necessities of life, that individual may take what he needs from the excess of another without incurring a moral penalty.[9] However, three conditions of taking must be met before such a course of action is morally permitted:

> (1) Every other means of acquiring the necessities must have been tried and exhausted.[10] This includes offering payment in a fair exchange, and begging for the necessities as alms.

(2) No more than the absolute necessities can be taken. Absolute necessities are defined as being those things which will keep the individual alive.

(3) The person from whom the necessities have been taken must not be left in as dire a situation as was the one who took his material goods.[11]

Nothing allows a person to take what rightfully belongs to another simply to increase his own comfort or quality of life. There is also the *caveat* that while a person who is thus engaged in acquiring the necessities of life may not incur moral guilt, he may very well run afoul of civil authority and incur penalties under law. In addition, "stealing to survive" is recognized as an extraordinary exception to how society should normally run—it is allowed, not recommended. Simply taking what is needed is no substitute for the opportunity to earn the necessities of life. Modelling a civil order on the principles of sheer survival would merely impede the productive efficiency of society and degrade the dignity of man.

Analogous to an individual in great need, a community in times of general emergency may morally take from an individual's excess to redistribute among those who are in danger of death as a result of the emergency.[12] This principle allows a government to alleviate conditions indirectly through the levy of additional taxes, or directly (e.g. through the requisition of food in time of famine).

Again, however, it is an emergency measure and cannot be taken as the norm for running a society. The same conditions must be met as for the individual, and the redistribution must last no longer than the duration of the emergency. Once an emergency is over and the conditions no longer exist, what was a just redistribution undertaken to keep people alive degenerates immediately into theft.

This principle may also be applied in cases of individual need, where a government may give assistance of a level sufficient to keep an individual alive—but no more. "Quality of life," "dignity of man" and other subjective rationales for increasing the level of assistance above what is needed to keep life in the body are not covered by this principle.

Where Redistribution Departs from Justice

Justice is concerned with the rights of all parties.[13] Forced redistribution of an individual's excess, except under the special conditions mentioned above, ignores the rights of the individual whose goods have been seized.[14] An individual has the right to preserve his own life, or those for whom he is directly responsible, but not to the extent of violating the right of another to life or property.[15] (War and self defense are separate issues.[16]) Simply taking what is needed constitutes theft,[17] which is an injury to another person, and a violation of both justice and charity.[18] Redistribution by the community through coercion to bring about an equality, or as an end in itself is also theft, however it be redefined or rationalized.[19]

Specifically, forced redistribution violates both commutative and distributive justice.[20] Commutative justice obliges transactions between individuals to be based on an equality of value given and received.[21] Distributive justice is exercised by the community towards the individual members of the community, bestowing on them material goods and certain intangibles relative to their contribution to the community.[22] Unlike the socialist aim of equality of results, based on the need of the individual, distributive justice is based on an equality of proportion.[23] Distributive justice operates on the recognition that an individual making greater input to the community should receive a proportional benefit from the community.[24]

Give-and-take is explicit in justice. Forced redistribution obviously violates commutative justice by taking from individuals and giving nothing in return. The violation of distributive justice is no less obvious. A community bestows wealth and benefits upon an individual based on the value of that individual's contribution to the community. The community may be anything from the city, to the state, to the corporation, but the principle is still the same: the community receives something in exchange for the wealth and benefits it bestows. Otherwise the wealth and benefits constitute almsgiving—which is charity, not justice.

The Demands of Charity

Some would make the argument that the community must, in the name of charity, confiscate individuals' excess for distribution among the needy. Forced redistribution, however, does not constitute any form of charity, although concern for the basic needs of man are the most often invoked justification for carrying it out. Since redistribution through coercion so blatantly violates justice, it also violates charity.[25]

There are four primary, or cardinal, virtues that are natural to man.[26] These are justice, fortitude, temperance and prudence.[27] They are a part of human nature, and a human being is in some way incomplete without them.[28] They do not rely on any outside agency for acquisition: to be human is to have a natural capacity for the cardinal virtues.[29] Foremost among these primary virtues is justice.[30]

In addition, there are the three theological virtues of faith, hope and charity.[31] As these virtues are not considered part of human nature, human beings rely on an outside agency to acquire them.[32] They are infused into man, not present naturally.[33] In Christianity, the outside agency which infuses these virtues is God, hence the designation as "theological" virtues. Foremost among these theological virtues is charity.[34]

Charity is thus "higher" than justice, but it in no way supersedes it.[35] If justice has been violated (thus in a sense rendering man less than human by transgressing his own nature), charity has been violated also. Committing an injustice in the name of charity is a serious error, and does not even minimally constitute an act of charity. Indeed, the needs of justice must first be served, or charity will never be achieved, for justice is the foundation of charity, underpinning and supporting it.[36] Charity fulfills justice, it does not eliminate it.

It is specious to argue that the social welfare system entrenched in so many countries is either justice or charity. It is neither. Redistribution through a social welfare system violates commutative justice in that the person taxed to support the system rarely receives equal benefit from his taxes. It violates distributive justice in that the individuals receiving welfare payments are not being rewarded for their relative input to the community.

Neither does a redistributive welfare state reflect charity. Charity, specifically almsgiving (which is what most people think of when charity is mentioned), has implicit in it the exercise of free will. Justice, as a moral virtue that concerns the actions between individuals and frequently involves transactions that can be measured objectively, may be legislated and forced.[37] Charity, as a theological virtue, may not.[38] Both are required of man. But while society may force or legislate justice, it cannot force or legislate charity.

It is sometimes argued that individuals have the right to receive a basic subsistence from the community (usually the state). Exercise of a right implies the functioning of justice,[39] and justice does not mandate that any individual or group has the right to receive a basic subsistence merely as the result of existence. The world owes no one a living—which is not the same as saying that no one has a right to life. Classical justice says that no one—including the unborn—may be deprived of life without just cause and due process,[40] but is silent about how that same life is to be maintained in the absence of the ability to make input into the economic system or even the physical ability to take nourishment without assistance. Charity, on the other hand, does insist that those with means care for those who are unable to care for themselves,[41] but the recipient of that care does not receive it by right, and thus out of justice (except from the parent or guardian in loco parentis/dependent relationship[42]). He receives it as the object of charity.[43]

A principle of distribution based upon classical justice, however, leaves unanswered the question of what to do about those individuals who lack the ability to make input into the system and participate as productive members of society. This is where charity functions in the classical framework.

An individual is obligated by charity to give alms when (1) he has an excess, and (2) another individual or group is dependent upon him for relief. Where either of these two circumstances are not met, there is no obligation to give alms, but it is advisable to do so anyway as a counsel of perfection. The rich have the obligation to contribute to the care of the poor out of their excess and according to the means available.[44] They are not obliged to contribute to the extent that they or their dependents are deprived.[45]

But if those who have an excess of material goods cannot be forced to distribute them to those with less out of either charity or justice, where is the possibility for the underprivileged to gain the basic means of subsistence and possibly strive for a better quality of life?

The classical virtues of commutative and distributive justice have been discussed and it has been shown that they deal with existing wealth of the individual or community. Both commutative and distributive justice are "output" or "distribution" principles. Commutative justice deals on an individual basis, and distributive justice deals on a "joint effort" basis.

Relating Justice to Social Institutions

The classical virtues are individual in nature. At best, they address the problem of man's interactions with his social institutions in an indirect way.[46] Once man begins functioning within an institutional environment, the classical virtues become inadequate with respect to the social nature of the situation. It becomes necessary at that point to develop a concept of social virtue.[47] The classical virtues of commutative and distributive economic justice are individual in nature, and require a social aspect in order to be complete. Another part of economic justice, participative justice, deals with the social aspect of economic justice, the as-yet uncreated future wealth of the individual or community.[48]

Social justice is a virtue, based on an individual's obligation to work in an organized way with other individuals to structure and continually perfect each of the institutions which he and others need for their common good.[49] The institutions themselves enhance or constrain the individual's rights of participation. A just institution provides each individual within that institution with an equality of opportunity and an equality of access to the means to contribute and thereby receive a fair distribution or return for one's input. Unjust institutions create barriers to equal opportunity and equal access to participation. Where an essential part of social justice—equality of opportunity—is missing, the institution will need to be rebuilt or improved in order to restore justice. It is only through concerted actions among people working for their common good—through "acts of social justice"—that unjust institutions can be changed.[50]

With respect to wealth and property, commutative and distributive justice deal with what is already owned or possessed by individuals. Participative justice, on the other hand, deals with what the individual has the opportunity and means to acquire at the present time and in the future while acting within a particular institution. It deals with intangibles, such as future uncreated wealth, knowledge, and technique—what is generally regarded as the common heritage of all men.[51]

It is important to distinguish between private goods and social goods. Confusion of the two becomes more pronounced as society tends towards either of the two extremes of socialism or capitalism. Capitalism tends toward the notion that all goods are private; socialism toward the notion that all goods are social, and belong to all.

Private goods are those that are owned by a particular individual, and that no one else may use without license. This category would include such things as productive land, machinery, private dwellings, clothing, food, tools, patents, copyrights, and so on. Social goods would include techniques, processes, knowledge—those things which no one person can own, and are open to free use by all. Money, credit, double-entry bookkeeping, even the political ballot, are examples of social goods. (Patents and copyrights involve special cases that will not be discussed in this article.) Sometimes a good that would normally be private, such as land, assumes the characteristic of a social good, as would be the case where a village common is open to all for livestock grazing.

For a community or institution to be just, the access to the social goods and common heritage of that institution must be available to every individual. Where some people are excluded from using the techniques, knowledge and means available to others within that institution, a violation of social justice exists.[52]

This does not mean, of course, that anyone who does not exercise his right to use social goods or knowledge available to all should receive the same reward as those who do. It is unjust to demand that the individual who has produced and accumulated wealth be stripped of, or forced to share his wealth with others who have not bothered to exercise their rights to use available knowledge and techniques.[53]

Where the community or individuals have actively or passively taken steps to prohibit the use of certain techniques or knowledge by various classes of people or have created a monopoly, steps must be taken to restore the principle of participation.

Violating Participative Justice

A significant example of how the participation principle is violated involves the use of self-liquidating credit to purchase productive assets. Given an equal ability to repay a loan (determined largely by the productive capacity of the asset itself), equal abilities, knowledge, in fact, equality in all relevant areas, a rich man would have far less trouble obtaining credit to purchase that asset than would a poor man whose only difference from the rich man is accumulated wealth.

Traditionally, in every economy of the world, there has been a monopoly which benefits the wealthy and inhibits or prohibits the accumulation of wealth by those with no past accumulation. As long as the community permits this state of affairs to exist, it engages in a violation of social justice, albeit in a passive way, insofar as it denies a certain class of persons ("the poor") access to the technique of acquiring wealth that pays for itself. This denies to the many access to the common heritage of man and to the means of economic self-sufficiency.

By permitting people to exercise their rights in participative justice, the community can go a long way towards providing true equality of opportunity, rather than a forced equality of results. The principle of participation, from which distributive justice naturally follows, solves to a large degree the problem of poverty (although it will never completely be solved). It provides an opportunity for people to make their way out of poverty through access to the various means and methods of wealth creation and accumulation. Since such an opportunity to create and accumulate wealth would not threaten the existing accumulation of the already wealthy, conflict is diminished between the rich and the poor. The demand to strip the rich of their wealth is then clearly seen for what it has always been: envy, not charity or justice.[54]

Eliminating Risk: The Wrong Emphasis

A culture of wealth (not to be confused with a culture of the wealthy) provides the opportunity for as many people as possible to become rich through the opportunities to acquire future wealth, but acknowledges the existence of risk. In a culture of socialism, however, every effort is made to do away with all imagined risk. A culture of socialism results in making everyone poor by concentrating on an equal distribution of currently existing wealth to ensure security.

But the problem of the world's desperate poor cannot be solved simply by making everyone poor. That would be neither justice nor charity. There can be a great deal done, however, to create a culture of wealth. Based on justice, such a culture would enable the poor who have the opportunity and means to make their way out of poverty. By making full use of opportunities to create and accumulate wealth, the poor within a culture of wealth can achieve the result of becoming one of the wealthy.

That those who are unable to care for themselves must be cared for is undeniable. Even in a perfectly just society there will be those who fail to accumulate wealth by one means or another or lose their accumulation, and thus have no way to sustain life by their own efforts. The virtue of charity, at a minimum, demands that those who have an excess care for those who have nothing.[55] What is so unsatisfying to those enmeshed in a culture of socialism is that the wealthy cannot be forced to act charitably—they must do so of their own free will, or it ceases to be charity and degrades both those who enforce such a redistribution and those who accept it.

Nor could a socialist equality of results ever be achieved. Those with the power to confiscate and redistribute will always use that power to their own advantage. Concentrated power corrupts, and wealth is power. But the way to minimize concentrations of wealth, and thus power, is to give everyone the opportunity to become wealthy and gain a measure of power for himself, not to concentrate all wealth and power in the hands of an elite group of redistributors.

Neither justice nor charity will ever give everyone the same degree of material wealth. Only tyranny can come close to this result, and then only by making everyone equally oppressed. The hope of the poor is in the application of a participative justice as it relates to the tools and institutions of the modern world. The hope of every person is a justice that provides an equality of opportunity, not in a pseudo-charity that imposes an equality of results.

Notes

[1] Thomas Aquinas *Summa Theologica*, IIa IIae q.58 a.1.

[2] Ibid. IIa IIae q.58 a.1.

[3] Ibid. IIa IIae q.58 a.2.

[4] Ibid. IIa IIae q.58 a.6.

[5] Ibid. IIa IIae q.58 a.11.

[6] Ibid. IIa IIae q.58 a.11.

[7] Ibid. IIa IIae q.58 a.11.

[8] Ibid. IIa IIae q.58 a.11.

[9] Ibid. IIa IIae q.66 a.7.

[10] Ibid. IIa IIae q.66 a.7.

[11] Ibid. IIa IIae q.66 a.7.

[12]Ibid. IIa IIae q.66 a.8.

[13]Ibid. IIa IIae q.58 a.2.

[14]Ibid. IIa IIae q.66 a.4.

[15]Ibid. IIa IIae q.57 a.2.

[16]Ibid. IIa IIae q.64 a.7.

[17]Ibid. IIa IIae q.66 a.3.

[18]Ibid. IIa IIae q.66 a.6.

[19]Ibid. IIa IIae q.32 a.7.

[20]Ibid. IIa IIae q.66 a.6.

[21]Ibid. IIa IIae q.61 a.1.

[22]Ibid. IIa IIae q.61 a.2.

[23]Ibid. IIa IIae q.61 a.2.

[24]Ibid. IIa IIae q.61 a.2.

[25]Ibid. IIa IIae q.32 a.7.

[26]Ibid. IIa IIae q.61 a.5.

[27]Ibid. IIa IIae q.61 a.1.

[28]Ibid. IIa IIae q.61 a.5.

[29]Ibid. Ia IIae q.61 a.5.

[30]Ibid. IIa IIae q.58 a.3.

[31]Ibid. Ia IIae q.62 a.1.

[32]Ibid. Ia IIae q.62 a.2.

[33]Ibid. IIa IIae q.24 a.2.

[34]Ibid. Ia IIae q.62 a.4.

[35]Ibid. IIa IIae q.23 a.6.

[36]Ibid. IIa IIae q.23 a.2.

[37]Ibid. IIa IIae q.57 a.4.

[38]Ibid. IIa IIae q.24 a.3.

[39]Ibid. IIa IIae q.57 a.1.

[40]Ibid. IIa IIae q.64 a.6.

[41]Ibid. IIa IIae q.32 a.5.

[42]Ibid. IIa IIae q.57 a.4.

[43]Ibid. IIa IIae q.31 a.1.

[44]Ibid. IIa IIae q.32 a.5.

[45]Ibid. IIa IIae q.32 a.6.

[46]Ferree, Rev. William J.: *Introduction to Social Justice*, (New York: Paulist Press, 1948) 3.

[47]Ibid. 6.

[48]Kelso, Louis O. and Adler, Mortimer J.: *The Capitalist Manifesto*, (New York: Random House, 1958) 53.

[49]Ferree, op. cit. 7.

[50]Ibid. 30-31.

[51]Kelso and Adler, op. cit. 75.

[52]Ibid. 74.

[53]Ibid. 74-75.

[54]Aquinas, op. cit. IIa IIae q.36 a.1.

[55]Ibid. IIa IIae q.32 a.5.

— 4 —

Economic Justice
in the Age of the Robot

by Norman G. Kurland
*(Excerpted from **Toward Economic and Social Justice**,*
Center for Economic and Social Justice, 1986)

Everyone has an inborn aversion to injustice. We can sense injustice in our daily lives, on the job, when we shop, and as we observe life in society. Justice, on the other hand, involves *discovered principles* which can be applied in practical ways to help us resolve and avoid human conflicts.

Throughout history many people have given their lives for "justice." But all too frequently the ideas of justice around which people have rallied were confused, superficial, divisive or just plain wrong. This led to tragic consequences for the heroes — and even worse for the victims — of what seemed to be a noble cause. Often the terms "economic and social justice" were misused describing, not justice, but what were really injustices or unresolved social problems.

In pursuing and implementing justice in today's world, the first challenge is to clarify these terms so that everyone can understand them. The next problem is to develop a conceptual framework and practical methodologies for applying in a practical way in their daily lives universal moral values. This new framework for action must take into account the reality that the Age of the Robot has the potential for expanding the world's productive capacity so that poverty can be eliminated.

Defining Justice

One definition of justice is "giving to each what he or she is due." The problem is knowing what is "due".

Functionally, "justice" is a set of universal principles which guide people in judging what is right and what is wrong, no matter what culture and society they live in. Justice is one of the four cardinal virtues of classical moral philosophy, along with courage, temperance (self-control) and prudence (efficiency). (Added to these are the three religious virtues of faith, hope and charity.) Virtues or "good habits" help individuals to develop fully their human potentials, thus enabling them to serve their own self-interests as well as work in harmony with others for their common good.

The ultimate purpose of all the virtues is to elevate the dignity and sovereignty of the human person.

Distinguishing Justice from Charity

While often confused, justice is distinct from the virtue of charity. Charity, derived from the Latin word *caritas*, or "divine love," is the soul of justice. Justice supplies the material foundation for charity.

While justice deals with the substance and rules for guiding ordinary, everyday human interactions, charity deals with the spirit of human interactions and with those exceptional cases where strict application of the rules is not appropriate or sufficient. Charity offers expedients during times of hardship. Charity compels us to give to relieve the suffering of a person in need. The highest aim of charity is the same as the highest aim of justice: to elevate each person to where he does not need charity but can become charitable himself.

True charity involves giving without any expectation of return. But it is not a substitute for justice.

Philosophical Developments of the Concept of Justice

The mandate "Justice, Justice, thou shalt pursue," we are reminded by the Old Testament, involves the highest duty each person owes to God. (Deut. 16:20). Pursuing justice is a moral imperative. It is not a zero-sum game where one gains only at the expense of another. By pursuing true economic justice, everyone can come out a winner, everyone gains dignity.

Aristotle in his *Ethics* divided justice into two parts: Commutative justice and distributive justice. (See *The Oxford English Dictionary*.) The first deals with exchanges of equal or equivalent value between individuals or groups of individuals. The second deals with a distribution or division of something among various people interacting together in shares proportionate to what each one deserves. These virtues impact directly on the behavior of individuals, not institutions.

The late Father William Ferree discovered in the writings of Pope Pius XI a major breakthrough in moral philosophy. (See works by Rev. William Ferree, S.M., Ph.D., including *The Act of Social Justice*, [Washington, D.C.: Catholic University, 1942] and *Introduction to Social Justice*, [New York: The Paulist Press 1948]) Pius XI pointed out that "social virtues" are separate but complementary to the "individual virtues." While individual virtues describe the moral quality of our individual actions, social virtues describe the moral quality of our *institutions*. For example, individuals may act justly within unjust institutions, and vice versa.

Thus, "social justice" focuses on human institutions and the principles of justice which guide their formation, development, and restructuring. Social institutions affect the behavior of individuals but they are not flesh-and-blood human beings themselves.

Defining Social and Economic Justice

Social justice is the broader concept and encompasses economic justice. Social justice is the virtue which guides us in creating those organized human interactions we call institutions. In turn, social institutions, when justly organized, provide us with access to what is good for the person, both individually and in our associations with others. Social justice also imposes on each of us a personal responsibility to work with others to design and continually perfect our institutions as tools for personal and social development.

Economic justice, which touches the individual person as well as the social order, encompasses the moral principles which guide us in designing our economic institutions. These institutions determine how each person earns a living, enters into contracts, exchanges goods and services with others and otherwise produces an independent material foundation for his or her economic sustenance. The ultimate purpose of economic justice is to free each person to engage creatively in the unlimited work beyond economics, that of the mind and the spirit.

What is Property?

Many people erroneously equate property with material objects, such as land, structures, machines, tools, things. In law, however, property is not the thing owned but rather the *relationships* an "owner" justly acquires (as a result of access to credit or previous creative activity) with respect to things. Private property is a set of rights, powers and privileges that an individual enjoys in his relationship to things. Under the law, these include the rights of (1) possessing, (2) excluding others, (3) disposing or transferring, (4) using, (5) enjoying the fruits, profits, product or increase, and (6) of destroying or injuring, if the owner so desires. These rights are only as effective as the laws which provide for their enforcement. The English common law, adopted into the fabric of American law, recognized that the rights of property are *subject to limitations* that (1) things owned may not be so used as to injure others or the property of others, and (2) that they may not be used in ways contrary to the general welfare of the people as a whole. As a functional matter and in the final analysis, property in everyday life is *the right of control.*

What is Private Property in Corporate Equity?

Next to the State itself, the corporation is one of civilization's greatest social inventions. In the modern world, the most important instrument for organizing private property rights in the means of production takes the form of corporate equity, represented by shares of common stock. These shares allow many owners to share individually and "jointly," not collectively, in the ownership, risks and profits of a modern corporation. The corporation in turn is a convenient legal vehicle which owns "collectively" the land, machines and other assets it needs to produce and market in the global marketplace. While individuals may own shares in a corporation, no shareholder has any legal title to the machinery or other assets owned by the corporation itself.

Why is Private Property Essential
to Economic Justice?

Joint or share ownership provides each shareholder his or her own *definable* private property stake in the corporation and thus decentralizes economic power. In contrast, collective ownership of an enterprise offers no definable stake for any individual owner and thus concentrates power in whoever controls the collective.

Property in the means of production is the primary social "link" between a particular human being and the process of producing and distributing wealth. Property determines who has the right to share in profits, the "wages of ownership." Assuming that economic values are set democratically and freely in a competitive marketplace and that unjust barriers to participation in work and ownership are lifted, property incomes become the key to distributive justice.

Power exists in society whether or not particular individuals own property. If we accept Lord Acton's insight that *"power tends to corrupt and absolute power corrupts absolutely,"* our best safeguard against the corruptibility of concentrated power is decentralized power. And if Daniel Webster is also correct that *"power naturally and inevitably follows the ownership of property,"* then democratizing ownership is essential for democratizing power.

Kelso and Adler:
An Expanded Ownership Theory of Economic Justice

Both the Marxist and the Kelso-Adler theories of economic justice recognize property as an institution essential to controlling income distribution patterns. (See Chapter 5 of *The Capitalist Manifesto*, Louis O. Kelso and Mortimer J. Adler [New York: Random House, 1958; reprinted by Greenwood Press, Westport, Connecticut].) Both agree that where a few individuals own and control industrial capital and the majority of workers own little or no capital, income patterns will become grossly distorted and lead necessarily to the abandonment of the orderly process of supply and demand, and eventually to a breakdown of the property system itself. And without the stability of property, force eventually is required to hold together the social order.

The Marxist and Kelso-Adler theories of economic justice differ mainly on where to place ownership powers and rights over productive capital, and on the best means for preventing ownership from becoming monopolized by a few. Also, Marx recognizes only property in labor (from Ricardo's labor theory of value), denying any personal right to acquire property in capital.

Where Marx, by abolishing private property in corporate equity, would make the State (or collective) the only owner of capital, the Kelso-Adler theory would diffuse access to private property broadly among all members of society. Thus, private property would serve both as the foundation for other fundamental human rights and as the ultimate check on the potential abuses by government or by any political majority against individual liberties and the rights of political minorities.

In the economic world, property performs the same power-diffusion function that the ballot does in politics. It does more. It makes the ballot-holder economically independent of those who wield political power.

The connection between widespread distribution of property and political democracy was evident to America's founders, as was reflected in the 1776 Virginia Declaration of Rights, the forerunner of America's Declaration of Independence and the Bill of Rights. Following John Locke's trinity of fundamental and inalienable rights, the Virginia Declaration of Rights declared that "Life, Liberty, *with the means of acquiring and possessing Property"* are the highest purposes for forming any just government. While access *to* property may be sacred and inalienable, as previously mentioned, the rights *of* property are not unlimited.

With the abolition of slavery and feudalism, the United States ensured that no person would ever again become the property of another. Through this and other limitations on the rights of private property, a just government transcends the weaknesses of a pure "laissez-faire" approach to ownership rights. But by fulfilling its duty to all its citizens to lift barriers to private property in the means of production, government builds a permanent political constituency for a free market economy.

Developing the Role of Private Property in Building a Just Global Marketplace

A major focus of moral philosophers in the Third Millennium should therefore be on the development of a system of economics and long-range strategy for restructuring the economies of the globe into a single common market based on private property, free markets, limited government and the modern business corporation. This strategy would not only restore the original rights of private property in corporate equity for present as well as new owners. It would also provide everyone, as one of the most fundamental of human rights, with the means—including more universal access to productive credit—to become an owner of privately-owned capital instruments.

The Three Principles of Economic Justice

The pursuit of justice is one of the ultimate ends of human life. Borrowing from the Kelso-Adler theory of economic justice (with a slight refinement of their third principle, that of "limitation"), we can see that there are three essential and interdependent pillars of the expanded ownership theory of economic justice: *The Principle of Participation, The Principle of Distribution,* and *The Principle of Harmony.* Like the legs of a three-legged stool, if any of these principles is weakened or missing, the system of economic justice will collapse. Like every system, economic justice involves input, output, and feedback for restoring harmony or balance between input and output.

The Participative Principle

The principle of participation describes how one makes "input" to the economic process, including the human right to private property as well as the right to work. The principle of participation requires

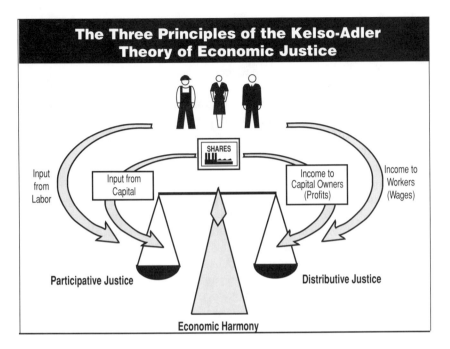

The Three Principles of the Kelso-Adler Theory of Economic Justice

SHARES

Input from Labor

Input from Capital

Income to Capital Owners (Profits)

Income to Workers (Wages)

Participative Justice

Distributive Justice

Economic Harmony

that every person be provided by society's institutions with equal access to make a productive contribution to the economy, both as an owner as well as a worker.

Participative justice is a humanizing alternative to institutionalized charity and governmental redistribution, which tend to become condescending and indifferent to human suffering and negate personal expressions of justice and personal charity. Participative justice is violated by institutions and laws that cause monopolistic or privileged access for a few to participation in ownership of modern instruments of production.

The following guidelines shape the participatory opportunities available to each person in contributing to the common good through the corporation, the labor union, the marketplace and in modern economic life in general:

- The right to life includes the right to earn a living. To enjoy a rich intellectual and spiritual life, each person must have a solid foundation in the material world.
- Both human dignity and equality of economic opportunity require that every person be given access to the means to participate in future private property ownership opportunities, as well as in creative work and self-management.
- The institution of private property — which guarantees a person access to the means to own and control capital tools

as well as the personal right to share in profits — is fundamental for building each person's material base in the modern world.

- New technology in the form of labor-saving and energy-sav-
ing capital tools is a prerequisite for human progress and
the source of material abundance. As human labor is liberated at the economic workplace by new technology, the contributions of workers to the man-machine mix must shift
from their labor inputs to their ownership of new capital
tools.

- In the modern corporation, each worker's property stake
should determine his personal right to share in the productivity gains and profits in the business that uses these tools.
His private property stake in corporate equity also should
determine his power to share in corporate decision-making
and in responsibility for those decisions.

- Participation is more than just gain sharing or profit sharing. It also involves self-governance, which depends on the
sharing of power, responsibility, access to information, accountability and risks.

- Power, responsibility and accountability over policy and operational decisions should always be decentralized and kept
as close as possible to those whose property is at risk. This
is the essence of democratic participation and the concept
of "subsidiarity". Subsidiarity requires that corporate decisions should never be made at higher levels when they
can be made prudently at the workplace. This follows naturally when full ownership rights are widely dispersed among
workers.

- Applied to corporate ownership, widespread citizen participation in ownership also broadens the social accountability of the modern corporation to an expanding base
of shareholders, laying the foundations for a genuine economic democracy, without which political democracy cannot long endure.

- No person should be required to do work that can be done
more efficiently by a machine that he can own.

- As each person becomes economically liberated through
ownership of advancing technology, education should be
provided to help him redirect his "free time" to acquire
knowledge and pursue creative work which enhances the
sovereignty and dignity of each person.

- Allocating among workers access to the capital credit needed
by business is the key to their participation in future ownership opportunities. Capital pays for itself out of future

profits. Thus, neither past savings nor wage reductions are necessary for workers to acquire future ownership.

* The democratization of credit for expanding capital ownership is therefore a fundamental human right, without which economic sovereignty for all is virtually impossible.

The Distributive Principle

The principle of distribution defines the "output" rights of an economic system matched to each person's labor and capital inputs. Through the distributional features of private property within a free and open marketplace, distributive justice becomes automatically linked to participative justice, and incomes to productive contributions.

Many confuse the distributive principles of justice with those of charity. Charity involves the concept "to each according to his needs," whereas "distributive justice" is based on the idea "to each according to his contribution." Furthermore, justice involves the sanctity of property, contracts and the free and open marketplace.

Distributive justice presupposes participative justice, especially the requirement that all persons be given equal opportunity to acquire and enjoy the fruits of income-producing property.

Originally understood as "to each according to his work," the post-industrial version of economic justice requires distribution *"to each according to what he contributes to production."* This modern guiding principle of distributive justice is also consistent with the traditional distributive attribute of private property, which is violated whenever an owner or worker is deprived of the fruits of his productive inputs.

The "private property" distributive principle is essential for motivating people to build and create abundance for all and for converting waste into useful production. Widespread access to capital ownership thus combines justice with efficiency, both at the workplace and in the world marketplace.

Where workers are deprived of equal ownership opportunities, have only their human inputs to contribute to production, and their incomes are threatened by industrial robots, artificial intelligence and other labor-saving technologies, the laws of supply and demand make their family incomes less secure.

But as all members of society, including the most handicapped persons, begin to derive ever-increasing incomes from their shares of ownership of industrial capital, the competitive market mechanism—instead of harming working people—can be allowed to operate as the most democratic and objective means for measuring just prices, just wages and just profits. Individual choice will govern in the marketplace.

Once consumer sovereignty can be expanded through rising ownership incomes and statesmen begin to favor greater reliance on a more just free market system, basic economic decisions of production, investment and resource allocation (subject to reasonable social regulation) can begin to be made on a more decentralized and personalized basis. Such democratic modes of economic decision-making would stand in sharp contrast to today's highly centralized, subjective, arbitrary, coercive, and bureaucratic mechanisms for guiding economic development.

The basic guidelines of distributive justice are as follows:

- An individual's earnings should be proportional to his or her contributions to overall production. Demanding to be rewarded for the labor or capital contributions of others is the equivalent of stealing. State-forced redistribution of income from one to another rests, therefore, on shaky moral grounds.
- One right of private property requires that an owner receive the free market-determined fruits of his human inputs as well as the free market-determined share of profits, reflecting his capital inputs.
- Distribution based on productive input (the distributive principle derived from private property) stands in sharp contrast to the principle, "to each according to his needs." The first distributive principle is indispensable for *justice* and for motivating people to produce wealth. The second is a guiding principle of *charity*, the necessity for which is reduced to the extent justice is realized for all.
- Where the ownership of a nation's wealth-producing enterprises is widely distributed throughout society, just prices, just wages and just profits are best determined by the free and competitive marketplace, not coercively or by mercantilist or protectionist government policies.
- Forced equality *of results* and artificial leveling holds back human development and causes human conflict. Equality *of opportunity*, on the other hand, is vital to the liberation and continuing perfection of each person.
- Under widespread capital ownership and a free market economy, capital incomes should automatically increase relative to labor incomes when capital productiveness increases faster than labor productiveness.
- All should pay fair value in exchange for what they receive in the economic marketplace. A global free marketplace should be actively encouraged so that consumers can receive the highest values at the lowest possible costs.

The Harmony or Balancing Principle

The principle of harmony encompasses the "feedback" or balancing principles required to detect distortions of either the input or output principles and to make whatever corrections are needed to restore a just and balanced economic order for all.

"Economic harmonies" is defined in *The Oxford English Dictionary* as "Laws of social adjustment under which the self-interest of one man or group of men, if given free play, will produce results offering the maximum advantage to other men and the community as a whole." This principle offers guidelines for controlling monopolies, building checks-and-balances within social institutions, and re-synchronizing distribution (outtake) with participation (input). The first two principles of economic justice flow from the eternal human search for justice in general, which automatically requires a balance between input and outtake, i.e., "to each according to what he is due." The principle of harmony, on the other hand, reflects the human quest for other absolute values, including Truth, Love and Beauty.

In the field of economics this balancing between input and outtake is reflected in Aristotle's commutative or "exchange" justice. Balancing principles are also incorporated in double-entry bookkeeping, the logic of an individual enterprise. It is also the logic of a market economy, as first suggested by the French 18th century economist Jean Baptiste Say. Say's Law postulated that in a free market economy, supply would create its own demand, and demand its own supply.

Notwithstanding the logic of Say's Law, *the history of politics is largely a history of ill-fated attempts to repeal the laws of supply and demand, alongside efforts of a few to monopolize economic power and privilege.* Historically political interferences with the market system seem to follow when the majority of citizens begin to perceive seemingly insurmountable institutional barriers to equal access to productive credit and expanded ownership opportunities. As a result, free market policies have seldom if ever been supported by a broad political constituency, with the rare historical exception in settling America's vast land frontier.

There is one thing Karl Marx and John Maynard Keynes agreed upon: they both condemned Say's Law, but for different reasons. Following either Marx or Keynes, most modern political economists (except for the modern followers of Adam Smith) also reject Say's Law.

Marx pointed out that Say's Law would not work in a market economy (1) where workers could only participate as workers, not owners (2) where there was a growing global supply of workers because of rising populations and lowered world migration barriers; (3) where emerging technologies continue to take over tasks formerly

performed by workers; (4) where new technology and expanding profits automatically flowed into the hands of a small ownership class;
and (5) where owners would be forced to invest any excesses in their
incomes into ever-larger accumulations of productive assets. "Capital breeds capital," as Marx described the traditional system of capitalist finance. "Supply could not create its own demand," as Say had
asserted. The purchasing power (demand) generated by the non-owning majority in any economy expanding under pure "laissez-faire capitalism" would never be enough to purchase all marketable goods and
services which an expanding industrial economy was capable of producing. Marx's logic was clearly right, "the rich would get richer and
the poor poorer" under monopoly capitalism.

On the other hand, Keynes, in trying to make capitalism work
without reforming ownership patterns, dismissed Say's Law by ignoring supply, at least for the short run. Keynes noted that a "free
market" economy failed to provide sufficient "elasticity" in prices
and wage rates to clear the market in times of massive unemployment and oversupply. Keynes thus focused exclusively on the demand side of the economic equation. The solution, according to
Keynes, was to "fine-tune" the economy by artificially increasing
mass purchasing power through governmental intervention in tax
policy, wage rates, interest rates, money and credit policies, welfare schemes and other public sector reforms, all aimed at generating "full employment", not universal participation in ownership
and profit distributions.

Perhaps the most important contribution made by Louis Kelso
was to revive the logic of Say's Law as a means for restoring an equilibrium between aggregate supply and aggregate demand (mass purchasing power) within the context of a market economy. Under
conditions of widespread citizen access to capital credit (in contrast
to consumer or nonproductive credit), leading to universal participation in ownership and profit distributions, Say's Law could be made
to work in an industrial world. Demand would create its own supply,
and supply its own demand. Capital growth would be matched by
consumer incomes ready to buy the marketable goods and services
produced by those new capital assets.

The following figure shows how Say's Law of Markets would work
under a system structured in ways consistent with Kelso's binary
theory of economics.

Widespread citizen participation as owners of capital would also
change politics by creating a political buffer against historic attacks
on free market principles. It would produce an expanding political
constituency necessary to shift control over the economy from government to a more dynamic, decentralized and just private sector.

Consistent with the principle of harmony are the following guidelines:

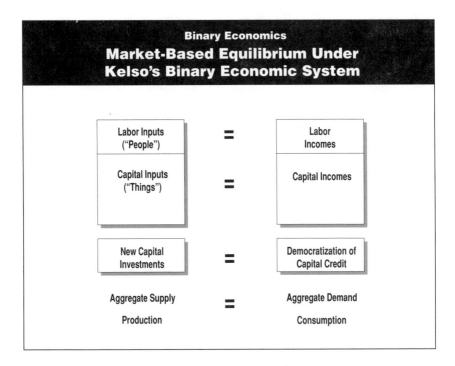

- Justice in distribution *follows* justice in participation. Where the Principle of Participation is violated, social pressures increase for arbitrary and subjective substitutes for private property for determining just income distributions. Thus, to safeguard property rights, the first social duty of every person is to work together with others to help change economic institutions which violate the Principle of Participation.
- As the most effective check on the State or on concentrated private economic power, private property should be made widely accessible, particularly to workers.
- All private property rights should be fully restored with respect to ownership shares in the modern corporation, society's most advanced social tool for organizing production and distributing incomes broadly. Since the right to property is an inalienable right, the derivative rights of property—e.g., rights to profits and shareholder voting—must not be violated either by government or by majority shareholders.
- In addition to its production and marketing functions, the most important social role of the corporation is to decentralize future ownership, especially among its own workers, and thus recapture from government the primary role for distributing mass purchasing power.

- The democratic labor union, whose primary social duty is to promote economic justice for workers, should undergo continual restructuring and self-renewal to gain for its members more just and widespread future access to private property rights in income-producing assets.
- The primary economic duties of the State are to respect and enforce contracts, to protect individual property rights, and to pursue economic justice by lifting all barriers to expanded ownership and free trade within a more participatory global enterprise system.
- Ultimately, the State, deriving its powers from the consent of the governed, represents two legitimate potential monopolies: one over society's instruments of coercion and the other in controlling the creation of money and credit. No other monopolies should be tolerated.
- The antidote for economic and other nongovernmental monopolies is competition. The key to competition is access to credit. To encourage new enterprises to compete with economic monopolies that may develop, the State must therefore ensure the availability of broad-based access to future capital credit for potential competitors.
- The power of government at any level to own or redistribute productive capital should be drastically curtailed. State-owned enterprises should be reorganized into profitable stock corporations and sold on credit to their employees and other citizens.
- Tax laws, inheritance laws, laws affecting corporations and unions, welfare and social security laws, public employee pension programs, antitrust laws and other laws reflecting national income and monetary policies should be reexamined and reformed to encourage maximum rates of private sector expansion, but through means that ensure expanded share ownership opportunities for all members of society.

Conclusion

In conclusion, we are reminded of the words of Pope Paul VI, "If you want peace, work for justice." While the elegance of the Kelso-Adler theory of economic justice offers much to guide us in restoring harmony to the social order, we should remind ourselves that the work of restructuring the social order is never finished. Social justice perfected is beyond human grasp. But since justice is a moral imperative, we are all called to pursue it endlessly.

— 5 —

Reevaluating Private Enterprise

by Lorenzo Servitje Sendra
(Extracted and edited from
"Reflections of a Latin-American Entrepreneur About Enterprise,"
Socio-Economic Papers No. 6, UNIAPAC, Brussels, 1991.
Original Translation by Laura de Laney and John M. Lamb.
Endnote Commentary by the Editor.)

Private Enterprise:
A Key to the Sustained Growth of Nations

The majority of Latin-American countries are hit by serious economic problems which express themselves by lowering the standard of living and by destroying hopes of recovery in the near future. In addition to exorbitant debt, other problems include inflation, high unemployment, government deficits, lowering of export prices, suburban and rural marginalization, grave delays in development combined in some areas with population explosions, and the barely realizable hopes of large parts of the populace.

In the economic recovery of Latin America, private enterprise and the entrepreneur have a role which is not only important, but decisive. Countries must increase their efficiency, productivity and productive investments, create jobs, improve the quality of their products, incorporate new technologies, and stimulate export activities. The experience of the last few decades demonstrates that private enterprise is all the better for accomplishing these tasks.

As the business enterprise is an essential social cell and the fundamental driving force of an economy, it is crucial to reexamine closely the enterprise and to promote it in light of this reappraisal.

Evolution of the Enterprise

There is undoubtedly, in general, a misunderstanding and even rejection of business. Nevertheless, there has been a change in perception over the last few years: more and more prevalent is the conviction that the entrepreneur is a professional, a creator of wealth and generator of jobs, and that society needs his entrepreneurial capacity. It is increasingly understood that, without the entrepreneur, society is condemned to underdevelopment.

Entrepreneurial activity is as old as human history. The elements of entrepreneurial organization (albeit in embryonic form) are evident in the hunts of primitive man: a group of men, the leadership of a chief, weapons as means of production, orderly assignment of tasks, division of work, and the corresponding remuneration by sharing the quarry.

In ancient times, particularly in Egypt, more sophisticated forms of business evolved. Later, the craftsmen of the Middle Ages comprised what would be called today "the small business." Where you had a business activity with the master craftsman owning the capital equipment and raw materials, while directing and carrying out a good deal of the actual work with the participation of the journeymen and apprentices, this would qualify that human group as an enterprise. The large commercial and maritime companies of the later Middle Ages could be considered enterprises in the broadest meaning of the term.

However, it is from the Industrial Revolution that business assumed the form recognized today. Its size increased, capital was aggregated and allowed for more important investments, products were standardized, specialization increased, surpluses were produced, and the division into capital owners, management and labor became more marked.

From the social point of view, the results of classic capitalist enterprise have been severely censured: long and exhausting hours in the field, factory, or mine; unhealthy and dangerous working conditions; despotic management; enfeebled day laborers; and constant insecurity. Countless men have had their lives consumed in hopeless misery.

Over time, there has been a reaction to this situation. Revolutionaries and social reformers have emerged. Exploited workers have started a slow and painful struggle to gain their rights. The workers' movements, often peaceful, sometimes violent, the political pressures and progressive introduction of labor laws have all had a decisive influence. Unions on the one side and the state on the other, have intervened in areas formerly reserved exclusively to owners and management.

Furthermore, some entrepreneurs who were embarrassed by the social upheaval and who had a vision of the future, introduced improvements in their businesses. Techniques for improving efficiency and job security made their appearance, and later, methods for strengthening human relations. Trade unionism and collective bargaining were solidly established. The institution of social security began to expand. From this developed today's labor relations which aim to give the worker more protections, higher wages, more humane treatment, and better working conditions.

Today we see a great variety of businesses in Latin America. These range from small, informal operations—a new world we have barely explored—to large corporations with many anonymous shareholders and which are run by professional management. Many of these enterprises are international in scope, and have at their disposal large accumulations of capital, many workers and advanced technology, as well as an interlocking network of businesses of diverse types, varying in size and in degrees of development.

Nature of Enterprise

But what, after all, is an enterprise?

Generally, we define an enterprise as a productive entity in which capital and labor combine in order to produce economic benefits. This is a true definition, but it is incomplete. A business enterprise is something more. It is a human invention, an instrument conceived by man to satisfy better his own needs and those of others.

An enterprise can be defined as a free association of persons who come together to produce saleable goods and services, bringing their capital, management skills and/or labor, with the objective of obtaining just returns for their contributions.

Put another way, an enterprise or business is a service instrument which has two basic and inextricably linked outcomes: (1) an external economic outcome which serves society outside the company by offering goods and services to the consumer; and (2) an internal economic outcome which serves those inside the company—investors, managers and workers—by producing wealth that is distributed through dividends and equity growth to the investors, and through wages, salaries, benefits and other forms of compensation to managers and workers.

Risk: A Seemingly Unknown Factor

An important characteristic of a business is that it finds itself almost permanently in a state of risk. Its products may not be able to compete in quality or price or may lose public acceptance; credit may be cut off; social upheavals may upset the market; its technology may become obsolete; it may fall victim to unrestrained competition; or price controls may be imposed. Unfortunately, neither government nor the general public have a sufficient understanding of the risk factor, which is, nevertheless, a critical element in the life of a business.

Capital and Work

One of the elements of business is capital. The material goods that the investors bring to the business are indispensable for making work more productive, whether the work is managerial or operational. Raúl Prebisch said, many years ago, that one of the causes of the underdevelopment in Latin America was under-capitalization.

In order for this contribution to the productive process to exist in Latin America, a high rate of savings is indispensable.[1] This, in turn, demands that chronic inflation be eliminated and that we create a culture which encourages high rates of savings. The role of savings and capital in business and in economic life is unfortunately little understood by the public.[2]

Work (also referred to as labor) is a vital factor in business. It is generally considered a simple resource—hence the term "human resource." It is with this concept of labor that ownership or management signs a contract, uses this "resource," manipulates it or dismisses it. In addition, there exists the so-called "adversarial" or "conflict" relationship, where workers view themselves as outsiders in the enterprise, and accomplish their tasks only by virtue of the authority and coercion of management.

The Entrepreneurial Spirit

The fundamental dynamic factor of a business is that of the entrepreneur, as understood in the Schumpeterian sense of the term. That is, the entrepreneur is the creator and promoter of the business, the one who sees the opportunities, fixes the objectives, assumes the risks, rallies and organizes his work force, locates and obtains the material resources, and thus renders more productive the labor used to produce goods.[3]

There is no doubt that, in reevaluating private enterprise, we need to recognize the vital initiative and key role of the entrepreneur in the process of production. Unfortunately, in many countries it is the merchant—he who seeks only to trade what others have produced—who prevails, rather than the entrepreneur, who usually has a broader and more creative view of his function.

What is the Image of the Latin American Entrepreneur?

By virtue of protectionist policies, the industrial sector in many Latin-American countries suffers from poor product quality, lack of innovation, and high costs. Frequently, the owners of an enterprise wish only to get rich quickly; they have only a short-term vision. As these owners view the enterprise as "just a business," they make no effort to improve conditions or to modernize. The enterprise exists precariously for a number of years, and finally disappears.

While there are prosperous family-owned businesses, they are far outnumbered by those that fail in the second generation. The majority of businesses continue to be the exclusive domain of their owners, with authoritarian management and a work force treated as outsiders, with no attempt made to integrate workers into the life of the company.

The concept of the social responsibility of the enterprise is little understood. Although there are national (state-owned) and foreign enterprises in existence—some of which play an important role in the economies of various Latin-American countries—many of them suffer from high fixed wages due to administrative inefficiencies or union pressures. In larger enterprises there is the risk of bureaucratization and wasteful spending, although bureaucracy and spending are indispensable in all business enterprises.

Up to this point we have referred to the enterprise mainly in terms of private enterprise. What about public enterprise?

Some Characteristics of the Public Enterprise

Without a doubt, some reasonably well-managed state-owned enterprises exist, comparable to many private ones. But, in general, it is true in many countries that public enterprises are less efficient than those in the private sector. There are many reasons for this. Notably, upper management in state-owned enterprises are appointed for political reasons, do not have the necessary entrepreneurial or management skills, and their tenure is usually short. Thus it is difficult for them to develop a long-term strategy. They are not bound to the results of the business, and are therefore not affected by mediocre performance or failure. Furthermore, in public enterprises, the possibility of bureaucratic inertia, weakness in the face of union pressures, unproductive practices, wasteful spending and corruption is much greater.

In order to survive and develop fully, private business needs to evolve in a free market system. What Winston Churchill said about democracy can also be said of the free market: "[I]t is the worst of systems, except for all the others." This suggests why the market economy should not be understood as merely a laissez-faire system. The modern and socially responsible view is that the market—an invaluable instrument for assigning resources with higher efficiency and greater productivity—may sometimes need some corrections, adjustments and complements as required for the common good, but which do not violate its fundamental precepts. If the free market is interfered with, the rational allocation of resources is distorted and black markets appear, as well as tax evasion, an underground economy, and other economic aberrations.

The Social Market Economy

Economist Wilhelm Röpke said of the market economy: "[I]t is a system of contractual relations of millions of isolated economies, which find themselves in complex relations one with another but which, thanks to the market mechanism, combine in a well-ordered entity. It is a combination of freedom and order which probably constitutes the largest measure of what can be obtained simultaneously from the two. In addition, this combination has brought humanity the advantage of an enormous augmentation of well-being."

Röpke maintains that a well-ordered free market economy needs a system of clearly delineated responsibilities assigned to the state: a sound monetary system and prudent credit policies; a legal system which prevents as much as possible abuses in the free market and which recognizes that success is only reached by the real performance of services; and, lastly, a multitude of means and institutions which minimize the numerous imperfections of the free market, with particular emphasis placed upon correcting the maldistribution of wealth, and on the safety and protection of the weak.

The efficient functioning of the market economy and its resulting productivity are due not only to its capacity to adapt to an infinite number of unforeseeable circumstances and unknown variables, but also to the enormous volume of information widely dispersed among millions and millions of people—the whole of society, in fact—which may never come under the control of the planning authorities. This mass of information, which the free market makes use of automatically, is never complete at any given moment. It constantly expands due to the diligence of millions of human beings who are motivated by the rewards to be gained for their intelligence and effort.

How do We Define the Enterprise?

Those who assume the responsibility of reevaluating the enterprise face the question of whether or not the concept of business as it exists today is the right one. Is it truly the form of business we want? Is it a good instrument in the service of man—of the whole human being? Does it answer his needs and favor his complete development?

In the exercise of economic activity, private business has produced some undoubted advantages. In general, it has offered the public sufficient goods when needed, and an efficient distribution of goods and services. Thanks to the diffusion of credit,[4] it has augmented the purchasing power of large sectors of the population and has brought them, through advertising, knowledge of new and useful goods. The economies of scale made possible through mass production have made higher quality goods available at a lower price.

Nevertheless, business is open to reproach for its obsession with profit, and for the fact that it does not take into account in its objectives and practices those values which are not strictly economic. Private enterprise can also be criticized for using workers as objects and deliberately exploiting them. In certain cases, profits result from simple speculation rather than from creative activity. In addition, business has often subordinated everything to economic measurement and technical processes while totally disregarding the deterioration or contamination of the environment.[5]

How Should We Define the Enterprise?

There exists in business a clear tension between moral and economic demands, which are implicit in free enterprise. But, all things considered, actions which are undertaken in business are human actions; they are therefore inevitably governed by ethics. This leads into a discussion about the work of man, freedom, responsibility, justice and solidarity.

It is said that business is private, but it is, at the same time, both public and highly social. It is an economic cell and at the same time a social one. The enterprise is tied to those who enter into contact with it in a more or less direct manner, such as shareholders, workers, clients, suppliers and competitors. But it is also linked to that extraordinary variety of groups and communities in society, such as the family, neighborhood, school, church, labor union, political party, cultural and athletic association, fraternal and charitable organization, and the state itself.

It has been said that behind the abstract concepts of capital and labor are concrete human beings. These are the investors and workers who wish to be treated as people, and rewarded in accordance with their respective contributions. In the same way, it can be said that behind the abstract "consumer" there exist real human beings who hope to receive real value for the price they pay, to be treated as people, and to be reasonably served.

The Social Responsibility of the Enterprise

A sense of service within business is essential. From that is derived the social responsibility of business. There is no doubt that the first social responsibility of business is to fulfill its economic role and purposes. But, at the same time, and inseparable from that economic function, is the responsibility that business has to realize its social objectives: to contribute to the complete development of its members and of society as a whole, not just by not undermining fundamental social values, but by actively promoting them as much as possible.

One economic aspect of business that has immense social impact is its capacity to create employment. Society expects much from business in this regard. In earlier times it was easier for man to engage in productive activity. In today's industrial society, which is predominantly urban, a man in most cases needs a job in order to earn a living. To do this, he asks an enterprise, which has at its disposal the means of production, techniques, organization and financial resources, to make use of his labor. There is a great responsibility for private enterprise to respond to this social demand. The entrepreneur (who has been defined as the person who has the ability to invest) is obliged to create sources of work, to expand and improve them, and to make them efficient and productive.[6]

Business has the responsibility of conserving and multiplying the human contributions and the material resources at its disposal; it must, as a consequence of its very nature, generate profits. Samuel Gompers, the American labor leader, said that the greatest crime that can be committed against a worker is for a business to lose sight of its need to earn profits, because when a business closes its doors, work disappears.

Closely related to this necessity of making profits is an enterprise's need to attain a high rate of productivity. An enterprise with high productivity (and thus, presumably, high profitability) not only pays a larger dividend to the shareholders, but can also offer better prices or higher quality products, pay its workers better wages, and pay more taxes.[7] Productivity is of such great importance that the Federation of Belgian Enterprises came to the conclusion in 1955 that it constitutes a moral obligation, not only for the owner and manager of an enterprise, but also for all those who work within it.

Emphasis on the Human Aspect

The view that the enterprise is not only an economic entity, but equally a social one—where a worker not only earns a living, but is also recognized as a human being and is given the opportunity to exercise his full potential—has long been a fundamental thesis of Christian social thinking.

It must be reaffirmed that the worker does not enter the workplace simply as a factor of production. He comes with all his being: body and soul, worries and illusions, strengths and weaknesses. The worker goes into the company where he spends the greater part of his day, with the hope that he will be taken into consideration as an individual, and will be given the chance to develop his abilities and give his best—in short, to be someone. The enterprise must respond to the need of every human person to participate with all his capabilities, not only to meet the demand for economic efficiency, but also as its moral duty.

In reevaluating business, it is first necessary to reevaluate the men who work in business. With this goal in mind, fundamental social principles must be maintained, among which are the dignity of the human person, the value and meaning of work, solidarity, subsidiarity and private property.

Dignity of the Human Person

By his rationality, free will and eternal destiny, man is a being whose dignity is superior to that of all other creatures. Thus it follows that there be a set of inviolable and inalienable rights for him. The dignity of man, which is also present in the most humble of workers, must be recognized and respected. The contribution of the worker to the enterprise is of a superior quality in comparison to that of the outside investor. The latter contributes what he possesses; the former contributes what he is. The encyclical *Laborem Exercens* clearly emphasizes this priority of labor over capital.[8]

Value and Meaning of Work

Work is integral to man. It allows him not only to earn a living, but also to realize his full human potential. Man develops by working. The principal alienation of the worker is, not that he is not the owner of the means of production, nor in not directing the work he carries out, but in considering his work as a necessary evil, as a simple means of subsistence. In order to liberate the worker from his contempt toward work, it is essential to restore the dignity and meaning of work in the greatest sense possible. Shigeru Kobayashi, author of *The Creative Administration*, says that work without meaning is a vice—that only work having meaning is virtuous, and that the mission of every business leader is to give dignity and meaning to work, even if only, at the very least, one wants the workers to carry out the work with interest and enthusiasm.[9]

Solidarity

Within an enterprise, solidarity refers to the interdependence of everyone who is engaged in that enterprise—investors, management and workers. They have many common and complementary objectives, as well as particular needs and divergent objectives. They will not be able to meet their particular needs in a reasonable way without a balanced negotiation between their divergent objectives.

Solidarity implies that each individual takes care of the whole, and that each one feels the necessity of contributing as much as he can to the common good. This presumes that everyone in the business is interested in its prosperity, in its realization of profits, in a fair level of salaries, in decent working conditions, in product quality, and in the profitability of the enterprise. Solidarity means that the worker becomes an integral part of the business, and that he commits himself fully to the extent he identifies fully with the company's objectives.

Subsidiarity

In an enterprise, the principle of subsidiarity refers to the willingness of management to promote the responsibility and development of those in lower echelons every day by giving them more information and delegating more decisions: "As many decisions as possible by subordinates, as many decisions as necessary by superiors." This rule, which actually is implicit in many participation programs, permits those who work in a business to develop and assume the responsibility of a greater contribution to the enterprise.

Private Property

The right to private property is the right of individuals and groups to possess goods in a private way. This is considered as the best means of preserving these goods, of retaining them, of increasing and distributing them in order to contribute to the development of man.

There is a clear social aim in the possession of private property which limits the arbitrary or absolute use of goods. The purpose of a real economy is the service of man, in which private enterprise occupies a fundamental position. This implies, of course, a harmonious interaction among the principles described above.

By virtue of his human dignity, man has to exercise his freedom, but he must do it in a responsible way. In other words, he must submit his freedom to the demands of the common good. To live in and enjoy the benefits of society, the individual must associate with other men. However, in his relationship with others, the individual must be subsidiary in order to help or let himself be helped (depending on the situation); and he must always take into consideration the needs and potentialities of others.

Private property is indispensable to man. It gives him the possibility of developing his dignity, freedom and growth to a greater degree. Private property must, however, also be submitted to the needs of others.[10]

Initiative and Responsible Freedom

The plan of an economy that is truly at the service of man must integrate in society the forces which give it balance, stability, and the capacity to resist destructive forces, both internal and external.

One of these forces, which arises from freedom yet has often been denied or repressed, is self interest. Carlos Llano said that there coexists in the human being, on the one hand, the propensity to acquire and accumulate (*desiderium*) and, on the other hand, to give and share (*effusio*). Although these two forces are often present in the same person, we must recognize that self interest is normally foremost. From self interest rises creativity, innovation, prudence, thrift, perseverance, and risk-taking—all qualities which develop as soon as freedom and initiative exist.

Freedom, the fundamental value of man, must be linked to his immediate interest if it is to be shown that it is a force worthy of a free and democratic society. Man has the freedom to attain something, to arrive at the goal he chooses. He is rewarded if the chosen goal is good and it is reached, just as he is penalized if the chosen goal is not good or is not reached. Responsibility—the ability to accept the consequences of one's acts—is the logical complement to freedom. And the concrete interests bound to private property are obviously more capable of instilling freedom and responsibility in the foundations of the social order.

Free initiative makes the role of the entrepreneur possible. Sombart, Weber and Strieder, the great sociologists and historians of the early twentieth century, noted that it is the modern entrepreneurial spirit nourished by multiple sources which has provided the impetus for present economic development.

Development and economic growth principally depend on the contribution of business. The natural creativity of man is reinforced by the entrepreneurial spirit. The enterprise which bases itself upon productive private property gives to an important sector of society something which remains alienated from the rest of society.

Progress and national development depend essentially on the existence of creative and dynamic business leaders. To claim that there would be productive activity without entrepreneurs is the same as saying that there would be medicine without physicians. A society which despises or is hostile to the entrepreneur seriously compromises its economic future.

Human Relations of Internal Collaboration

Understanding and cooperation between the entrepreneur and the workers is also a fundamental necessity. Much has been said about the existence in business of the "adversarial relationship." This idea was developed by those who think that the class struggle is always the rule, and that the worksite is more a battleground which separates, than a meeting place which unifies. The truth, most entrepreneurs would state, is that while tensions and conflicts do exist in business, the prevailing spirit is that of cooperation and harmony. A permanent task of every business leader is precisely to see that the "adversarial relationship" does not become part of his enterprise, and to strive to create a spirit of unity and cooperation.

The human aspect of the enterprise must be emphasized in order to revive relations between supervisors and subordinates at all levels by introducing in these relations the respect that each person merits as a human being. Everyone in an enterprise must be imbued with the strictest sense of justice and mutual confidence. Each must be inspired with the esteem and affection that is owed to a neighbor, including that neighbor in our professional life who is an employee, colleague or supervisor.

This recognition of common humanity must reach its culmination in one of the great aims of Christian social thinking, which is to convert workers from simple factors of production into real associates within the enterprise. In this way workers can identify themselves completely with the enterprise, assuming as their own its objectives, ideas, problems, projects and results.

What we seek to embody in the enterprise is eloquently described by Lawrence Miller in his recent book. When workers at the Preston Trucking Company were asked if they worked for the company, they responded: "Listen, my friend, we don't work for Preston Trucking. We are Preston Trucking."

The Enterprise Devalued

Many governments in their economic policies seem to forget the potential which exists in private enterprise, and relegate it to a secondary or lower role in a program of national economic recovery. This is due to the fact that these policies are dictated by incomplete and even erroneous conceptions of private enterprise. It is not uncommon for these misconceptions to result from many diverse radical ideologies, which contribute to the discrediting of private enterprise. Sometimes these misconceptions of private enterprise are also based on experiences of businesses which carried out their function in an irresponsible, harmful, or antisocial manner. Additionally, the public often has an equally incomplete and distorted view of business—its aims, the necessary profitability, and the role of the entrepreneur.

Thus we have an urgent duty to rehabilitate the view of the private enterprise held, not only by governments and many parts of society, but also among entrepreneurs themselves. But what should we do, and what specifically can we do?

Hope

First and foremost, we must have hope. Recently, John Paul II said, "After years of open or subtle conflict, more and more segments of the population are about to discover the indispensable contribution that the entrepreneurial risk and professionalism of business leaders bring to social progress. It is recognized that without entrepreneurs and leaders no modern organization of enterprise is conceivable. Nor without them can there be constant adjustments between the demands of the market, the hopes of the workers and the requirements of proper entrepreneurial management—on which depends the health of the economic and social system."

Recognition of the Social Value of Economic Benefits

It is imperative that we as entrepreneurs reflect more upon the nature of our enterprise. We must understand that the obligation of the entrepreneur to obtain economic benefits is indissolubly linked to the performance of a service to society, to such an extent that it cannot be said which takes priority. We must understand that entrepreneurs are not alone in business. An enterprise is in no way a means solely for personal enrichment, but it constitutes a human group to which each one can contribute by giving of his best, if it is directed in an appropriate way. We must understand that an enterprise starts, grows and develops within a given society, and that it inevitably has a social responsibility. From this viewpoint, creating a conscience within the world of business leaders is fundamental.

Broadening Our Horizons

It is also indispensable that business and its leaders have a broader vision of their role in economic and social life. Gabriel Zaid, in a recent article, wrote that the advanced countries have converted themselves into nations of wage earners; that business, in its intense desire for economic growth, removes more and more opportunities from the small and medium entrepreneurs who continue to be the most efficient in the use of capital; and that a proliferation of small and medium-sized enterprises, as well as of one-person enterprises, is radically necessary for a healthy economic and social life.

Every day we learn more about the importance of the informal economy with its hundreds of thousands of small owners. Japan has a widespread network of small businesses, and Italy is also well known for the economic strength that its small businesses represent. Opportunities must be offered to allow new entrepreneurs to appear. Businesses should, where possible, turn more frequently to subcontracting, and facilitate the birth and development of secondary industries, or support industries which have a greater possibility of efficiency and economy.

Teaching the Meaning of Business

An important task for the entrepreneur is to strive to teach the worker about the nature of business in general, how it works, the role of capital, the costs, taxes, and what brings about productivity, profitability and economic benefits. It is indispensable that every employee in every company know the objectives, policies, work plans, risks, problems, and results. It is worthwhile teaching this material in training courses offered to employees.

A similar communications strategy must be used to educate the public in general, and students in particular. What has been realized in Mexico by an institution named Desarrollo Empresarial Mexicano (Mexican Business Development) is remarkable in this regard. This institution promotes the creation of small experimental enterprises among the young while they are still studying. It encourages them, supports them and orients them in their projects.[11]

Interaction With Other Sectors of Society

Another important element in restoring the full social value of the enterprise is promoting contact between businesses and other social groups, as well as with the government. This is with a view to contributing not only to the solution of problems which directly affect the enterprise, but also to those which have a higher social and economic significance.

The enterprise is not an island. Communication, negotiation and dialogue are more and more concerned with human relations. In Latin-American countries, there is a great deal to be learned in this area. We should also take note of Japan, a country in which the entrepreneurs, the workers and the government arrive at mutually profitable agreements, which reflect a clear vision of common interests.

To arrive at this, governments must cooperate with the business community and become aware of the fact that by reducing the regulatory burden and encouraging enterprise, they contribute to the development and prosperity of the people. A program to bring together entrepreneurs and officials who are responsible for the economy is indispensable. The barriers of ignorance and of mutual distrust must fall.

The same effort must be carried out with the workers. The "adversarial relationship" must be eliminated. A new climate must be established in our enterprises. Communication must always remain open. Solutions must be sought by patient and sincere dialogue—in accepting agreements, partial agreements if necessary, which are bringers of hope.

The Great Potential of Business

We must have a high and noble concept of enterprise; We must have the capacity to spread this ideal among others in society; we must convince them. Business is, and can be, many things:

- A place where workers are trained and where they develop; a place where they may gain, not only the means of subsistence, but also the possibility of, and help in, growing and improving themselves;

- A center of freedom where people can express themselves in a responsible way, act on their initiative, make use of their faculties, and realize their potential as human beings;
- A fundamental social organization which gathers together people in a productive activity and which, on the whole, contributes to integrating a growing and viable private sector into society; this constitutes a legitimate counterweight to the often intrusive action of the state;
- A community where the virtues of solidarity and fraternity are exemplified. As work becomes more and more separated from the family, it demands sentiments of confidence and affection as profound as those that bind the family together. Each person must feel totally a member of the business; he must feel that he is appreciated and taken into consideration.
- An active center of production where a spirit of creativity and progress exists; where efficiency and profit have a high and worthy rank; where work—a profound vocation of mankind—is not considered as servitude, but as a full and free exercise of his best abilities; and, lastly, a center of production where everyone contributes to the measure of his capabilities, so that it becomes more efficient, and it consolidates and develops itself; and, finally,
- A model for society. People look more and more to business as a place to work or to invest their savings. A business, through the consistency of its objectives, the complete development of its employees, its constructive prosperity and its profound sense of the human spirit, must exhibit an exemplary nature to the community, in order that other professional groups may receive guidance and encouragement from it.

Beyond Wage Earning

We have already seen that non-ownership itself is not the cause of worker alienation since the real cause is a contempt for work and dependence on a unilateral authority which is based on the possession of capital. We have also seen that participation in the decision-making process attempts to remedy the situation. The ownership of a few shares in a company will not necessarily cause a worker to develop a totally different attitude towards the firm for which he works. On the other hand, *there can be no doubt that if a coherent policy of profit-sharing and participation in the decision-making process has been pursued within the overall context of the real integration of a worker into his firm, his part-ownership of it will strengthen the whole process.*

Being Authentic Entrepreneurs

We must revalidate the enterprise, but to do this in a real way, business itself will most certainly have to be transformed. The task of transformation inevitably belong to the entrepreneur. Thus we must be authentic entrepreneurs.

In conclusion are offered the words of an Argentinian entrepreneur. He wrote the following about the authenticity of the entrepreneur:

> If there are no sales, if the prices are not fair, if bureaucratic difficulties block this or that way, it is exactly at that moment that we feel we are entrepreneurs, and to act as entrepreneurs. One of the most remarkable industrialists of the province where we find ourselves said recently: "There are enterprises which develop, even in times of crisis. Its leaders are crazy. I am crazy." He was referring to the specific lunacy of genius, to that fervor that no one can retain. The geniuses who look for new roads, who do not waste time in complaining, who do not resign themselves, who do not hope that the state or luck will comfort them—these are entrepreneurs. Our challenge today is to be authentic entrepreneurs.

Comments by Editor:

[1] Servitje makes his case for increased capital investment financed solely through past savings without reference to the role that productive credit (which is repaid with future savings, or profits) plays in this process. In the Kelsonian economic model, it is possible to finance capital investment totally with credit, linking creation of all new money to the creation of the new wealth. This would result in an asset-backed currency, zero inflation, elimination of monetized government deficits and a constriction of nonproductive (consumer) debt. For a discussion in this book of the role of credit, see the articles in "Section Three: Rebuilding Basic Economic Institutions." A blueprint for applying the Kelsonian economic model as a means for economic recovery in Latin America and the Caribbean is found in *High Road to Economic Justice: U. S. Encouragement of Employee Stock Ownership Plans in Central America and the Caribbean,* Report to the President and the Congress by the Presidential Task Force on Project Economic Justice: October 1986. (Published by the Center for Economic and Social Justice, Washington, DC, 1986.)

[2] As little as the connection between savings and investment is understood by the general public (and by governments), the role of productive credit, as opposed to consumer and other nonproductive credit, is even less understood. Relying on past savings amassed through accumulation to fuel economic growth, as opposed to future savings generated by productive assets acquired through the use of productive credit, inhibits the development of a full-growth economy and concentrates the opportunity for acquiring the new wealth in the hands of the already-wealthy. See "Charity or Justice, Where is the Hope of the Poor?" and "Capital Credit, A New Right of Citizenship" in this book.

[3] Clearly, "the entrepreneur" need not be a single individual, even in a single business. Without denying the vital role of the visionary leader, we find that the organizing and managerial functions of the entrepreneur can be shared among many people combining in an organized way for their common good. Even what is considered the unique "catalytic" and risk-taking nature of the entrepreneur can be found in varying degrees within most, if not all, people, and can be encouraged within the corporate culture. While traditional economists extend a special status to the entrepreneur, the Nietzschean "superman" or single leader who dominates all others within the group (and thereby maintains sole ownership of an enterprise) is the direct antithesis of the "servant leader" view of the entrepreneur.

[4] Servitje speaks here of consumer (nonproductive) credit, which, in reality, does not expand an individual's or society's purchasing power. This type of credit merely shifts payment for the purchase of a current good or service to a future period, with the consumer generally being charged a fee for this service. Judiciously used, consumer credit does have the short-term advantage of giving the consumer immediate use of a good or service while paying for it over a period of time, instead of delaying purchase until sufficient savings are accumulated, or income is increased. Yet nonproductive credit is by its nature ultimately counterproductive in that it actually reduces future purchasing power by at least the amount of interest and fees charged for the current consumer credit, and at most by the lost productivity which results when credit is allocated to nonproductive instead of productive uses. Where overall credit in the market has been limited, as in most economies today, using what credit exists in the system for consumer spending and funding government deficits creates a credit "drought" which inhibits investment by business.

[5] That is, in the short run. In the long run, environmental damage is counterproductive and does not result in maximizing profits over the longest period of time. And someone eventually has to pay to repair the damage, either the perpetrator or the members of the general public who are victimized by environmental abuses.

[6] In this discussion of the social responsibility of business to create jobs, Servitje seems to suggest that ordinary workers can only derive a living income from wages paid in exchange for labor—that the ordinary, presently non-owning person can only contribute to business through his labor inputs. The argument that business exists primarily to supply people with jobs, taken to its logical conclusion, results in the creation of jobs for the sake of jobs, not jobs for the sake of producing value in the form of goods and services for the customer and profits for the owners of the business. Making workers into owners of capital assets can free a business from the "jobs for the sake of jobs" trap, which leads to gross economic inefficiencies as well as social inequities. Louis and Patricia Kelso also make the point that where people can derive most of their incomes from capital ownership, the focus of human work will begin to shift from economic toil (i.e., jobs) to that of "leisure" work which is engaged in, not for pay, but for personal fulfillment and social development.

[7] While a business often has little trouble paying higher wages when profits are high, increasing fixed costs can be detrimental to the economic survival of the firm should profits not remain at a level sufficient to cover fixed labor costs. Tying worker compensation to profitability, instead of increasing the fixed wages paid to labor, maximizes the possibility of increased profits, while minimizing the possibility of layoffs or company bankruptcy in the event that profits fail to keep pace with increased fixed wages.

[8] This seems to reflect David Ricardo's "Labor Theory of Value," which was also embodied in the writings of Adam Smith, as well as all economic theories underlying the modern welfare state. (Witness President Clinton's continuing advocacy of "jobs, jobs, jobs," with no mention of wealth creation with expanded capital ownership.) This theory states that capital in and of itself contributes nothing to production, but serves only to enhance the productivity of labor. On this theoretical basis some economists have asserted that profits ("excess labor") belong by right to the workers and not the capital owners.

Servitje is actually pointing out that in the larger social context, labor or human work is more important than capital, or things. The reader will note that while this argument is valid from a spiritual standpoint, it may run counter to the economic disciplines of the free market, where the relative contributions of capital and technology are rapidly outpacing those of human labor. How can this apparent conflict between economic and spiritual concerns be resolved? The priority of labor (people) over capital (things) can best be realized by recognizing every person's right to own capital, thus giving the worker a legitimate economic, as well as moral, claim to the earnings of and control over capital.

[9] Unstated here is that "work" has taken on many meanings. Most people see only its most narrow definition, where work refers only to "mental or physical labor carried out in exchange for wages." This ignores the possibility of the owner of capital who is economically freed to engage in uncompensated work for the betterment of all, such as teaching, studying, healing, leading, praying, or pursuing social justice. Working for subsistence is the most urgent, but also the lowest, form of work.

[10] Where such a submission of one's private property rights to the needs of the common good is not done voluntarily out of a sense of moral obligation, there is a danger that the individual's rights of private property will be subverted or eliminated by the state or society (as under socialism). This danger diminishes as we focus not on redistributing property, but on enabling every person to possess it. As George Mason reminds us in the May 1776 Virginia Declaration of Rights, we must not only safeguard each person's rights *of property*, we must also extend to each person the rights *to property*, including the means and opportunity to acquire and possess productive wealth (the theoretical basis and practical means for which Louis Kelso later developed).

[11] This is similar to the "Junior Achievement" program carried out in many places in the United States of America.

III

Rebuilding Basic Economic Institutions

Rebuilding Basic Economic Institutions

Having established a sound set of universal moral principles upon which a viable cure for poverty can be developed, the next step is to determine the economic and political policy framework for applying those principles. What are the essential social innovations and policies needed to construct a more just social and economic order? Can these tools be articulated in such a way as to render them, not only consistent with principles of social and economic justice, but also consistent with the workings of "the real world"?

The articles in this section, "The Binary Economics of Louis Kelso: A Democratic Private Property System for Growth and Justice;" "Capital Credit: The Ultimate Right of Citizenship;" and "Beyond ESOP: Steps Toward Tax Justice" give such a tool kit. Reflecting basic principles of justice outlined in earlier sections, these articles address current economic and political realities in their proposals for restructuring existing economic institutions better to serve their original social purposes.

Challenging established economic paradigms, in "The Binary Economics of Louis Kelso," Syracuse professor Robert Ashford examines the premises and logic of Louis Kelso's economic theories of expanded capital ownership. Ashford poses the pivotal elements of Kelso's binary economic theory in light of arguments raised by traditional economists such as Nobel Prize winner Paul Samuelson. The article focuses particularly on how the Kelsonian framework restores the real-world relevance of Say's Law, which was rejected for different reasons both by Karl Marx and John Maynard Keynes. Say's Law, which states that in a private-property, free-market economy, the production of a given output necessarily generates aggregate income sufficient to purchase that output, is a law of economics which seems to defy the workings of the real world. Where Keynesian economists merely discard Say's Law, Kelso's theory brings to light the crucial role of expanded ownership in restoring equilibrium between aggregate supply and demand in a truly free market economy. Another important ad-

vance of Kelso's economic paradigm is refuting the notion of "productivity" and replacing it with the concept of "productiveness."

The net economic effect of the Kelsonian system is to stimulate
faster rates of economic growth, without inflation and with less control by government over the lives and well-being of every household
in society. The net political and social effect of Kelso's system of logic
is to offer a sounder theoretical foundation for policy-makers and moral
leaders committed to decentralizing economic power into the hands
of all citizens.

Clearly, in posing some fundamentally new assumptions which
challenge the intellectual status quo (whether of the various capitalist or socialist schools), the article seeks to promote serious dialogue
and raise the level of debate. This is not easy. Traditional economists
have vested career interests in maintaining the validity of what they
have learned and taught.

To the extent that it is indoctrinated with traditional economic
ideas, the general public, too, is challenged by binary economics. Basic assumptions are overturned about how people can and should earn
an income in a world of advancing technology. This may evoke a natural disturbance at change, but also a deeper confusion resulting from
the fact that many basic traditional economic assumptions are so
engrained as to have achieved the status of unquestioned postulates.
There is nothing so hard to question as something that "everybody
knows."

Despite the complexity of the task, Professor Ashford establishes
a common ground between traditional economics and binary economics, while challenging the economic assumptions of the academic elite
and the general public. Ashford's outline of binary economics is useful to its understanding and for providing a conceptual tool and more
accurate predictive model for the politicians, lawyers and economists
charged with implementing economic, legal and social reconstruction.

"Capital Credit: The Ultimate Right of Citizenship" addresses
quite another issue: that of the political acceptability (legitimacy) to
the policymaking community of universal access to widespread ownership of productive assets. Here, Dr. Friedman presents the reader
with both a philosophical and a practical argument.

While the other articles in this volume predicate the prospect of
widespread ownership upon natural law considerations, Dr. Friedman
selects an avenue grounded in the Sociology of Law. Drawing upon
her earlier work, *Legitimation of Social Rights and the Western Welfare State*,[1] in which she applied Max Weber's notion of rational legal
authority to show how the social rights of the welfare state became
acceptable, she develops the legitimation rationale to cover yet another right of citizenship: economic rights.

On the practical side, she outlines the content of those economic rights in terms of universal access to productive assets, referencing the Industrial Homestead Act.[2] She reinforces her practical argument by placing the present earning power of individuals in technological society against the historical backdrop of the industrial revolution when "work" became associated with "wages," and when the notions of wage income and property income became more clearly differentiated.

She concludes with the observation that our present shareholder and credit systems make possible the enlarging of the numbers of individuals in society who may derive property income (i.e., interest and dividends), and she makes the case that a specific *political* mechanism for such an eventuality would be *economic rights* in capital credit. The economic rights would be a fourth right of citizenship—a status that has gained increasing content over the last three centuries, beginning with civil rights, continuing through political and social rights, and potentially encompassing economic rights.

Once the soundness of Kelsonian economics has been established and the propriety of universal access to capital credit accepted, it will be possible to begin rebuilding basic economic institutions so as to promote social and economic justice. "Beyond ESOP: Steps Toward Tax Justice," the third article in this section, was originally published in 1977 and reflects the economic and political situation in the United States of America at that time. The author has added a number of notes to the original text to point out Congress' piecemeal acceptance of some of the article's recommended reforms. However, the actual overall tax system has remained basically unchanged. As President Carter is quoted in the beginning of the article, "Our [the United States of America's] tax system is a national disgrace."

That theme has been repeated by all candidates for public office in the U.S.A. in every race since 1976, including the presidential campaign of 1992. Every candidate has promised to eliminate budget deficits. None has offered a comprehensive, just and broadly appealing plan to eliminate fiscal deficits or to make the tax system of the United States of America work. While the numbers have changed and the crisis has worsened since this article was first published, the analysis and prescription for change remain unaltered. While focusing on the tax system of the United States of America, this article is based on universal principles and a systems logic consistent with the framework established in "The Binary Economics of Louis Kelso" and "Capital Credit: The Ultimate Right of Citizenship" that could be applied to any nation's tax system.

Norman Kurland begins by contrasting the Marxist redistribution principle of taxation with a justice-oriented approach. He asserts that the State should focus on equal distribution of the opportunity for ownership of productive assets, rather than on equal redistribution of wealth confiscated from producers through taxation. A new tax system is outlined that is designed to eliminate budget deficits and encourage broadly owned capital growth. Applying the Kelso-Adler principles of justice to restructuring the tax system, Kurland's reforms counter the largely accepted and implemented tax proposals of Karl Marx. Vehicles for ownership opportunity, particularly the Employee Stock Ownership Plan (ESOP), are outlined and related to this justice-oriented taxation philosophy.

However, Kurland's paper is not limited to a strict delineation of the role of taxation in an expanded ownership economy. Tax reform is seen in context with credit and monetary reforms, and the problems associated with government debt and deficit spending. Fitted into a comprehensive national program of expanded capital ownership (not to be confused with capitalism), the proposals in "Beyond ESOP: Steps Toward Tax Justice" offer a realistic and attainable goal for the American people without overturning the current political or economic structures of the nation. They represent a return to the principles upon which the United States government was founded, and would lead to profound changes in the distribution of wealth and power, from a plutocratic concentration to a democratic decentralization of economic power. Other countries can also use the precepts contained in the article to investigate and develop rational and just principles of taxation, along with national policies for promoting widespread ownership in the means of production.

Notes:

[1]Dr. Kathy Friedman, *Legitimation of Social Rights and the Western Welfare State,* University of North Carolina Press, 1981.

[2]"The Industrial Homestead Act" by Norman G. Kurland. See pages 123-147 of *Every Worker an Owner* (Washington, D.C.: Center for Economic and Social Justice 1987). For a discussion of the Industrial Homestead Act in this volume, see "Beyond ESOP: Steps Toward Tax Justice" by Norman G. Kurland, and "The Third Way: America's True Legacy to the New Republics" by Norman G. Kurland and Michael D. Greaney.

— 6 —

The Binary Economics of Louis Kelso: A Democratic Private Property System for Growth and Justice

by Robert H. A. Ashford

© *1994 Robert H. A. Ashford. Reprinted with permission of the author.*

Introduction

B inary economics[1] is fundamentally different from modern capitalist and socialist economic theories in all of their forms. It may be properly viewed as classical, free-market economics modified to reflect the post-industrial age.[2] It is also a different system of private property—distinct from all private and public property in all existing capitalist and socialist economies. The word "binary" is an all-inclusive term. It views all factors of production as falling under one or the other of two mutually exclusive categories, "labor" or "capital." Binary economics embraces all types of labor input (physical and mental) and all types of capital input (i.e., things like land, tools, structures, and processes) and describes how to match production and consumption most efficiently and justly under free-market, private property conditions.

Binary economics was advanced to correct what the Kelsos, Louis and Patricia, regard as a factual error: "the labor theory of value" in the assumptions of Adam Smith's *The Wealth of Nations*.[3] To that end, binary economics is based on a fundamental mathematical relationship between human beings and nonhuman factors of production when they are used to produce goods and services—a relationship which traditional economics ignores or trivializes. This relationship is captured in the term "productiveness" which is conceptually distinct from "productivity" as that term is employed in traditional economics. A system based on "productiveness," as distinguished from "productivity," provides a paradigm as different from modern capitalist or socialist economics, as heliocentric astronomy is from geocentric. Binary economics provides a new explanation for poverty in an industrial economy[4] and suggests a new strategy for making all people self-sufficient *without taking property from others.*[5]

People are poor because they have not acquired the capital necessary to supplement their labor input, and they can become economically autonomous only with a private property system that enables them to acquire this capital. Rather than socializing private capital ownership, a binary system democratizes access to credit as an indispensable social means to enable everyone to acquire private capital.[6]

To correct discrepancies in income distribution, the logic of binary economics reveals that nations must revamp the traditional strategies of both capitalist and socialist economies. They must eliminate their virtually exclusive dependence on employment, welfare, and traditional growth strategies, and initiate a program to achieve universal capital ownership according to binary economic principles. Only through such an approach can the autonomy that families enjoyed in the preindustrial world be restored in the current industrial era.[7]

Binary analysis proposes that the most fundamental economic problem to be solved is how to empower every family and single individual to equip itself with a viable and adequate holding of capital. Although advancing technology (capital) has become the dominant means for producing goods and services, a tiny percent of the population owns virtually all nonresidential capital in every nation. This problem is the direct result of a misguided national economic policy founded on a defective private property system that effectively enables only those who already own capital to acquire additional capital. Traditional governmental solutions—such as stimulation of traditional investment through tax, credit, and regulatory incentives, job creation, minimum wage laws, or transfer payments—are counterproductive in the long run. The effect of such programs is the further concentration of the capital ownership base, thereby increasing people's dependence on jobs and welfare for survival, and suppressing the true growth potential of the economy.

Binary economics shares two assumptions with classical economics:

(1) the purpose of production is consumption, and
(2) in a market economy real earnings must compensate only for real production.[8]

Thus the Kelsos reason that to maintain a market economy in the context of industrialization, increased productive power of capital must be linked with increased consumer power through ownership. Relegating most people to what they can earn by selling their services in the labor markets and to what they can appropriate and redistribute through welfare legislation effectively precludes their right to acquire capital ownership on market principles. In an industrial context, some "capital-less"[9] people may fare handsomely for a time without substantial capital ownership, but the vast majority's participation in the production of society will diminish unless the private property system provides them with an effective opportunity to participate in the capital markets to acquire on credit a share of capital wealth.

Other approaches are incomplete because they fail to deal adequately with the problem of concentrated ownership distribution caused by traditional capital financing.[10] Also defective are approaches which attempt to deal with distributional problems by instituting taxes and transfer payments that redistribute income after it has been earned,[11] or by government appropriation and ownership of capital. Such approaches either distort or eliminate the market for capital and labor. They disassociate production from consumption and suppress growth.

Because the purpose of production is consumption, binary economics holds that to maintain a market economy, the question of appropriate distribution of consumer income must be addressed in the process of capital formation itself and in all voluntary changes in the ownership of existing capital. Further, to achieve sustained growth, productive power represented by capital must be linked through property rights to those whom society expects to purchase what it produces.

Binary economics rejects the strategies provided by traditional economic theory by which people are to acquire capital. Traditional capitalist theory suggests a simple solution: people must decrease consumption (save) and invest wisely. The Kelsos find such a strategy wholly unrealistic because most people have insufficient savings and earnings to meet their consumption needs. Dependence on current earnings and savings for capital formation ensures that almost all new capital will be acquired by existing capital owners. Convinced that the existing private property system limits to the already-wealthy the right to acquire capital, the Kelsos advocate an alternative binary private property system that democratically extends to all people the effective right to acquire capital on market principles.[12]

Therefore, the Kelsos propose a comprehensive, but wholly voluntary, legislative program of economic reform intended to make "capital credit" available to all, enabling them to buy corporate stock in productive enterprises and pay for it out of the pre-tax income it generates. With borrowed money, stock ownership trusts (or similar capital credit devices) would acquire stock on behalf of constituent beneficiaries including employees, consumers, the unemployed and welfare recipients.[13] Investments would be limited to self-financing capital with projected income sufficient to amortize the acquisition debt within a reasonable cost recovery period. Through a system of private "capital diffusion" insurance and government reinsurance, banks and other qualified lenders would be insured against loss on acquisition loans to the ownership trusts.[14]

The stock held by the trusts would be a special "full property rights" stock, paying its full net return[15] as income to the trust. In turn, the trust would first repay the acquisition loan and then pay all income to the beneficiaries. Congress would effectively authorize the Federal Reserve Board ("the Fed") to monetize new capital formation by discounting capital credit loan paper held by lenders at its administrative cost. Monetized capital credit, low interest rates, loan insurance, and benefits to employee and consumer shareholders would provide incentives for companies to adopt a binary financing program to meet their future needs for capital.

The Kelsos have illustrated the institutional infrastructure of a binary economy (Figure 1).

Although sweeping in their national scope and complicated in their detail, these proposals all derive from a few premises and principles— far fewer than those applied today by either socialist or capitalist economics to explain and predict economic behavior and to formulate national economic policy. Further, the system would operate only in a wholly voluntary manner.

The Kelsos maintain that the voluntary operation of a national binary economy will yield a number of benefits. A national financing program based on binary economic precepts will broaden the distribution of income and also produce increases in economic growth far exceeding forecasts based on traditional economic strategies. It will also tame, if not eliminate, business cycles and inflation; reduce government deficits and taxes; and restore the international competitiveness of American industry.[16]

The effect of these proposals is not to socialize private capital, but to democratizes access to the credit needed to acquire private capital.[17] By enabling people without capital to acquire capital on credit, these proposals create a different system of private property—a system that may be seen as limiting the collateralization rights of existing owners, to extend *effective* acquisition rights to all, whether or not they have wealth to place at risk. However, if the binary growth predications based on productiveness materializes, there will be no effective limitation on the collateralization rights of existing owners. Rather, the investment opportunities of all owners will increase.

Yet many economists fear that monetization of productive credit might produce an inflation that would swamp any real growth. Un-

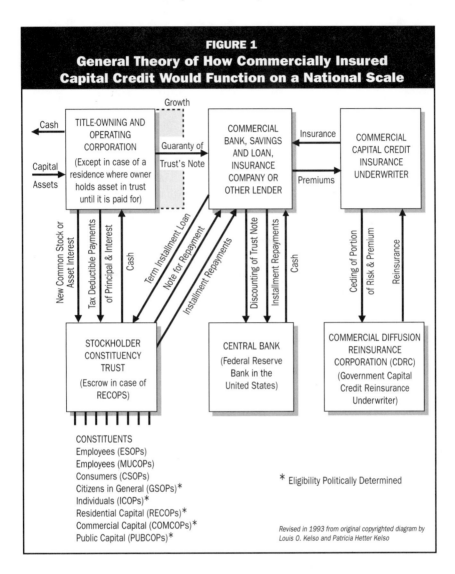

FIGURE 1
General Theory of How Commercially Insured Capital Credit Would Function on a National Scale

Growth

Cash

TITLE-OWNING AND OPERATING CORPORATION
(Except in case of a residence where owner holds asset in trust until it is paid for)

Capital Assets

Guaranty of Trust's Note

COMMERCIAL BANK, SAVINGS AND LOAN, INSURANCE COMPANY OR OTHER LENDER

Insurance

Premiums

COMMERCIAL CAPITAL CREDIT INSURANCE UNDERWRITER

New Common Stock or Asset Interest

Tax Deductible Payments of Principal & Interest

Cash

Term Installment Loan

Note for Repayment

Installment Repayments

Discounting of Trust Note

Installment Repayments

Cash

Ceding of Portion of Risk & Premium

Reinsurance

STOCKHOLDER CONSTITUENCY TRUST
(Escrow in case of RECOPS)

CENTRAL BANK
(Federal Reserve Bank in the United States)

COMMERCIAL DIFFUSION REINSURANCE CORPORATION (CDRC)
(Government Capital Credit Reinsurance Underwriter)

CONSTITUENTS
Employees (ESOPs)
Employees (MUCOPs)
Consumers (CSOPs)
Citizens in General (GSOPs)*
Individuals (ICOPs)*
Residential Capital (RECOPs)*
Commercial Capital (COMCOPs)*
Public Capital (PUBCOPs)*

* Eligibility Politically Determined

Revised in 1993 from original copyrighted diagram by Louis O. Kelso and Patricia Hetter Kelso

der traditional economic theory, monetization, preferential interest rates, and assumption of investment risk by the government do not result in new capital without savings. Rather the effect is to form new capital by appropriating or reducing the wealth of those not benefitting from the program (e.g., other investors and consumers) by reducing their claim on societal output. Many economists would therefore dispute the assertion that the Kelsonian system promotes real growth, maintaining that it merely provides an alternate means of redistributing existing wealth. They may also argue that the binary system may reduce incentives for efficiency and productivity and thereby promote recession rather than growth. These concerns will be discussed presently. Significantly, from a binary perspective, they fail to comprehend the principle of binary growth.

The Principle of Binary Growth

The most remarkable aspect of binary analysis is the principle of binary growth. Stated perhaps oversimply, the more broadly capital ownership is acquired by individual consumers on market principles, the larger will be the resulting economy. This proposition is either a grand illusion whose underlying fallacy has eluded me and a growing number of scholars throughout the world, or it is one of the most important discoveries of the twentieth century. Stated more broadly, the theory of binary growth holds that economies grow on market principles, not only with increases in investment and worker productivity and decreases in transactions costs, but also as an independent (and much more potent) function of the distribution of capital acquisition on market principles. This proposition is exactly the opposite of the claims of traditional capitalist economic theory. In traditional capitalist theory, economic growth results from increases in productivity and investment and decreases in transactions costs; but in terms of economic growth, it makes no difference who owns the capital (absent gains in productivity resulting from motivational or other factors). "Redistributing capital," the traditional argument goes, "merely spreads around pieces of the same pie; it does not create a larger pie. And worse yet, it may distort market incentives for productivity and efficient resource allocation, and therefore may result in a smaller pie."

Yet, intuitively, the binary theory of growth seems to square better with the facts. On the individual level, it makes a big difference who owns the capital. Generally, it is the difference between being rich and poor. The more capital you own, the greater your ability to participate in the economy both as a producer (owner) and as a consumer. Likewise, on the national level, all the world's large economies are capital-rich economies. Both individually and nationally, affluence is the product of capital, whereas jobs and welfare rarely produce more than subsistence. What is true for rich people and nations is true for the poor. The more fully each individual provides productive input in the economy not only as worker but as owner, the more fully he or she can participate as a consumer, and the larger the economy will be. Furthermore, as an economy industrializes, the importance to the individual of participating in a balanced way in production and consumption both as an owner and a worker becomes increasingly important. Likewise, as an economy industrializes, it becomes increasingly important to the economic growth of the entire society that capital is increasingly acquired on market principles by all people, not merely by existing owners, so that its incremental income may be used to purchase the incremental output.

Thus, in binary terms, it matters greatly whether capital acquired competitively on market principles is acquired increasingly by the poor and middle class rather than almost exclusively by a small percentage of the population. If capital is increasingly acquired by the many poor and middle class people (paid for by its own earnings), and if capital's income is thereafter required to be distributed to the poor and middle classes, they will spend more money on goods and services, and thereby fuel a larger economy than if the capital were acquired by the few rich. Unlike the poor and middle class who have many unsatisfied needs and wants, the rich will seek to invest their capital earnings, but in an economy characterized by comparatively less consumer demand.

In short, sustained economic growth on market principles requires that incremental productive power provided by capital must be acquired broadly by the masses of people expected to purchase what it produces. If capital acquisition is restricted by a closed private property system for the benefit of existing owners, the distribution of capital income will be insufficient to support consumption, and growth will be suppressed.

Binary economics thus provides a conceptually distinct alternative to traditional capitalism and socialism, worthy of serious consideration in its own terms. As such it should be explored, not ignored, as a theory of law and economics.

Binary Economics and Employee Stock Ownership Plans

Although Louis Kelso has gone generally unrecognized by modern economists in influential positions, he had remarkable success with the United States Congress in fashioning a legislative program for the Employee Stock Ownership Plan ("ESOP"), the vanguard of his system of ownership trusts. The essential Kelsonian feature of the ESOP is its ability to acquire in trust for employees stock in their companies on nonrecourse credit, and to pay for it with the stock's pretax income.[18]

In response to Congressional encouragement, the number of ESOPs has increased substantially in the last decade. The General Accounting Office estimated that there were approximately 4,800 active ESOPs in 4,700 companies in 1986, covering approximately 7.1 million employees and $13 billion in assets.[19] According to the National Center for Employee Ownership, in 1993 there were between 9,000 and 10,000 active ESOPs covering approximately 11 million workers with over $60 billion in assets.[20]

However, studying ESOPs in the present economic environment is somewhat like studying the first horseless carriages before systems of roads and service were established. Inferences to be drawn from current studies may not be applicable within the context of a binary economy. Analyzing the full potential of ESOPs and other binary financing proposals requires a calculus that adequately reflects the economic infrastructure designed to support them and the alternative private property rights system on which they are predicted.

Say's Law in an Industrial Economy

Central to the Kelsos' binary analysis is a highly controversial law of classical economics known as Say's Law of Markets ("Say's Law").[21] Say's Law holds that in a private-property, free-market economy, the production of a given output necessarily generates aggregate income sufficient to purchase that output.[22]

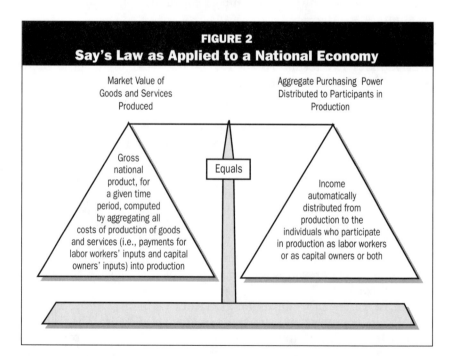

FIGURE 2
Say's Law as Applied to a National Economy

Market Value of Goods and Services Produced

Aggregate Purchasing Power Distributed to Participants in Production

Gross national product, for a given time period, computed by aggregating all costs of production of goods and services (i.e., payments for labor workers' inputs and capital owners' inputs) into production

Equals

Income automatically distributed from production to the individuals who participate in production as labor workers or as capital owners or both

For the last two centuries, economists have debated whether Say's Law establishes a principle on which, on an economy-wide basis, supply will create its own demand,[23] and demand its own supply. The Kelsos acknowledge this controversy:

> Economists have been at loggerheads over Say's Law ever since its promulgation in 1803. One of its implications is that the phenomena variously known as depressions, panics, and recessions cannot occur. But they have occurred, and with ever deepening severity, from the inception of the Industrial Revolution. Say's Law has remained a riddle to conventional economists because they approach it with a wrong assumption: that there is only one way that individuals can make productive input and earn income—through labor.[24]

Unlike anyone before them, however, the Kelsos apply their concepts of productiveness and private property rights to Say's Law to derive several conclusions not found in traditional economic analysis.

"Supply-side" or "trickle down" economists accept Say's Law and recommend government policies to stimulate investment, with the expectation that increased capital investment will create a larger economy, a greater pool of jobs and a larger tax base for welfare distribution.[25] Keynesian economists, on the other hand, reject Say's Law,[26] claiming that demand is demonstrably insufficient to clear supplies at market prices.

Contrary to classical and neoclassical theory, Keynesians support their contention by citing endemic unemployment, unsold inventories, and unutilized production capacity which manifestly would not persist if supply had created its own demand.[27] Many Keynesians advocate a "trickle-up" policy: one that stimulates demand largely through jobs and welfare.

In its embrace of Say's Law, binary economics takes exception to both approaches, maintaining that questions of consumer supply and demand must be addressed simultaneously in the very process of capital formation and capital transfers.[28]

Underlying binary economics, Say's Law provides the fundamental economic restraint and basic logic in a market economy: production must be financed to generate the consumer income to purchase the consumer goods produced. Say's Law also provides the formula and requirements for a steady-growth, noninflationary economy that increasingly matches unsatisfied needs and wants with the productive means to satisfy them.[29] If mass production is not financed to generate mass consumer purchasing power, vast inflationary and redistributionary measures, accompanied by recurrent booms and busts, must follow, as indeed they have.

Given binary economic suppositions and logic, a number of propositions follow from Say's law:

(1) An industrial economy must not limit workers' participation in the economy to their productive labor input alone; they must participate through both their labor and ownership of capital.

(2) As technology advances, increased productive input of capital must be linked with increased consumer income from capital ownership.[30]

(3) In an industrial economy, only through broadening capital ownership may consumers "participate in production [on market principles] to an extent sufficient to provide them automatically with adequate purchasing power"[31] to consume what the economy produces.[32]

(4) More economic growth will result if capital formation and transfers are financed on market principles to broaden the ownership base, so as to generate the consumer income necessary to purchase the consumer goods produced. (This proposition is a restatement of the principle of binary growth.)

Economists ignore these imperatives, which in binary economics follow inescapably from Say's Law. Furthermore, whatever they think of Say's Law, most economists would contest the idea that alternative financing designed to produce alternate ownership distribution will, of itself, create growth. The question of whether broader capital ownership, financed according to binary principles, will promote substantial economic growth, impede growth or leave it unaffected is thus crucial to an evaluation of binary economics.

Say's Law is important as one of the few points of common reference between Kelsonian and traditional economics. However, before understanding the binary application of Say's Law and the objections that might be premised on traditional economic theory, one must consider concepts of independent productiveness, ownership, insured capital credit and other aspects of binary theory in greater detail.

The Concept of Independent Productiveness

Both socialist and traditional capitalist theories make a foundational error in their analyses of the productive input of capital and labor. In the last two hundred years, in physical terms, the economies of western nations have grown many hundredfold, vastly outstripping previous per capita economic growth. The increasing capacity to produce has been accompanied by an increasing reliance on capital in the productive process. However, when people interact with capital to form an inseparable product or service, how should its market value—the return on production—be allocated to the capital and the labor inputs?

The neoclassical economic approach looks at what labor and capital earn and conclude that their relative returns are a function of the marginal value of their inputs. This approach assumes a more or less competitive market for capital and labor. Yet it is doubtful—given the multiplicity of worldwide political barriers to, and interferences with, the free operation of the laws of supply and demand—whether existing markets are competitive.[33] In traditional economics, the generally accepted conditions for competitive markets include:

(1)　barrier-free market entry;
(2)　a sufficient number of buyers and sellers so that no single participant can substantially affect the market prices; and
(3)　freedom from collusion among market participants.[34]

Consistent with these conditions, the binary view is that markets for capital and labor cannot be competitive so long as people without capital are effectively restricted from acquiring capital.[35] Traditional economic theory, on the other hand, ignores the consequences of the substantial barrier that stands between most people and effective participation in the capital markets, and rather frequently assumes (inconsistent with these limitations) that capital markets are efficient.

Traditional economic theory assumes that the most important productive relationship between capital and labor is the one described by the concept of "productivity." Productivity is output per unit of input.[36] Economists calculate labor productivity by combining production of labor and capital with respect to per-hour or per-dollar input of labor alone.[37] Capital productivity, more usually expressed as the rate of return on investment, may be similarly calculated.[38] "Marginal productivity," the first derivative of productivity, expresses the marginal increase in output per additional unit of input. According to neoclassical economic theory, marginal productivity signals to managers how much capital and labor to employ in the productive process and thereby to optimize output for any level of available inputs.[39] In judging the relationship among capital, labor and production, traditional economists agree that capital increases labor productivity.[40] Although productivity stands at the foundation of traditional economics, there are serious "productivity measurement problems"[41] which burden the effectiveness of traditional economic analysis.

In binary terms, the concept of "productivity" as applied in traditional macro-economic analysis is incoherent. It ignores and obscures a more important relationship among labor, capital and production:

productiveness. Productiveness can be thought of as the quantifica-
tion of "independent factor input" of each factor as a percentage of
total output of both factors.

An example will help quantify the conceptual differences between
traditional economic productivity and Kelsonian productiveness: A
person can dig a hole in four hours by hand. After the invention of
the shovel, he can dig the same hole in one hour. In traditional economic terms, labor has four times the productivity because four times
as much work can be performed in the same time period. In binary
economic terms, the productiveness has changed from 100% labor
before the invention of the shovel, to 25% labor and 75% capital input
with the shovel. Thus the Kelso system views the laborer as having
only one fourth the productiveness rather than four times the productivity. Capital has not "amplified labor productivity," which would
be the view of traditional economics, but has "replaced labor productiveness" per hole, and therefore requires a reduction in labor's claim
on the income earned from each unit of output.

In traditional economics, productivity is the foundational mathematical concept for organizing, analyzing and explaining growth and
participation in that growth. In binary economics, productiveness is
the fundamental concept, and productivity plays only a second-order
role. The productivity concept in traditional economics induces the
worker—or the government or labor union acting on his behalf—to
compensate for the threatened erosion in his income by demanding
more pay for less productive labor input. The productiveness concept, however, highlights the worker's need to acquire the capital that
has replaced his labor productiveness, in order to preserve and enhance his earned claim on the increased aggregate output.

Consider now the example of a company that owns a building
with ten manual elevators and employs ten elevator operators to run
them. On a trial basis, the company replaces five of the ten manual
elevators with automatic elevators and all operators are put on half-
time to operate the remaining manual elevators. Operators must input only half as many operator labor hours to maintain the same
output of ten elevators available for service. Yet few, if any, economists would conclude, as they might in the shovel example, that the
elevator operators are twice as productive. Rather a traditional economic analysis would consider the elevator operators' productivity to
be unchanged because the output of each has not changed with respect to the labor input of each.

If half the operators are retained full-time and half are fired, the
theoretical productivity of the remaining operators does not change.
However, the discharged operators, who retain the same potential
productivity as those still on the job, cannot earn a living on this "potential productivity" if they remain unemployed. Their former labor

productiveness has been replaced by capital productiveness. In binary terms the productiveness of "capital workers" (i.e., capital owners) has replaced the productiveness of labor workers.[42]

When all the operators are replaced by automatic elevators, labor input has been reduced to zero, and the productivity of labor, in traditional economic terms, is infinite. (Productivity is measured by dividing output by input; as the denominator approaches zero, the value of the fraction becomes immeasurably large.) In Kelsonian terms, the important conclusion is that capital worker input has totally replaced labor worker input. For that task, labor productiveness is zero; capital productiveness is 100 percent.

As new labor-saving technology is implemented within a Kelsonian framework, workers' percentage claim on total output arising from labor's productiveness is reduced because the productiveness of the workers' capital has replaced correspondingly the productiveness of their labor in aggregate production. Demands for higher wages based on "increased productivity" do not obviate the need for workers to participate legitimately in the acquisition of capital that has replaced and supplemented their labor productiveness in today's high technology world.

While increased capital productiveness may spawn a larger economy and create more jobs, the invariable effect of new capital formation is to replace labor productiveness with capital productiveness. Consequently, as technology advances, labor workers can legitimately claim from their aggregate labor only a decreasing percentage of total output.

In terms of independent productiveness, there is no difference in principle between the shovel and the elevator. Each replaces and supplements labor productiveness in the same way. The only difference is that automated capital generally replaces and supplements vastly more labor productiveness than manual capital. In binary economics, a shovel, though physically dependent on human labor to realize its productive input, is as independent a wealth producer as the person who digs a hole, with or without the shovel. The shovel is also as economically independent of the human factor as the automatic elevator. The economic independence of capital productiveness exists without regard to the person-hours needed to maintain or operate the capital.[43]

To illustrate productiveness over time, the Kelsos use Figures 3A and 3B.

These charts show increasing capital productiveness and decreasing labor productiveness as a percentage of total output. As a result of our closed private property system, which limits capital acquisition to existing owners, Say's Law requires a redistribution of capital income illustrated in Figure 4.

Thus according to binary economics, capital now accounts for eighty to ninety percent of the total productiveness of any of today's

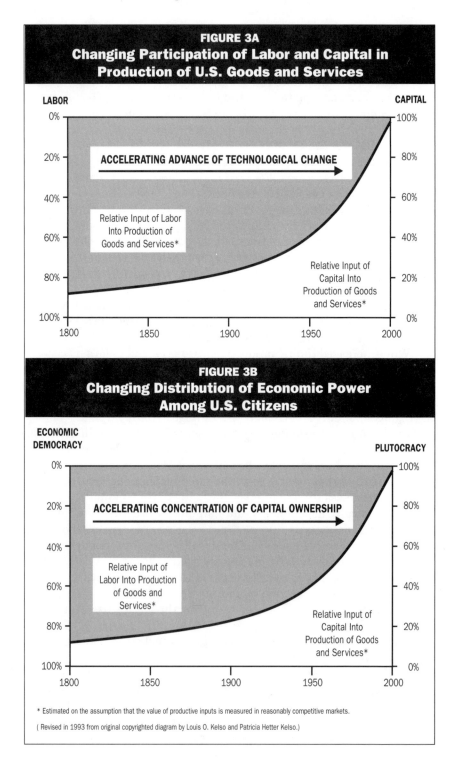

FIGURE 3A
Changing Participation of Labor and Capital in Production of U.S. Goods and Services

LABOR   CAPITAL

ACCELERATING ADVANCE OF TECHNOLOGICAL CHANGE →

Relative Input of Labor
Into Production of
Goods and Services*

Relative Input of
Capital Into
Production of Goods
and Services*

1800   1850   1900   1950   2000

FIGURE 3B
Changing Distribution of Economic Power Among U.S. Citizens

ECONOMIC
DEMOCRACY   PLUTOCRACY

ACCELERATING CONCENTRATION OF CAPITAL OWNERSHIP →

Relative Input of
Labor Into Production
of Goods and
Services*

Relative Input of
Capital Into
Production of Goods
and Services*

1800   1850   1900   1950   2000

* Estimated on the assumption that the value of productive inputs is measured in reasonably competitive markets.

(Revised in 1993 from original copyrighted diagram by Louis O. Kelso and Patricia Hetter Kelso.)

FIGURE 4

Distortions in the Property System of the U.S. Economy in Order to Distribute to Non-Capital-Owners Income Generated by the Production of Goods and Services Through Capital

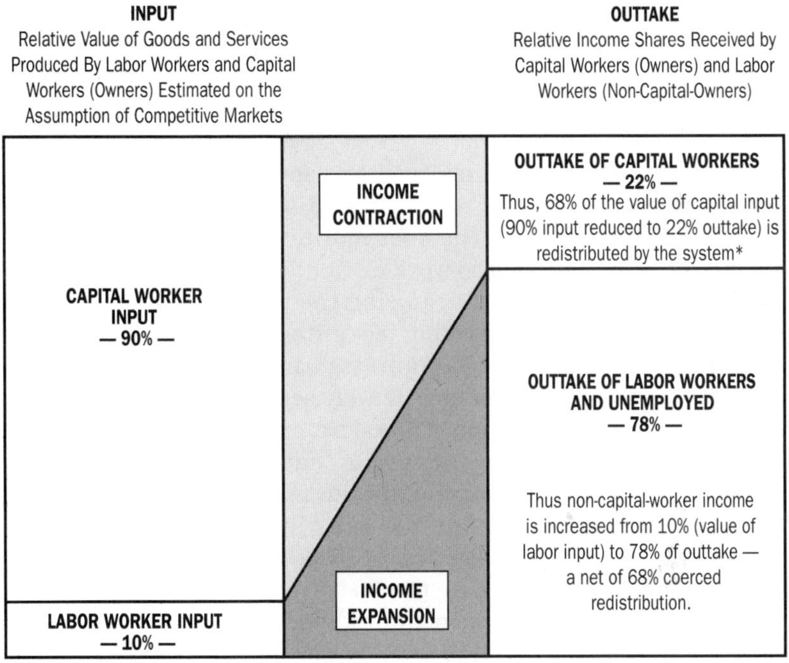

INPUT
Relative Value of Goods and Services Produced By Labor Workers and Capital Workers (Owners) Estimated on the Assumption of Competitive Markets

OUTTAKE
Relative Income Shares Received by Capital Workers (Owners) and Labor Workers (Non-Capital-Owners)

INCOME CONTRACTION

CAPITAL WORKER INPUT
— 90% —

OUTTAKE OF CAPITAL WORKERS
— 22% —
Thus, 68% of the value of capital input (90% input reduced to 22% outtake) is redistributed by the system*

OUTTAKE OF LABOR WORKERS AND UNEMPLOYED
— 78% —

Thus non-capital-worker income is increased from 10% (value of labor input) to 78% of outtake — a net of 68% coerced redistribution.

INCOME EXPANSION

LABOR WORKER INPUT
— 10% —

*Transfer payments, mandated increases in minimum wages, coerced redistribution of progressively more pay for less work input, etc.

modern industrialized economies; but much of that income is necessarily distributed to people through inflated wages or welfare payments to maintain consumer demand, as required by Say's Law.

People Are Poor Because They Do Not Own Enough Capital

Productiveness and its relationship to labor, capital and technological advance provide a different, more fundamentally helpful explanation of why most people are poor in an industrialized economy. People are poor not because their labor wages are low or nonexistent, but because they cannot acquire the capital that has replaced their labor productiveness and the additional capital necessary to earn an income that will allow them to consume at a level that amounts to living well.[44]

Simple logic tells us that as the production of goods and services changes from labor-intensive to capital-intensive, as it has been doing since the beginning of the industrial revolution, the way in which every consumer in a free, democratic society participates in production . . . must synchronously change from labor-intensive to capital-intensive.[45]

The Kelsos note, "If under free-market conditions 90 percent of the goods and services are produced by capital input, then 90 percent of the earnings of working people must flow to them as wages of their capital and the remainder as wages of their labor work."[46]

If the reader accepts the alternative foundation that productiveness offers for analyzing the productive input of capital and labor, then to improve the lot of the poor and to provide an alternative to demanding more pay for less work or welfare payments, society must afford a practical means of acquiring the capital whose productiveness produces an ever-increasing percentage of total societal output.

Apart from inheritance and gift, traditional economic theory provides one principal means of legitimately acquiring capital: work hard to earn enough from labor to withhold from current consumption, and invest wisely. Binary economics posits that this solution is irrational and ineffective; the solution is simple but impossible for most people.[47] Those without capital already have too little consumer income because capital productiveness has overtaken their labor productiveness. Further withholding by the poor from their consumption will worsen the growth-stifling consumption deficit that results from the concentration of capital ownership. For sustained growth, Say's Law requires a private-property system that enables people lacking appreciable productive capital to acquire it on market principles without reducing their already inadequate consumer income. To solve this problem, binary economics turns to another discipline: corporate finance.

A Democratic System of Corporate Finance

One cardinal principle of business finance, sometimes referred to as the "feasibility principle," is to invest only in capital that pays for its own acquisition cost in a comparatively short period of time, generally under five years.[48] Included within the projected income necessary to meet the feasibility requirement is an amount sufficient to provide reserves for depreciation, research and development so that worn or obsolete capital can be replaced with new capital.[49] Thus capital both pays for its acquisition and generates a perpetual, self-financing return.[50]

To acquire new capital, corporate managers retain earnings, issue stock, or borrow money. As traditionally structured, each technique's primary effect is to finance new ownership into existing owners. Of the three techniques, only debt financing has the systemic potential of enabling people to acquire capital without prior ownership of capital.

To meet their capital needs, large corporations rely most heavily, if not primarily, on borrowed money. Under traditional financing approaches, however, the growth potential of corporate debt is ultimately available only to existing stockholders: the people with savings to place at risk in the event of business failure. In effect, the binary approach extends the corporate advantages of debt financing to people who have no savings to place at risk. It creates an open, democratic system of corporate finance.

Universal Collateralization Requirement Keeps Most People Poor

To insure against business failure, commercial lenders require not only that the proposed financing meet the feasibility requirement; they also require some satisfactory form of collateral or guarantee with which the loan may be satisfied to protect the lender against the borrower's failure to meet the feasibility requirement. This almost universal collateralization requirement explains why, to confirm the old adage, it takes money to make money.

Because existing owners of capital already earn more than they consume, the purpose of their incremental production is no longer consumption. Rather, "income *in excess* of that used for consumption . . . can and will be used only to acquire additional capital productive power, which in turn will produce further excess income, which in turn will be used to acquire further excess capital productive power, etc., ad infinitum," causing a progressive distributional variance with the balance between producer input and consumer income required by Say's Law.[51] Exclusive reliance on the financing practices that promote this imbalance thwart the goals of economic growth and equal opportunity.

Satisfying Collateral Requirements With Capital Credit Insurance

To satisfy the security requirements that stand as a barrier between most people and the ownership of capital, binary economics proposes a system of commercially insured, and governmentally reinsured, capital credit. To initiate the system, the government would establish the Capital Diffusion Reinsurance Corporation (CDRC) to facilitate the provision of private capital insurance and to stand as the insurer of last resort. In effect, it approaches the problem of business failure as a casualty loss problem and therefore seeks to insure the business risk at competitive prices. The success of binary proposals depends on the proposition, yet to be fully explored, that the risk of business failure customarily borne by equity investment can be competitively priced and included in the cost of borrowed capital. If this is feasible, then effective acquisition rights need not be essentially restricted to those who already own substantial assets, but can be extended democratically to all.

Binary economics' recourse to capital credit is not a facile or naive reliance on a pyramid scheme of easy credit policies associated with subsidized financing for consumption or for any particular business purpose. On the contrary, credit is available for any capital needs, as determined by private firms, but only for self-financing investment that meets standards of market discipline required for all financially sound capital investment.[52] If the investment fails, there is no income for the beneficiaries.

Nor is the binary approach an attempt to undermine incentives to encourage efficiency, industry, cooperation, competitiveness and inventiveness. On the contrary, binary economics would extend capital credit to reinforce incentives for all such human input. But even operating optimally such incentives cannot inspire human input or yield labor earnings beyond the limits of its economically productive input. Thus given the import of productiveness, insured capital credit is simply the only means yet proposed to enable people without capital to acquire capital on market principles so that within a binary time frame,[53] increasing consumer income is distributed to balance increasing capital productiveness as required by Say's Law.

Because binary financing does not resort to traditional equity investment, it cannot require such investment to assume any of the risk of business failure associated with binary financing. Thus the practical efficacy of binary financing programs depends on the proposition that the risk of business failure, customarily borne by traditional equity investment, can be commercially insured. To facilitate the provision of private insurance, the specifically established Capital Diffusion Reinsurance Corporation (CDRC) would stand as a reinsurer and the insurer of last resort. In answer to objections to such a governmental assumption of responsibility, the Kelsos have argued that with reference to the financial well-being of the top two thousand or so United States companies, since the New Deal, the federal government has already assumed the risk of their aggregate failure. Witness the governmental response in bailing out two such "too big to fail" companies": Chrysler Corporation and Continental Bank. The major differences are that the risk is presently indirectly mediated politically by monetary, taxing and fiscal policies rather than explicitly as a market decision under the binary approach, while the government promotes the financing of new productive capacity so that it is owned by people with few, if any, unsatisfied needs and wants. The binary proposal does no more than capitalize the risk already assumed by the government, and facilitate its pricing and financing on market principles, for the productive and consumption needs of all.

In 1986, the Kelsos estimated the insurance costs in the range of two percent. Shortly before his death, by reason of the deteriorating economic conditions, he increased this estimate to the range of five percent. Any particular estimate is of course debatable, and the question is worthy of serious study. As a corollary to the binary growth effect, however, binary logic suggests that much capital formation fails to proceed on a self-financing basis because of a systemic failure to distribute to consumers enough earnings from capital. Thus the financial feasibility of capital credit insurance must be judged consistently with the prospects for binary growth.

Binary Growth in Binary Time Frame

To explore the long-term dynamics of binary growth, it is helpful first to focus on a time horizon of ten years and to assume a competitive capital cost recovery period of five years. The ten-year horizon may then be bifurcated into a "binary time frame" consisting of two five-year segments. Because the beneficiaries of binary financing cannot begin to spend their binary income until after the capital has paid for its acquisition cost, new capital financed in the first year will not produce spendable capital income for its beneficial owners until the sixth year; but thereafter, it will produce that income indefinitely.[54] The new capital formation of the second year will produce an additional increment to the beneficiaries' income in the seventh year, and so forth. By the tenth year, five full years of binary financing will be providing the full payout of the equity return to the beneficiaries. By reason of their higher marginal spending rate, more of the additional income earned by the new owners (who have many unsatisfied consumer needs and wants) will be spent on consumption than if the income had been earned by existing owners (who have few, if any, such needs and wants).

This broad-based incremental consumption will fuel a demand for greater investment, and therefore a larger economy, than would be financially feasible if capital had been traditionally financed. If traditionally financed, the capital would have earned its income for people with few, if any, unsatisfied consumer needs and wants, who would thus seek more investment opportunities, but in the context of weaker consumer demand. Viewed from a ten-year perspective, more consumer demand and therefore more growth will materialize over the ten-year period to the extent that new capital formation and capital transfers are financed on binary principles rather than with traditional collateralization requirements. In binary terms, the incremental consumer demand giving rise to the growth is not inflationary because it is linked through property rights to the production of goods and services of equal value. Consumer income for the binary beneficiaries is limited at all points by the antecedent earnings of the underlying capital.[55]

If one extends the time horizon to twenty and fifty years, one sees a basis for sustained, non-cyclical economic growth.[56] This basis for growth continues to increase indefinitely as more capital is financed on binary principles. This is a growth connection that is not the result of the increased productivity of any particular workers, nor of increased investment or technological gains, nor of reduced transactions costs, nor of any other traditionally advanced basis for growth. *It is a long-run self-sustaining connection between production, ownership, consumption and growth that exists in a binary time frame. It is unique to binary financing, and is at the heart of the binary private property solution for the economic well-being of the poor and middle class, without taking from the rich.*

Viewed in a binary time frame, the effect of the program is to finance the basis for both increased supply and demand. In this sense, binary economics offers an economic strategy fundamentally distinct from both the right-wing, supply-side, trickle-down strategies and the left-wing, demand-driven, Keynesian governmental approaches of taxing, fiscal, and monetary policy. Binary economics is neither a right-wing nor a left-wing theory. It rejects both approaches because, in their long-run analyses, they make the fatal error of disassociating production and consumption. To achieve sustained economic growth, the basis for production and consumption must be simultaneously financed within an appropriate binary time-frame for economic planning.

Thus, in utter conflict with traditional economic thinking, according to binary economics, in the long run, it matters greatly whether capital bought competitively on market principles is acquired increasingly by the poor and middle class rather than almost exclusively by a small percentage of the population. Therefore, one important message of binary theory to those concerned with the welfare of all people, is that it may matter greatly whether our private property system restricts acquisition rights to the existing owners or extends them universally to all people.

Binary Growth Is Not Traditional Redistribution

When exploring the implications of binary growth, one should note a number of remarkable features regarding binary growth and binary income. First, in an economic sense, if it exists, binary growth is not redistribution, at least not in any traditional sense. In comprehending the binary long-run approach to growth, one must understand the source of the incremental consumer demand. It only exists if the underlying capital has paid for its acquisition costs and then produces additional income. In any year, binary income is paid as dividends to its beneficiaries only if in that year the underlying capital has produced goods and services equal in value to the income distributed. To the extent of aggregate binary growth in any year, binary income is not compensation for labor, including human capital; and it is not income redistributed from the productive input of others (either as workers or owners). Further, to the extent of aggregate binary growth in any year, it cannot be fairly said that the provision of insured capital credit for binary beneficiaries has crowded out existing owners of their rightful investment opportunities (which they might have enjoyed under the present closed property system) because the binary growth investment opportunities would not have materialized but for the binary property system. Moreover, all of the transactions will have occurred voluntarily by principals and agents acting on behalf of private companies and their traditional and binary shareholders. Any binary income is likewise wholly the result of voluntary transactions in response to market forces. Thus to call the benefits of binary growth, if any, "redistribution," as that term is traditionally conceived, is a fundamental misnomer.

The fact that the long-run capital-based binary income, if any, is not redistribution in any traditional economic sense has important economic, political, and jurisprudential implications. Most significantly it disposes of all the volumes of literature against traditional redistribution on grounds that it is a distortion of the efficiency of market forces. If valid, binary growth uniquely eliminates the supposed conflict between efficiency and distributive justice. The binary growth generates market-based capital income that replaces and supplements command-based traditional redistribution.[57] Further, the distributional income benefits derive from lowering the substantial barriers that now stand between most people and the capital markets in the name of trickle-down theory. Thus it creates the private property foundation for even greater market efficiency.

In other words, granted that the theoretical prospect of binary growth may yet be unproven in practice, and may be yet disputed on a number of grounds, nevertheless if it exists, binary growth is not objectionable as redistribution or as an abandonment of market principles. If binary growth materializes, it will do so because Louis Kelso discovered a more efficient private property system that connects people more directly with market forces by providing them increasingly with the production-based capital income to purchase what society produces.[58]

Capital Formation Without "Financial Savings"

Perhaps the most difficult aspect of binary growth theory from a traditional economic perspective is the explicit relationship assumed by binary economics among savings, consumption, and growth. "Sustained economic prosperity in a market economy requires that earners and their dependents devote currently earned income to current consumption."[59] Under a binary economic system, economic growth will be great enough to allow simultaneous increases in both personal consumption and capital investment, without forcing people to choose between savings and consumption.[60]

From a traditional economic perspective, these binary growth predictions are problematic because they seemingly ignore the necessity for savings to provide the capital investment deemed necessary for growth. The idea that a higher marginal spending rate for consumer-owners will provide the basis for sustained economic growth contradicts the very definition of savings. In traditional economics, savings requires a reduction in consumption. Expressed society-wide as an equation, savings (S) equals total output (O) minus consumption (C):

$$S = O - C$$

Furthermore, according to traditional economic theory, the way to promote economic growth is to increase productivity. Increases in productivity require investment, which requires savings. Growth requires incentives to save more, not spend more. Thus new capital owners' increased marginal spending will reduce rather than increase investment and stifle rather than promote long-term growth.

In an important sense, however, this traditional analysis is static, not dynamic. It assumes the "O" is a quantity that does not grow with a broader distribution of wealth. Given the time horizon of business managers, however, "O" depends not primarily on consumer demand at the time of investment (t - 1) but on anticipated consumer demand at the projected time the investment will begin producing goods and services (t - 2).

The Kelsos do not deny that increased capital investment has historically accompanied economic growth that would not have materialized without the new capital formation. Indeed, the concept of productiveness is an expression of that relationship. Productive capital at t - 1, however, is not feasible without correlative consumer demand at t - 2. Because binary financing produces more real consumer income at t - 2 than traditional financing for any given amount of capital formation, it provides greater incentives for investment than traditional "savings-based" financing.

To understand the "savings controversy," it is important to recognize that there is in part a definitional difference, and a difference in the analysis of growth ultimately traceable to the difference between productiveness and productivity, and to their relationship to growth. Louis Kelso and Mortimer Adler distinguish between two meanings of the word "savings": "physical savings" and "financial savings." "In a physical sense, 'saving' is simply the use of goods or services to produce capital goods rather than for immediate consumption."[61] In contrast, Kelso and Adler define "financial savings" as "money or credit diverted from immediate use for consumption."[62]

In law, the distinction between financial and physical savings rests on the difference between "property" and "things." Property is not things, physical or intangible, but rights with respect to those things. Financial savings are claims on physical savings. The individual allocations of financial claims on physical savings depend on the rules of the prevailing property system. A private property system with unlimited collateralization rights will produce one allocation of financial claims, whereas one based on binary financing with commercially insured capital credit will produce another.

In traditional economic terms, however, viewing the binary system as an appropriation or dilution of the property of non-benefiting investors and consumers (and therefore as a reliance on savings in the physical sense) does not negate the potential growth that binary economic theory has predicted. To the contrary, the validity of those growth predictions does not depend upon whether or not binary financing is viewed as an appropriation or dilution of existing savings of persons not commensurately benefiting from the extension of credit.

Although it has received little attention in recent times, an examination of the savings-investment-growth question by economist Harold G. Moulton corroborates the binary economic premises and supports binary growth predictions.[63] Moulton, then president of The Brookings Institution, published his analysis in 1935, when the United States was struggling to understand the causes of the Great Depression and discover the way to economic recovery.

The relevant portion of Moulton's analysis is set forth below:

> According to the traditional viewpoint, an expansion in
> the rate of capital accumulation can be accomplished only by

a reduction in the rate of output of consumption goods—because labor and materials have to be transferred from one type of activity to the other. Evidence shows conclusively, however, that consumption and capital formation do expand and contract together.[64]

In considering whether consumption or investment leads the recovery-growth process, Moulton presented the conflicting theories of those who advocate stimulation of consumer demand and those who stress capital investment as the necessary starting point for growth.[65] Moulton found that rise and fall in economic growth "appear to have originated in forces affecting the output of goods destined for consumption. . . ."[66]

The motivating force in all economic activity, under a system of private initiative, is the wants and demands of people. The base of the economic pyramid is the production of consumption goods—primary necessities, first and comforts and luxuries later. In the ascending scale of goods that are relatively indispensable we find new plant and equipment at the top. This is simply because the demand for plant and equipment is derived from the demand for the consumption goods which such plant and equipment can produce.[67]

Foreshadowing binary financing theory, Moulton later concluded:

. . . the best hope of success in stimulating a strong recovery movement through concerted action would be to operate on both the consumption side and the capital side simultaneously, for each might be expected to reinforce the other.[68]

To operate on both the consumption and capital sides, Moulton would resort to the banking system to expand credit, but, unlike Kelso, he did not focus on the concept of productiveness or the need for restructuring private property rights. Nevertheless, his defense of the use of such credit is instructive:

. . . it is possible to increase the supply of capital goods without an antecedent or concurrent restriction of consumption. The truth is that the accelerated capital expansion and increased productivity result in an increased output of both capital goods and consumer goods. Thus real wages are increased. The history of capital expansion and wage and price trends in the United States affords no support for the theory that bank credit expansion merely means *involuntary* savings. Nor do the facts support the thesis that savings in the sense of positively reducing consumption is essential to the formation of capital.[69]

Several points deserve emphasis. First, when the Kelsos and Adler maintain that individuals and society need not choose between consumption and investment, they do not claim that the same item of resource or human service may simultaneously be expended in providing a consumer and a producer good or service. Their growth theory does hold, however, that an alternative property system based on binary economics would produce a broader distribution of ownership, which will in turn create noninflationary real market demand for more resources and services that would not be feasible for investment without the broader distribution of capital ownership. Second, the fact that the institution of the binary alternative system may be viewed in traditional economic terms as an appropriation or dilution of the property of non-benefiting investors and consumers (and therefore a reliance on a redistribution of their savings for the investment benefit of the new binary owners) does not negate the predicted binary economic growth potential resulting from a broader distribution of ownership. To the contrary, nothing in the savings-investment-growth controversy undermines the prospect of binary growth or, therefore, the reality of the economic choice offered by the Kelsonian economic and private property system, which up to now has been virtually ignored by traditional economic scholarship.[70]

Choosing Among Paradigms

The Kelsonian conception of economics and property rights provides a foundational challenge to the traditional paradigm for the analysis of economic behavior.[71] The organizing vision of productiveness-based economic analysis is not congruent with traditional productivity-based economics. There are important differences between the two in terms of the meanings of important variables and the mathematical relationships among those variables.[72]

Beyond the formal discipline of economics, the conception of what is theoretically possible and the expectation of what is reasonably achievable are both bounded by the limitations and experiences of the traditional approach to economics. To evaluate binary economics fairly, one must consider it in a context that neither excludes it theoretically from the realm of the possible, nor dismisses its predictions because they far exceed the boundaries set by predictions based on traditional theory or on experience in an economy structured on prevailing private property rights.

Pursuing an inquiry consistent with traditional economic theory, however enhanced it may be by other disciplines, may not prove anything to a Kelsonian. Conversely, such an inquiry, if it is consistent with binary theory, may be equally fruitless to a traditional economist. Because proof is itself paradigm-specific, the preference for one paradigm over another may result from judging a newly presented paradigm against one generally accepted as true, rather than evaluating both from neutral principles. The shift in preference from one paradigm to another may be more likely the result of an inductive leap than a proof.

Over time, however, society does make foundation-altering choices regarding paradigms as dramatic as the one characterized by the shift from geocentricism to heliocentricism, known as the "Copernican Revolution."[73] Thus the history of ideas may inform an exploration of binary proposals from competing frames of reference.[74]

In retrospect, replacing one paradigm with another may be explained in part by the operation of three principles of preference that *may* be capable of prospective application in a paradigm-neutral, albeit subjective, way:

(1) *Utility*: Which paradigm accomplishes more of what is desired by description, prediction, and control of the environment?

(2) *Facility*: Though the same events might be described or predicted—and the same results achieved—with the application of different paradigms, which one is easier to apply to achieve the desired ends?

(3) *Simplicity*: To achieve description, prediction, and control, which paradigm requires fewer foundational assumptions and corrective exceptions not implicit in the assumptions?[75]

Although these principles of preference may not be susceptible to easy application, they may provide helpful guidance in evaluating supposedly objective information that alternative models offer to describe and shape our perception of reality. The principles may also have the virtue of being paradigm-neutral, as well as the vice of being ill-defined within the terms of competing paradigms. For these qualities to be embraced and advanced as comparative advantages of any particular paradigm, their necessary definition for the purposes of argument will serve to highlight any paradigmatic bias.

Values beyond the theoretical and empirical operation of the paradigms may be decisive for different evaluators as they apply these principles, particularly the "utility" standard, to paradigms for describing economic behavior.[76] Moreover, when paradigms conflict, empirical measurements designed to "verify" one or another approach may require adjustment for paradigm bias to the extent they are grounded in a methodology favoring one paradigm over another.

For example, Keynesian Paul Samuelson offers as proof that binary theory is an "amateur and cranky fad," the discrepancy between "productiveness" and "productivity" generally reflected in the divergent percentages of productive input assigned to capital and labor.[77] Notwithstanding its "empirical content," this "scientific evidence" of Kelso's so-called "error" merely begs the question because it is premised entirely on the validity of the productivity paradigm that binary economics has drawn into question, and on the present closed private property system rather than the open, democratic private property system that a binary economy would establish.

The relative utility of competing paradigms, particularly new ones offered to challenge existing ones, is not always immediately discernible. The superiority of the Copernican system[78] to the geocentric alternative, in terms of utility, could not have been fully understood for at least 140 years after it was advanced. It set the stage for the work of Johannes Kepler,[79] and, ultimately, to the formulation by Sir Isaac Newton of his general laws of motion for both celestial and earthly bodies.[80] These laws could not have been inferred from the "reality" of an earth-centered solar system.

Thus in evaluating competing paradigms with regard to their social utility, one must counteract the inherent prejudice of accepted paradigms. One must suspend adherence to preconceptions and "avoid mistaking an organizing construct for a structural reality that, by defining the possible, limits vision and deadens will."[81]

Conclusion

The Kelsos thus maintain that a democratic private property system structured to achieve universal capital ownership on free market principles should be our national goal. The Kelsos' binary vision offers the prospect of general affluence, leisure, and individual economic independence in an increasingly democratic, privatized, and capital-rich economy. All of the old seemingly insolvable problems that have pitted left against right are swept away. Dedicated scholars should not dismiss binary theory without giving it a careful, rigorous consideration.

For a fair consideration, it is necessary to understand binary theory in its own terms, in a paradigm-neutral context, before judging it, and to evaluate binary proposals not only with respect to traditional economic suppositions based on productivity, but also with respect to binary suppositions based on productiveness.

For years, binary economics has been shut out of an economics discipline that has proven unable to solve persistent problems of poverty and cycles of depression and unwilling to examine an alternative promise to do so. But given a binary property rights system, an alternate theory of economic production and distribution, and the altered institutional and decisional environment, there is much in the proposals and theory of binary economics to be explored by people of good will from all disciplines and callings.

Notes:

[1]The theory of binary economics, originated by Louis O. Kelso, was first published in L. Kelso & M. Adler, *The Capitalist Manifesto* (1958). Since then it has been developed and explicated in L. Kelso & M. Adler, *The New Capitalists* (1961); L. Kelso & P. Hetter, *Two-Factor Theory* (1967); L. Kelso & P. Kelso, *Democracy and Economic Power: Extending the ESOP Revolution Through Binary Economics* (1990), recommended by Kelso as his most definitive statement of binary economics. For a more complete statement of the author's views see "The Binary Economics of Louis Kelso: The Promise of Universal Capitalism," published in *Rutgers Law Journal* 22: 3, (1990) and "Louis Kelso's Binary Economic Democracy," presented to the Fourth Annual Conference of the Society for the Advancement of Socioeconomics (1991).

Binary economics has also been referred to as "two-factor theory," *Two-Factor Theory*, 3; "social capitalism," Kelso & Hetter, "The Right to Be Productive," (pts. 1 & 2), *Financial Planner*, August 1982, 50, 51 (part 1); *Financial Planner*, September 1982, 86 (part 2); and "universal capitalism," *Two-Factor Theory*, 3-8. "In the phrase 'universal capitalism' the word 'universal' means approximately what it does in the phrase 'universal suffrage'" (Ibid. 7).

[2]The Kelsos, Louis and Patricia, take exception not only to Marxist theory, as originally proposed by Karl Marx, but also to all of its revisions and applications of socialism around the world. Likewise, they reject all forms of modern capitalist economic theory including laissez-faire classical economics, Keynesianism, monetarism, and supply-side economics. They embrace Adam Smith and his contemporary, Jean-Baptiste Say, but maintain that *The Wealth of Nations* must be purged of a factual error which became apparent only after the full bloom of the Industrial Revolution. Specifically, traditional economic theory fails to comprehend and properly account for the increasing productive input of capital.

[3]Smith assumed that the only way people can engage in production is to perform labor work. "The real price of every thing, what every thing really costs to the man who wants to acquire it, is the toil and trouble in acquiring it" (A. Smith, *An Inquiry into the Nature and Causes of the Wealth of Nations* [E. Cannan ed. 1937] 30). His writings evidence no anticipation of how extensively people could engage in production through the ownership of private capital. This assumption permeates the socialist and capitalist economic literature, (Kelso & Kelso, "Afterword: The ESOP as a First Step in New Age Economics," *Employee Stock Ownership Plans* [R. Smiley, Jr. & R. Gilbert eds. 1989] AF-2; Accord *Dictionary of Business and Economics* 259 [C. Ammer & D. Ammer eds. 1984]. The binary concept of productiveness belies Smith's assumption.

[4]People are poor because they have not acquired the capital needed to supplement their labor productiveness.

[5]Whether the proposals based on binary economics involve the taking of existing property is subject to controversy and depends upon one's analysis of growth and upon the definition of private property.

[6]This approach should not be confused, however, with those advanced in the social credit movement of Major Douglas. See note 17.

[7]"The theory of universal capitalism challenges the classicists, the Marxians, . . . the Keynesians, [the monetarists, and the supply siders] precisely on the point on which they all agree: the goal of full employment. Universal Capitalism rejects this goal as (1) humanly repugnant, (2) functionally inadequate, and (3) socially perilous" (L. Kelso & P. Hetter, *Two-Factor Theory* [1967] 31). Such a goal elevates work to an end in itself, rather than as a means to enjoy consumption, and thereby promotes unnecessary toil and suffering (Ibid.). Indeed, in an Aristotelian sense, full employment is a formula for enslavement of the citizenry (L. Kelso & M. Adler, *The Capitalist Manifesto* [1958] 13-29). Rather, the goal of the economy should be universal capital ownership (Ibid.). "A capitalist society would cast out the irrational doctrine of full employment. As more and more of its wealth is produced by capital and less by labor, more households would participate in the production of wealth as owners of capital and fewer as owners of labor" (L. Kelso & M. Adler, *The New Capitalists* [1961] 87). For an increasing number of the population, employment through capital ownership and "[u]nemployment . . . [as a laborer] is natural and desirable in technically advanced economies" (Ibid.) 4).

[8]A. Smith, op. cit. 30-33.

[9]L. Kelso, "Poverty's Other Exit," *41 North Dakota Law Review 147* (1965) 152.

[10]In assessing economic proposals, "universal capitalism . . . asks *whose* private ownership? *whose* free enterprise?" L. Kelso & P. Hetter, *Two-Factor Theory*, 4 (emphasis in original).

[11]See, e.g., L. Thurow, *Generating Inequality: Mechanisms of Distribution in the U.S. Economy* (1975) 196-202, explaining Dean Thurow's taxation strategies for "Altering the Distribution of Physical Wealth"; Gramlich, "Economists' View of the Welfare System," *Am. Econ. Rev.: Papers & Proc., May 1989* 191, including references to works by, inter alia, Alan S. Blinder, Milton Friedman, Arthur M. Okun and James Tobin.

[12]*Democracy and Economic Power*, 11-47.

[13]The best known of these trusts is the Employee Stock Ownership Plan (ESOP).

[14]*Democracy and Economic Power*, 108-109, 111.

[15]Here "net return" is income net of reserves for depreciation and research and development, but no additional retention of earning for new capital formation.

[16]At the heart of these predications is the premise that binary financing will effect a broader distribution of capital ownership, as compared with traditional financing, and that this broader distribution will produce a larger economy. Given binary premises, traditional economic strategies continually fail to exploit the full growth potential of the economy by failing to apply financing techniques that promote a broader distribution of capital ownership. However, the idea that broader distribution of capital ownership will, in itself, generate a larger economy conflicts with the dominant approaches of traditional economic theory, and provides perhaps the most difficult conceptual problem for those relying on traditional theory to judge binary theory and proposals. This subject is developed further, infra, at notes 7, 43, 46, 52, and accompanying text.

[17]To avoid confusion with the analysis of Major Clifford Douglas (which they reject) the Kelsos do not use the term "social credit," but rather "commercially insured capital credit." See, e.g., L. Kelso & P. Kelso, *Democracy and Economic Power* (1986) 105. See generally C. Douglas, *Credit-Power and Democracy* (1921); C. Douglas, *Economic Democracy* (1920); C. Douglas, *The Monopoly of Credit* (1931); C. Douglas, *The Nature of Democracy* (1934); W. Hiskett, *Social Credits or Socialism: An Analysis of the Douglas Credit Scheme* (1935); E. Holter, *The ABC of Social Credit* (1934).

[18]For a description of the ESOP and a practitioners handbook, see R. Smiley and R. Gilbert, *Employee Stock Ownership Plans.*

[19]*General Accounting Office, Employee Stock Ownership Plans: Benefits and Costs of ESOP Tax Incentives for Broadening Stock Ownership* (1986) 18-19. The GAO estimated that "the cost of ESOP tax incentives averaged between $1.7 billion and $1.9 billion per year during the period from 1977-1983, for a total of $12.1 billion to $13.3 billion over that period" (Ibid. 5).

[20]As verified via telephone communication with the National Center for Employee Ownership.

[21]*Democracy and Economic Power*, 31. French political economist Jean-Baptiste Say (1767-1832) developed the principle.

[22]Say's Law "holds that in a market economy the aggregate market value of the wealth produced is equal to the aggregate purchasing power created by the process of production" (*Two-Factor Theory*, 10).

[23]T. Sowell, *Say's Law: An Historical Analysis* (1972) 3-4. Accord T. Sowell, *Classical Economics Reconsidered* (1974) 37-45. Professor Sowell has described the controversy:

"The idea that supply creates its own demand—Say's Law—appears on the surface to be one of the simplest propositions in economics, and one which should be readily proved or disproved. Yet this doctrine has produced two of the most sweeping, bitter, and long-lasting controversies in the history of economics—first in the early nineteenth century and then erupting again a hundred years later in the Keynesian revolution of the 1930's. Each of these outbursts of controversy lasted more than twenty years, involved almost every noted economist of the time, and had repercussions on basic economic theory, methodology, and sociopolitical policy. The shock waves from these controversies were felt well beyond the confines of economics, and evoked powerful emotions among people unacquainted with the technical issues involved or even with economics in general. In retrospect it is clear that the history of Say's law is an important part of intellectual history generally, and has important implications for the dynamics of controversy, the nature of intellectual orthodoxy and insurgency, and the complex relationships among ideology, concepts, and policies.

. . . [T]he two great controversies over Say's law which shook the foundations of economics were . . . different in one crucial respect: the supporters of Say's law won a resounding victory in the nineteenth century, while its opponents triumphed in the twentieth century. In each case the victory was followed by intellectual guerrilla warfare. The most prominent of the later nineteenth century opponents of Say's law was Karl Marx. The Keynesian ascendancy, after dethroning Say's Law in the 1930's and 1940's, has been challenged even more effectively—to a point approaching a counterrevolution, in which the most prominent name has been Milton Friedman."

[24]*Democracy and Economic Power*, 34. Others have recognized the controversy: "Historically, Say's Law emerged in the wake of the industrial revolution, when the two striking new economic phenomena of vastly increased output and the economy's cyclical inability to maintain sales and employment led some to fear that there was some inherent limit to the growth of production—some point beyond which there would be no means of purchasing it all" *(4 The New Palgrave, A Dictionary of Economics* 249 [J. Eatwell, M. Milgate & P. Newman eds. 1987]). But see *Dictionary of Business and Economics* op. cit. 415 acknowledging the controversy but denying the validity of Say's Law.

[25]See, e.g., I. Magaziner & R. Reich, *Minding America's Business* 2-3 (1982); *Dictionary of Business and Economics*, 451.

[26]In his break with classical economics, John Maynard Keynes rejected Say's Law. T. Sowell, *Say's Law*, 201-07. Accord Power, *"The Economics of Keynes," Economics and Human Welfare* [M. Boskin ed. 1979] 321, 331). According to the Kelsos, the idea that Keynes was free to reject Say's Law "is as naive and groundless as asserting that the National Aeronautics and Space Administration has repealed the law of gravity" (*Two-Factor Theory*, 187-88 n.10).

[27]Markets are not efficiently able to facilitate a drop in prices to clear supplies according to Keynesian theory, largely because money supply prices, particularly money wages, are "sticky" downward (Wells, *"Money and the Money Wage Rate," in Economics and Human Welfare*, 393-98; see also *The New Palgrave*, 4: 251, explaining post-Keynesian criticism of Say's Law).

[28]L. Kelso & P. Hetter, *"The Right to be Productive," Financial Planner*, (August 1982) 31-38.

[29]*Democracy and Economic Power*, 31-38.

[30]Ibid. As a result of this linkage, the Kelsos frequently refer to binary financing as "simulfinancing" (Ibid 47, 61-62, 130-31, 151, 157-58, 169-70).

[31]*Two-Factor Theory*, 62.

[32]Ibid. See also 10, 60-61.

[33]*The New Palgrave, 3:* 831, 837-38. Accord *Dictionary of Business and Economics*, 383. Reliance placed by traditional economics on competitive market theory is probably best explained by the perceived weakness of analyses based on imperfect competition rather than on the inherent strength of competitive market theory (*The New Palgrave, 3:* 837-38).

[34]*The New Palgrave, 3:* 838.

[35]See, e.g., *Democracy and Economic Power*, 17.

[36]*Dictionary of Business and Economics*, 369.

[37]Ibid.

[38]Ibid.

[39]Ibid. 286; Accord, *The New Palgrave, 3:* 323.

[40]"Labor productivity increases because of improved technology, improvements in labor skills, or capital deepening" (P. Samuelson & W. Nordhaus, *Economics* [12th ed. 1985] 912).

[41]*The New Palgrave, 3:* 1010-13.

[42]"The Right to Be Productive," 54.

[43]In understanding the binary vision of capital as an independent instrument of production, like labor power, one might imagine every piece of capital as an unattended robot, regardless of the degree or kind of human input required to create, operate, maintain it, or otherwise make it continually productive. In this sense, one can see productiveness as a complete rejection of the labor theory of value.

[44]"The Right to Be Productive," 93. Poverty is a relative concept. A middle class home may seem sparse to the rich and opulent to the poorest among us. According to the Kelsos, people are poor in an industrial economy if they do not receive a substantial portion of their consumer income through their capital ownership.

[45]L. Kelso & P. Hetter, "Recommendations by Louis Kelso and Kelso & Company to the U.S. Department of Labor Concerning the Governance of the Corporation" (Jan. 15, 1985) 5-6, unpublished, emphasis in original.

[46]*Democracy and Economic Power*, 138-39. Kelso's claim that capital accounts for 80-90% of societal productiveness seems to contradict consistent empirical findings, based on modern economic theory premised on marginal productivity, that labor claims between 70% and 80% of the income. Binary economics does not dispute those findings, but takes issue with the premise that the market for capital and labor can competitively value the respective inputs when most people are effectively barred from acquiring capital. In the binary view, much modern economic theory disregards the redistribution inherent in the legal and social structure which is designed to give more pay in return for less work from laborers. As industry changes from labor-intensive to capital-intensive, traditional financing does not provide an effective way for most people to acquire a viable share of the capital that produces an increasing proportion of total societal output.

[47]If one defines a capitalist as one who earns least one-half his or her consumer income from capital ownership, then in even the largest and most successful of capitalist economies, the traditional approach has produced many workers and welfare dependents, but few capitalists. See *Two-Factor Theory*, 5; *The New Capitalists*, 10. Studies on the distribution of wealth and income show that a disproportionately large amount of income is concentrated in the hands of a small percentage of the population.

[48]It is the feasibility principle that makes binary financing practicable: "New Capital formation in well-managed businesses (e.g., the top 2,000 U.S. corporations) does not come into existence unless it will pay for itself in a reasonable short period of time—generally under five years. One of the key responsibilities of management is the enforcement of this rule. *Newly formed capital is therefore inherently financeable*" (*Two-Factor Theory*, 61, emphasis in original). The Kelsos continue: "Well-managed businesses rigidly subject the nonhuman factor to 'birth control.' The human factor, by contrast, comes into existence without reference to the economy's physical need for labor" (Ibid.).

[49]The federal government taxes income from capital net of deductions for depreciation and research and development. These deductions indicate the cornerstone of national economic policy to encourage the perpetual maintenance of the capital estates of existing owners, but no comparable facilitation policy enables people without capital to acquire an estate worth preserving.

[50]Managers, of course, do not always succeed in their feasibility judgments. For reasons of poor planning or management, as well as unforeseen circumstances, ventures fail. Hopefully, in a competitive environment, managers who fail do not remain managers. On the other hand, the risk of failure can be calculated and offset through the application of insurance principles. See Kelso and Hetter, "Uprooting World Poverty: A Job for Business" *Business Horizons*, Graduate School of Business, Indiana University (1964), and *Democracy and Economic Power*, 42, 44, 105, 106, 108-109, 111, 164.

[51]'The Right to Be Productive," 54 (emphasis in original). "Such excess productive power we call 'morbid capital,' because its nature, like that of cancer, is to grow without symbiotic relationship to the organism to which it is attached."

[52]All proposed binary financing would be reviewed "first by corporate management, then by commercial lending institutions, then by commercial capital credit insurance underwriters, and, finally, perhaps by the CDRC and/or the [Central] Bank (*Democracy and Economic Power*, 113).

[53]As explained more fully below, a binary time frame is the time it takes capital to pay for itself and then begin earning a spendable income for its owners. See discussion, infra, under the heading "Binary Growth in a Binary Timeframe."

[54]Self-financing capital acquisition requires sufficient gross income for depreciation and research and development reserves to restore capital perpetually to a technologically current state.

[55]Note, further, that the growth effects of Kelso's capitalization process may start before the fifth year. First, with a five-year capital planning horizon, the anticipated increase in consumption may be reflected in additional capital spending as early as the first year. Second, to the extent the return on the equity represented by the binary stock exceeds the debt-servicing requirements, income will be available for payment to the binary beneficiaries before completion of the capital recovery. Third, to the extent that consumers feel wealthier by reason of their capital ownership, their marginal savings and consumption rates will shift toward more consumption even before they begin to receive binary income.

[56]In twenty years, three-fourths of the annual binary capital acquisitions will be generating an income for their new owners. In fifty years, ninety percent. In the long run, the portion of binary capital that, having repaid its acquisition cost, is generating current income for its beneficiaries approaches 100%.

[57]As people derive increasing income through their capital acquisition rights, they will be less dependent on traditional welfare and make-work employment.

[58]Note here the implicit distinction between efficiency and productivity. If productiveness has economic significance, it produces an efficiency (more growth) not caused by increased productivity considerations.

[59]*Democracy and Economic Power*, 36.

[60]"New capital formation—economic growth—has been artificially and needlessly limited by the availability of savings or existing capital ownership. . ." (*The New Capitalists*, 105). The proposition that the economy must "choose between current consumption and capital investment [is] an artificial necessity that has long depressed market demand in Western industrial societies" (*Democracy and Economic Power*, 37). "The logic of . . . insured capital credit financing eliminates institutional limits on the availability of capital credit, which are mythical except when based upon shortages of physical ingredients to production and consumption of goods and services." (Ibid. 113). "Only where a shortage of labor, raw materials, or know-how exists would there be any reason to choose . . between increased consumption and new capital formation. In all other instances, new capital formation and personal consumption would normally expand simultaneously" (*The New Capitalists*, 101).

[61]*The New Capitalists*, 9-10.

[62]Ibid. 9.

[63]H. Moulton, *The Formation of Capital* (1935).

[64]Ibid. 43. Moulton then offers analysis of the period from 1901 through 1932 to establish his empirical assertions. (Ibid. 43-47).

[65]Ibid. 49-55.

[66]Ibid. 71.

[67]Ibid. 71-72.

[68]Ibid. 73-74.

[69]H. Moulton, G. Edwards, J. Magee & C. Lewis, *Capital Expansion, Employment, and Economic Stability* (1940) 26, emphasis in original.

[70]For a survey of the meager analysis of binary theory by professional economists, see Robert Ashford, "The Binary Economics of Louis Kelso: The Promise of Universal Capitalism." *Rutgers Law Journal 22:1* (1990), 75-96.

[71]See T. Kuhn, *The Structures of Scientific Revolutions* (1962). In this context, a "paradigm" is an analytical system of rules used for description, prediction, and verification. "Description" includes definition of fundamental entities, variables, and dynamic relations among them; verification includes empirical techniques and rules of proof.

[72]As an example of an important difference in the mathematical relationships among variables, consider the concept of "underutilization." For the traditional laissez faire microeconomist, underutilization of resources is a special case because generally efficient markets operate to employ all resources to the level of their marginal product. In binary economics, underutilization is the general rule so long as savings-based financing is the dominant technique for capital acquisition because market-generated consumer purchasing power is thereby suppressed (*The New Capitalists* 114).

[73]See J. Dreyer, *A History of Astronomy from Thales to Kepler (2d* ed. 1953) 240-344; A. Koyré, *Astronomical Revolution* (1973) 57; T. Kuhn, *The Copernican Revolution* (1957) 74-75.

[74]The analogy to epicycular revision in astronomy may offer insight regarding the current state of economics. For least the last decade, popular print media have offered a steady stream of articles, essays, and editorials decrying the failure of predictive accuracy of economics. See, e.g., Gelman, "What Good Are Economists?," *Newsweek* (Feb. 4, 1984) 60. "Within the profession, the unifying Keynesian consensus has given way to a fractious squabble, as old theories and established models seem to square less and less with reality. Respected theorists line up on opposite sides of central questions, such as whether budget deficits affect interest rates" The article emphasizes the inability of professional forecasting firms, independent consultants and university professors to predict quarterly economic results with consistent accuracy. See also Brock, "Seeing the Economy's Future with a Shattered Crystal Ball," *Insight* (June 30, 1986) 42, 43: "'Macroeconomic theory is in absolute shambles' says William A. Niskanen, Jr., former chairman of President Reagan's Council of Economic Advisors. . . . 'The standard models, used to predict the economy for decades have been discredited. . .'"; Van Dyke, "Why Economists make Mistakes," *Bankers Mag.* (May-June 1986) 69, 69: "Lately it is difficult to pick up a newspaper or magazine without an article on economists' inability to forecast." Silk, "Economic Scene: Where did We Go Wrong?,"*N.Y. Times*, (Jan. 1, 1982) 36, describing economists' concern about the failure of modern economics to address contemporary problems.

[75]See Eichner, "Can Economics Become a Science?,"*Challenge*, (Nov.-Dec. 1986) 4, 5-6, offering "coherence," "correspondence," "comprehensiveness," and "parsimony" as four factors by which economics and alternative paradigms might be judged in terms of scientific rigor.

[76]Thus an economic approach that creates a smaller pie might still be preferred if it achieves a larger real distribution to those most needy, or makes good character by providing more equal property acquisition rights.

[77]118 *Cong. Rec.* 20,207 (1972): statement of Paul Samuelson, read into the record by Sen. Harris.

[78]See generally Copernicus, *The Revolution of Heavenly Bodies* (1543).

[79]Johannes Kepler (1571—1630), after twenty years' observations of the sun and planets, crystallized his observations into three laws. The first placed the earth and other planets in elliptical paths around the sun, with the sun one focus; the second held that if a line were drawn between each planet and the sun, the line sweeps equal areas in equal time intervals; and the third stated that the square of the period of each planet's revolution around the sun is proportional to the cube of its distance from the sun (T. Ashford, *The Physical Sciences: From Atoms to Stars*, [2d ed. 1967] 54-55).

[80]"[I]n a single law, Newton synthesized all the motions and regularities of the solar system[.]" and "showed that the heavenly bodies obey the same laws as here on earth" (Ibid. 56). See I. Newton, *Philosophiae Naturalis Principia Mathematica* (1687).

[81]Michaelman, "Reflections on Professional Education, Legal Scholarship, and the Law-and-Economics Movement," *Journal of Legal Education, 3:* (1983) 201.

— 7 —

Capital Credit:
The Ultimate Right of Citizenship

by Kathy V. Friedman
(Presentation at 86th Annual Meeting of the American Sociological
Association, August 23-27, 1991, Cincinnati, Ohio)

"The first task of the problem-solver is to persuasively define the problem."
—Stephen L. Esquith, Professor James Madison College,
Michigan State University.

Introduction

This work presents the case for modernizing the rules of society that govern access to future wealth, and institutionalizing those rules as economic rights for citizens of constitutional, democratic regimes. These economic rights would parallel the civil, political, and social rights that have been created—respectively—during the eighteenth, nineteenth, and twentieth centuries in the West.

As we stand on the threshold of the twenty-first century, we—by which I mean the world in general and America, in particular—do so with some outstanding social inventions. From them, we may construct even more outstanding social institutions to enter the new age. The two social inventions that could result in the further embellishment of the institution of citizenship are technology and capital credit. Institutionalizing a new relationship between these two phenomena could revolutionize the relationship between the citizen and the state for all time.

I would like to show that access to "capital" credit—also called "self-liquidating" credit (to be defined below)—would be the ultimate property right, the ultimate citizenship right, and—in fact—a highly plausible institutional device for bringing sufficient income into the households of tomorrow's citizens without further income redistribution.

In 1981 I wrote a book on the relationship between the citizen and the state, *Legitimation of Social Rights and the Western Welfare State: A Weberian Perspective*, University of North Carolina Press. In it, I applied Weber's sociology of law, using his types of authority to analyze the rise of the modern welfare state. I showed, specifically, the rationale by which the modern democratic state legitimated itself when taking on the function of income redistribution—without appearing to reduce the status of citizens by patronizing them. I traced, therefore, the process by which the social rights of the welfare state were created and legitimated as part of the status of citizenship.

After publication of the book in 1981, I moved to Washington, DC, and worked on Capitol Hill for several years. It became apparent to me that, despite the rise and expansion of the welfare state, Americans were still having trouble bringing sufficient income into their households from labor force participation.

From my vantage point as a Legislative Assistant in a Congressional office, I saw many types of legislation introduced to address this problem: extended unemployment compensation, trade adjustment assistance, individual training account, import quotas, extended health benefit coverage for employees laid off from firms, advance notice of plant closing, increases in the minimum wage, and the like. Although in the mid-1980's, 42% of every U.S. budget dollar went as a direct transfer to individuals, Americans were suffering from a declining standard of living relative to the immediately preceding decades. Why?

I began to rethink the rise of the welfare state. While in *Legitimation of Social Rights* I was concerned with the *justifications* that were articulated by policymakers in order to make the welfare state possible, I am now concerned with the *distributional* problem that the welfare state was instituted to address. That problem is the relationship among people, work, and income, and specifically, the social institutions for allocating wealth to societal members in an age of increasing technological advance and attendant economic dislocations.

From a distributional standpoint, the welfare state was a response to the declining opportunity for people to derive income from labor force participation. Due to the intense productivity generated by the application of technology, Western economies began undergoing vicissitudes in the business cycle, vicissitudes that periodically threw people out of the labor force because their productivity was not needed. Then, the enormous societal wealth generated by the application of technology was taxed by the welfare state and redistributed through an increasing series of programs to individuals, households, and communities in American society.

To be sure, when the welfare state was instituted, policymakers assumed it would be a temporary phenomenon, redistributing income until economies "righted" themselves. Economies did not do so. In fact, the issue of income distribution in American society grew more complicated with the rise of robotics, increasing international competition, and the deterioration of economies worldwide due to inflation and debt. Moreover, income inequalities have not substantially narrowed for the last few decades. Finally, the political popularity/legitimacy of the welfare state has declined, though not the actual dollar volume of redistributions. Where do we go from here? Have we been trying to solve the wrong problem?

It was with this question in mind that I began "Capital Credit: the Ultimate Right of Citizenship" to provide an innovative framework for a new connection between the worker and the economy, the citizen and the state under democratic regimes. The social institution which would embody this new, unique, original relationship would be the economic right of citizens to access "capital" or "self-liquidating" credit.

The Nature of "Capital" or "Self-liquidating" Credit

"Capital," "self-liquidating," or "income-producing" credit (terms to be used interchangeably throughout this document) must first be distinguished from "consumer" credit—the latter of which is already widely distributed throughout America. Consumer credit is the kind "we don't leave home without." It confers the right to spend resources we do not have, but expect to have in the foreseeable future. It dares consumers to bite off more than they can chew.

From 1980 to the present, the outstanding consumer credit loans of Americans have escalated from $300 billion to $795 billion.[1] According to the Credit Research Center at Purdue University, the average American household now holds $7,500 in consumer debt, including car loans. This amounts to 18 percent of after-tax income, the highest consumer debt figures since World War II. Consumer credit creates debt.

By contrast, capital credit or self-liquidating credit is that which is extended to buy a commodity that will pay for itself, an apartment building, for example, from which rents would pay the mortgage. The debt incurred through borrowing "self-liquidates." Moreover, an income-producing commodity is left in place of what was formerly the debt, and the commodity continues to produce income or its owner. Capital credit, therefore, creates wealth.

Before continuing, let me interject two important points: first, there are many people in the U. S. who already have access to capital credit. Second, all rights—civil, political, and social—first start out as attaching to a very small sector of the citizenry, and then end up by being expanded, successively, to everyone. Taken together, these two premises foreshadow the feasibility of the argument that I will be making. Namely, the institutional framework already exists for economic rights in capital credit, and for their democratization as part of the rights attaching to the status of citizenship.

We are now ready to ask: who are the people in today's society that already have access to capital credit, and how did they gain access? What income-producing commodities do they buy with their credit?

Credit Buys Technology

Today, the chief income-producing commodity bought on capital credit is technology. According to a recent Plant and Expenditures Survey conducted by the U. S. Census Bureau, $476 billion was granted in loans—that is to say, on credit—for the expansion of America's business and industry in 1989. [2] This figure is 10.8 percent higher than the credit extended the previous year, 1988. The projected figure for 1990 was $513 billion, 7.8 percent more than in 1989.

Capital credit is readily extended for the purchase of technology because technology is the ultimate wealth-producer in the history of civilization. The overwhelming percentage of a modern industrialized nation's GNP is the result of the application not of human sweat and toil, but of technology. Thus the chief category of people in society whose status permits purchases of income-producing technology are the stockholders of business and industry. By virtue of being stockholders, their access to capital credit is automatic: they need not put up their own assets in order for the company in which they own stock to take out loans for corporate expansion.

After a loan is repaid from a company's profits through expansion, subsequent profits accrue for time immemorial to the stockholders and, if they will it, their descendants. These profits reflect themselves in dividend checks and in increased value of the stock. The usual names for this type of income are "property income" or "unearned income." I also will refer to this as "income from ownership."

The irony here is that neither property income nor income redistributions are "earned" in the sense of pay for work. Yet the early redistributions of the U.S. welfare state were legitimized as rightful because they were "earned" by paying part of one's labor earnings into the Social Security system (Friedman, 1981). We, as a society, have found many ways to institutionalize "unearned" income through redistribution. Yet, we have not thought to institutionalize access to the "unearned" income that results from property ownership, and in particular, ownership of wealth-producing technology.

By institutionalizing—through economic rights in capital credit— access to the enormous wealth that technology creates, wealth could be allocated to society's members through the *primary* income distribution (i.e., property income or income from work), vastly reducing the politically tenuous income *redistributions* of the welfare state. Moreover, I shall argue that if human labor power is not the chief factor of wealth creation, it makes income from work very tenuous, and it makes income from redistribution increasingly problematic as those redistributions continue to escalate.

This takes us to the next, and most crucial part of this argument: how did those who today have access to income-producing credit— and who thereby receive income from ownership—get into that fortunate position? To answer this question, it is necessary to step back into the early stages of history to study the evolving relationship between technology and the creation and distribution of wealth. Then we will see how that relationship could be re-institutionalized in order to disseminate widely the future wealth that technology will create. The following exposition of how we arrived at our present paradigm will clarify why we have chosen—to date—to redistribute income rather than to redistribute ownership opportunities.

Technology Creates Wealth

As human history has progressed from its dawn to the present, the relationship between human energy, machine energy, and the production and distribution of wealth has undergone vast changes. In his 1966 book, *Power and Privilege: A Theory of Social Stratification*, Gerhard Lenski showed how the production of wealth increased exponentially with the application of new technologies—at first in the agricultural sector, next in the manufacturing sector, and finally in the service sector of human societies.

While societies remained at the subsistence level, there was very little inequality in the distribution of wealth: scarcity equalized the position of each societal member relative to the others. Technology, at this stage, consisted in rudimentary tools to work the land. The tribe—as a unit—reaped its meager rewards.

As technology became more efficient, particularly with the harnessing of animal power, a societal surplus developed. A "surplus" refers to that which was not immediately consumed for survival. As the surplus increased, it did not reach the hands of each societal member in equal shares. Rather, social classes emerged according to their differential command over, and enjoyment of, the surplus societal wealth. Accordingly, the political, military, and religious elites and the artisans and others who attended to their needs were the first to occupy the higher rungs on the ladder of social stratification. These elites lived in the first cities.

In exchange for their status and command over wealth, the urban classes provided a certain degree of service to those who produced the surplus. Namely, the urban elite organized and protected the society from outside predators. They also initiated the arts and those aspects of civilization that unfold when some members of society are freed from the relentless toil of working the land.

Thus, during the early stages of human history—up until the Industrial Revolution—ownership of land, or rights to that which was produced on the land, brought wealth to certain members of society, i.e., the landed gentry or the urban elites. Land was the chief source of wealth. Those who were in the best position to put up money for the new machine technologies that constituted the Industrial Revolution, therefore, were the landowners. Just as this class had been receiving income from ownership of land, it began to receive income from ownership of mechanization. (To anticipate my later argument, in nineteenth century America, land was again the chief form of national wealth, and in order to develop this valuable resource, the 1862 Homestead Act was passed to disseminate access to land to all Americans. Here the argument will be advanced that equivalent legislation is needed today to disseminate access to machine wealth—a dissemination that has not been made since the Industrial Revolution.)

Wealth Distribution Falls into an Immutable Pattern

The rank and file, on the other hand, continued to receive their income from work: formerly working the land, many shifted to the factories. *Thus the Industrial Revolution crystallized the pattern of income from ownership and income from work that had been, and would continue to be, the major paradigm for the distribution of wealth in human societies for the ensuing centuries.*

This paradigm—pejoratively known as "capitalism"—provided the definition of the situation from which arose the institutions of the welfare state. Namely, when income from work became insufficient as a result of economic depressions in Western nations throughout the twentieth century, the legislation that created the welfare state was geared toward the prevailing paradigm: replacing lost income from work, saving jobs, protecting jobs, training or retraining people for jobs, creating jobs, instituting a minimum wage for job performance, and the like.

In the short term, this made sense: indeed, the welfare state was presumed to be a temporary institution until Western economies righted themselves. (And here an old Russian saying is applicable: "Nothing is so permanent as something that was meant to be temporary.") However, in the long term, it is clear that the U.S., and Western economies in general, are fighting a losing battle. Work, as we know it, is simply not bringing sufficient income into households to provide a standard of living commensurate with the enormous wealth of the nation as a whole. *The Washington Post* has reported that

> Young families with children suffered a 24 percent decline in median income between 1973 and 1987, a figure that approaches the 27 percent decline in per capita income in the Depression years following the 1929 economic collapse. The mortgage payments on a typical house were 21 percent of a young family's average income in 1968, and 51 percent in 1986.[3]

We have been fighting a distribution problem since the initiation of the welfare state. And now, it is clear that the size of the welfare state cannot be increased, expanded or otherwise amplified to correct what remains of the distribution problem. We continue to have the identical problem that we had when the welfare state arose.

The distribution problem rests, ultimately, upon a participation problem: namely, it is not people, through their work, that are the major producers of national wealth. It is technology. Therefore, we have taxed technology and redistributed the wealth that flowed *from* it to those whose *work participation* was replaced *by* it. We have taxed—sometimes doubly and trebly—the wealth that machines produce and redistributed it through the extensive set of rules, regulations, and justifications that together make up the enormously complex welfare state and its various constituencies (the bureaucrats who give and the clients who receive).

Economic participation of most of the populace has been replaced by participation in an *administrative* apparatus. Conversely, the participation of capital—or, more accurately, the participation of those with access to capital investments in technology—is very limited in its distribution to "players" in today's economy. Limited access to ownership opportunities (of modern technology) has been cutting more and more of society's members out of the participation game.

Not really understanding that capital participation is now the name of the game, policymakers have been successively supplementing income from work without reexamining the validity of the assumption that income *should* continue to be inextricably associated with work participation for most of the people most of the time. Our allocative principle needs rethinking. But the immutable habits of human history have overshadowed the initiative needed for institutional change. Instead, policymakers have drifted along—somewhat automatically—on the income-from-work mind-set, backing themselves into a corner from which this paradigm cannot release them.

In the meantime, job opportunities for many categories of workers may continue to diminish. In *The Work Revolution* (1983), Gail Schwartz and William Neikirk hypothesize that the electronics revolution may do for (or to) the work force of the next century what the agricultural revolution did in this century. The agricultural revolution ultimately threw about 97% of the people off the land. Whereas the late stages of the Industrial Revolution threw people out of the factories and into the service economy, the electronics revolution is overtaking the service economy.

Although there are those who are optimistic about the thousands of new jobs that will be created in the future, can we really afford—as students of society, and as policymakers—to overlook the long historical trend of the replacement of human effort by machines, a replacement which has been removing the legitimate basis of income from participation in productive work?

There is no question that the centuries-old pattern is losing its shape: wealth distribution cannot conform—and indeed, has not conformed—immutably to the paradigm of income from ownership and income from work, crystallized earlier in history. The rise and prodigious expansion of the welfare state—which institutionalizes income from redistribution (i.e., neither ownership nor work)—proves that the old pattern can no longer hold. Tomorrow is here: can we formulate a new paradigm?

Credit: The Basis for a New Pattern

We are now at a juncture in human history where the revolutionary ramifications of capital credit could conceivably extricate us from our old income-from-work paradigm. Credit is a remarkable human invention. Just as the invention of money was an abstract form of wealth, and made possible all kinds of transactions that would have been impossible without it, so too, credit is an abstract form of money—and makes possible a whole new pattern of ownership of wealth in society.

First, what is credit? Credit is an agreement between parties that something of immediate value may be conceded to one party in exchange for a promise—from the other party—to return something of equal or greater value at a later time. Extended wisely, credit enriches both lender and borrower.

Today, as the twentieth century draws to a dramatic close, the sophisticated technology that creates our goods and services is bought—as mentioned—predominantly on credit. No longer is it necessary, as it was at the time of the Industrial Revolution, for "real money" to be advanced at the time of purchase.

The implications of this simple fact are astonishing. If making a purchase does not require prior ownership of some form of wealth, then those without wealth could make purchases of commodities that pay for themselves. What they could purchase would be parcels of technology as measured by shares of corporate stock, and they could make these purchases "on credit." Instead of using money in hand to buy parcels of land or the machines in factories, they could use access to capital credit to purchase stock shares in wealth-producing, high-technology enterprises.

This situation would change entirely the sociological characteristics of who in society may own wealth and income-producing property. As political sociologists, we may ask: "What legitimate rationale might our society formulate to institutionalize this possibility as one of the rights of citizenship?"

Democratizing Access to Capital Credit

It should not come as surprise to learn that—in the U.S.—institutional precedents already exist that could serve as a basis for creating such a right. New institutions are often emerging in the wings before receiving society's cue to take center stage. Theory, legislation, and practice have been combined—since the 1970's—to confer on 11 million working Americans today the economic right to capital credit for the ownership of income-producing technology. How did this happen? Could the process be generalized to include more people in American society? The answer to the second question is "Yes!" Now, let us deal with the answer to the first question.

In 1956, Louis Kelso—the late corporate and finance lawyer—articulated an intriguing principle to allocate future corporate wealth without confiscating wealth from those who already had it. He embodied this principle in a legal device which he called the Employee Stock Ownership Plan (ESOP). ESOPs are formal arrangements in which employees in a firm are entitled to acquire and own stock in that firm without putting up their own cash. The viability of the stock rests on the firm's own solvency as collateral, accompanied by the capacity of the firm's technology to pay for itself through greater productiveness and profits.

ESOPs disseminate ownership opportunities in productive technology as follows: under the terms of an ESOP, loan money obtained for company expansion is used to issue new shares of stock, which are then apportioned to eligible employees. This is done through a "leveraged" ESOP. A "leveraged" ESOP is one in which the stock purchased with borrowed money goes into a "suspense account," from which it is gradually "released" into employee accounts as the loan is repaid to the lending institution.

ESOPs also can be used to finance the purchase of outstanding stock, that is, as a device for transferring existing assets to employees. Indeed, in the 1950's Kelso applied the ESOP principle successfully to a small chain of California newspapers, in which the employees became the owners of the firm and collected the dividends of ownership in addition to their regular paychecks.

Nevertheless, the argument has not proceeded all this way just to discuss ESOPs. There is a far larger point, and the point is this: the ESOP is but a specific manifestation of an abstract principle—a very ingenious principle—that could be generalized in order to *distribute directly* to a nation's people the new wealth that future technology will generate, without its first being laundered through a vast welfare state.

We may think of the generalization of the ESOP principle as "the democratization of credit." That is, just as our democracy has measured itself and defined itself by the widespread distribution of civil rights, political rights, and social rights, we are now in a position to create and to disperse economic rights whose content would be access to capital credit.

Consider, for a moment, what this would mean from a historical standpoint: *if* today's policymakers articulated a justification for every member of society to have the right to own shares of stock in profit-making enterprises, *then* we, as a society, would have come full circle to the time in history when—once again—we are all sharing in what is generated by people working together as a social unit (see diagram on p. 149). Only this time around, there is more for society to share among its members than subsistence equality—the wages of a primitive technology of plowshares. The sophisticated technology of today produces wealth, stupendous wealth.

Rather than continue along the path that history pursued after the Industrial Revolution—a path on which wealth generated from the application of an increasingly complex technology became concentrated in the hands of a small percentage of the population called "stockholders"—why not redistribute the status of stockholder as an economic right?

Why continue the cumbersome redistribution—through a welfare state—of a wealth that is in any case generated by machines, by technology (the productive power of capital), not by (the labor power of) stockholders? The welfare state made sense only if it *was* to be temporary. As a permanent social institution, it has shown itself to be inappropriate to the recurring task of leveling out consumption patterns indefinitely.

Justifying Access to Capital Credit

If an entire nation, an entire society of individuals became stockholders in the technology of that society, would that not be unfair to present stockholders? Who would agree to such an idea, and under what conditions? Who would be in charge of creating and granting economic rights in capital credit? Whose are they to give away?

First, the same questions might have been asked earlier in history about the universal bestowal of civil, political, and social rights. Moreover, except for the civil rights that were extended in a sweep with the democratic revolutions (though, to be sure, the evolution of civil rights had a lengthy history before bursting indelibly onto the historical canvas with those revolutions), bestowal of rights is not, at first, universal: political and social rights were granted incrementally to more and more sectors of the populace. By whom were they bestowed? They were granted by political institutions, through the passage of laws, in response to circumstances generated by social change.

As societies undergo change—whether through evolving environmental circumstances, the introduction of a new technology, through newly emerging social values or the like—new institutions are usually established to bring order and predictability to the uncertainty caused by social change. New institutions are tested. If they work, they are often extended in scope.

A case in point was the evolution of the right to vote. At first, the Constitution granted the right to vote to all citizens who were property-owners in post-revolutionary America. Eventually the right to vote was granted, successively, to all citizens who were white males, who were people of color, who were female, and who were eighteen years of age and over.

Similarly, the social protections of the welfare state, as such, began in the U.S. with the passage of the Social Security Act in 1935. At first, the Act covered just the worker himself or herself, and the chief contingencies covered were unemployment, disability, and old age. Since the Act proved itself a workable institution for addressing in an orderly fashion the problem of interrupted or terminated income, benefits were extended to other household members of the wage-earner (spouses, children). Next, benefits covered more contingencies, and finally, benefits were increased (for example, cost of living increases take effect automatically as a result of the 1972 Amendments to the Social Security Act).

To return to the potential parallel of economic rights to civil, political, and social rights as part of the rights of citizenship, we see that once a justification has been articulated, it can be extended almost indefinitely. Logic alone forms the upper limit of extension. Civil, political, and social rights were created directly as citizenship rights with a specific content. Rationalization of the law subsequently extended the scope of content of these rights, and by so doing, enlarged the perquisites of citizenship, a topic I treated extensively within a Weberian framework.

The same process could apply to right creation for economic rights in capital credit. The purpose of the present exposition has been to argue that perhaps the time has come for economic rights in income-producing credit to be considered as a possible citizenship right. Perhaps the time is ripe for policymakers to articulate a principle (or principles) of justification—as was done to create and legitimate the emergence of the welfare state—that could be extended in scope to cover more and more of the citizenry until "capital self-sufficiency" became a universal right.

Economic rights in income-producing credit would alleviate the financial burden upon the redistributional state. By bringing dividend income into households, such rights would create a rationalized principle of income distribution—using the modern corporation to utmost societal advantage as an organizational nexus for the generation and dissemination of wealth.

Current Access to Income-Producing Credit

Economic rights in capital credit—although they already exist in American society, and in many other societies throughout the world—*are not currently the result of laws to create the rights of citizenship.* Rather, they are the result of laws governing *tax policy.* Tax laws—of which the chief tools are tax incentives and tax disincentive—are a society's way of reinforcing certain economically-oriented behaviors and discouraging others. Thus the tax laws that have created economic rights in capital credit for employees in companies where ESOPs are in place were not *intended* to expand the rights of citizenship, *per se.* They were simply meant to create tax incentives for corporations or businesses to structure the distribution of company profits in new ways.

However, if our society were to decide that such rights would be desirable on a universal scale, then I am arguing that the corporate, tax, and legal frameworks (the "infrastructure") already exist to elevate economic rights in capital credit to the status of a right of citizenship. Let us examine the current infrastructure of access to income-producing credit in the U.S. today.

Since the 1970's, 17 tax laws have been passed in the U.S. providing incentives—both to lending institutions and to companies—for the formation of ESOPs. For example, banks, insurance companies, and other institutional lenders may exclude from their taxes half of all interest they receive on loans to ESOPs used for acquiring employee stock. From the standpoint of the company using an ESOP to take out a loan, there are also advantages: the company can negotiate a lower interest rate from the lending institution, which, after all, is receiving half of its interest payments tax-free. Moreover, company contributions to leveraged ESOPs are tax deductible.

There are various reasons why companies may form as ESOPs initially, or convert to employee ownership—sometimes called the "worker owned firm" (WOF)—at some point in a company's life cycle. Advantages accrue to the company, employees, and the economy when the company is a healthy one. (The negative publicity that has attached to recent worker buyouts of companies that have deteriorated beyond redemption—leaving employees holding an empty shell—does not detract from the principle itself. All institutional innovations have negative applications quickly discovered by opportunity seekers, but these can be countered through law as the new institution evolves.)

As indicated earlier, in the U.S. today, over 11 million working Americans share in the profits of stock they own in the companies for which they work. The justification for the employee privilege of owning the technology that (in combination with their own labor power) produces their company's profits is that the employees work there. But what about the self-employed, government employees, housewives and househusbands, and those who have retired? How can access to income-producing credit be extended to these categories of citizens, if such access is to qualify as a truly "universal" citizenship right?

Potential Access to Universal Self-liquidating Credit

Here is where Kelso's initial ESOP principle shows its ingenious quality as an institutional device applicable to the social organization of any society. That is, the principle is amenable to the clear identification and justification of other constituencies—beyond workers in firms—as stockholders in the technology of our times. This qualifies the principle as capable of becoming a right of citizenship, i.e., it can be universalized. Specifically, three other types of stock ownership plans already have been enunciated beyond the original ESOP, each with a definitive constituency that can be legally identified, each with precedents in today's U.S. tax code:

- The Individual Stock Ownership Plan (ISOP)
- The Consumer Stock Ownership Plan (CSOP)
- The Community Investment Corporation (CIC)

The ISOP has been put forth as the type of access to capital credit that could be made available to the self-employed, government workers, retirees, housewives, the handicapped, and certain others. Through minor reforms in the tax code governing Individual Retirement Accounts (IRAs) and Keogh Plans, ISOPs could be institutionalized. Under this tax arrangement, the above-mentioned categories of people would be eligible for credit to purchase stock in the continued growth of American industry as outlined above. If just a small percentage of the $513 billion in capital expansion projected for 1990 were targeted—under the tax code—toward reinforcing decentralization of stock ownership, a substantial deconcentration of wealth could take place within a few generations—reducing or nearly eliminating reliance on today's multifarious income transfers.

The CSOP would pertain to regular customers of electric utilities, mass transit systems, cablevision systems, and the like. These plans could be structured to extend access to capital credit for the purchase of stock by regular customers. Such utilities and systems frequently need to take out loans for expansion of services. These loans could serve as the vantage point for broadening the ownership base of these systems.

The Community Investment Corporation (CIC) is the plan that would cover residents of communities for large scale land development projects in those communities. Residents would become shareholders in planning and development corporations responsible to the shareholders. The corporations would plan and develop land for commercial, industrial, and residential uses. (The Alaska Pipeline was the largest such proposed project in American history that fell into the category of decentralized ownership with dividends for residents. What was proposed was that British Petroleum's stock in the pipeline project would be made available under the terms of a General Stock Ownership Corporation, and ownership would have been allocated on a statewide basis. The plan did not materialize, but the principle is captured in the tax code. The CIC is oriented more toward establishing claims for residents in local communities, rather than claims on a statewide basis.)

An "Industrial Homestead Act" for America

Recall our earlier reference to the $513 billion to be loaned in 1990 for the expansion of business and industry: until the last few decades, it was usual for a company's *current* stockholders to be the chief beneficiaries of any greater profits that flowed from company expansion. Throughout the 1980's, the richest one percent of the American population increased their income by 75 percent, while the bottom 40 percent of the population experienced no income growth at all (Mishel and Frankel, 1991).

This finding—by the Economic Policy Institute in Washington, DC—hints at the chief source of income growth in today's world: *returns on investments, not wages and salaries.* Those who already own stock in a company profit as the company profits, particularly when the company successfully expands. *If the return on investments is the newly emerging form of economic participation to derive income in advanced industrial economies, then, in a democracy, this new basis of participation needs to be broadened to include the citizenship at large.*

In 1982, Norman G. Kurland—an attorney and longtime associate of Louis Kelso—articulated a framework for our nation to universalize the principle of extending ownership opportunities to citizens through broadening access to capital credit. He called his framework "The Industrial Homestead Act," and aptly so. This Act would be the twenty-first century counterpart to the 1862 Homestead Act, and would serve the identical function: to widely disseminate national wealth in an orderly fashion, and to enormously strengthen and develop the American economy by so doing.

Today, the source of wealth is no longer land, but capital credit. The frontier is now technological, not terrestrial. The new wealth (self-liquidating credit) is as abstract as the old wealth (the good earth) was concrete. And—like access to land—access to capital credit would rejuvenate America's economy were it democratized.

An *Industrial Homestead Act* would comprise these elements:

- A *rationale*: to institutionalize the economic right of all citizens to participate in an economy in which capital participation is successively replacing labor participation.
- The establishment—through the tax code—of a *system of individual accounts.* This would, in effect, be a tax shelter for each American *to accumulate sufficient capital credit to provide capital self-sufficiency.*
- The stipulation of a capital credit *amount* that each account could accumulate. (In the 1970's, Representative Bill Frenzel introduced H.R. 462, "The Accelerated Capital Formation Act" which specified an amount of $500,000.) *Dividend income* would flow from these accounts and would ultimately replace income transfers.
- A *system of allocating shares of stock into the accounts.* This would require *development of a set of criteria* for allocation. The criteria would be related to whether the account was an ESOP, ISOP, CSOP, or CIC. These criteria would be *key*

to the legitimacy of the allocation process, and would be the functional equivalent to the legitimation process that predicted the rise of the welfare state.

- The establishment of *Federal Reserve policies* to support and reinforce the system of national accounts in capital credit. The chief feature of such Federal Reserve policies would be the creation of a "two tiered" interest rate structure. A lower interest rate would be made available for all borrowing for objectives related to increasing national productivity. This would include capitalizing citizens through democratizing access to self-liquidating credit. A higher interest rate would apply for all borrowing that does nothing to increase national wealth. This includes inflationary borrowing such as that to pay interest on the national debt, a type of borrowing that currently "crowds out" private sector borrowing for productive purposes by driving up the interest rates.

Legitimation of the Potential

In sum, in our respective roles as workers, consumers, or residents, we *could* become the legitimate claimants of access to the income-producing credit that is enjoyed today by the very few, but is theoretically available to the many. Through the articulation of justifying principles, and the rationalization of law to protect these principles, economic rights in capital, self-liquidating credit could become a basic component of the status of modern citizenship. The corporate structure is in place. Practical applications of the principle have worked. Legal precedents have been set. Philosophical roots exist for broadening the privileges of citizenship, and for raising the standard of living of citizens in affluent America.

What is at issue here is simply the modus operandi of improving the allocation of resources to those our society calls "citizen." We have already admitted—through our institutionalization of an enormous welfare state—that resources are not well allocated through the primary income distribution, and that this is a problem we have defined as worthy of solving. We have chosen redistribution as the method of addressing the problem, but our virtually insurmountable budget deficit forecloses further steps along this path.

Extending access to capital credit as a citizenship right, by contrast, would prune the complex growth of the welfare state, and would simply mainline income to citizens through logically extending the functions of the modern corporation in a democratic society. It is a choice of justifying the *dividend* check over the Social Security check,

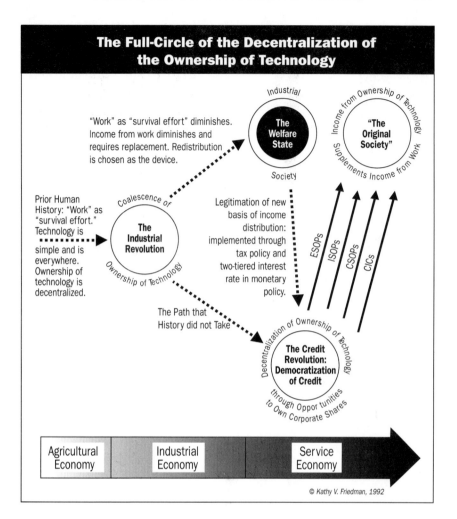

The Full-Circle of the Decentralization of the Ownership of Technology

"Work" as "survival effort" diminishes. Income from work diminishes and requires replacement. Redistribution is chosen as the device.

Prior Human History: "Work" as "survival effort." Technology is simple and is everywhere. Ownership of technology is decentralized.

Coalescence of

The Industrial Revolution

Ownership of Technology

Industrial

Society

The Welfare State

Income from Ownership of Technology

Supplements Income from Work

"The Original Society"

Legitimation of new basis of income distribution: implemented through tax policy and two-tiered interest rate in monetary policy.

ESOPs   ISOPs   CSOPs   CICs

The Path that History did not Take

Decentralization of Ownership of Technology

The Credit Revolution: Democratization of Credit

through Opportunities to Own Corporate Shares

Agricultural Economy	Industrial Economy	Service Economy

© Kathy V. Friedman, 1992

the unemployment check, food stamps, and education vouchers. It is a choice to rethink the utility of endless forms, bottomless bureaucracy, and an infinite regress of new constituencies discovering "rights." We are *all* entitled. Access to capital credit would simply *systematize* it. Or—in Max Weber's language—it would be a further rationalization of the law that creates the status of "citizen."

Notes:

[1] J. G. Brenner, "Where Consumer Credit Is Due," *The Washington Post* (October 21, 1990) A1 and A22.

[2] "Business Will Spend $513 Billion on Capital Improvements," *Census and You*, June 1990.

[3] Vobejda, Barbara, and Taylor, Paul, "Suddenly, a Pessimistic America," *The Washington Post* (November 6, 1990) A1 and A9.

— 8 —

Beyond ESOP:
Steps Toward Tax Justice

by Norman G. Kurland

> *"Our tax system is a national disgrace."*
>
> (President Jimmy Carter, during his 1976 Presidential Campaign)

> *"The Congress in a series of laws . . . has made clear its interest in encouraging employee stock ownership plans as a bold and innovative method of strengthening the free enterprise system which will solve the dual problems of securing capital funds for necessary capital growth and of bringing about stock ownership by all corporate employees."*
>
> (Section 2701, U.S. Tax Reform Act of 1976)

> *"To begin to diffuse the ownership of capital and to provide an opportunity for citizens of moderate income to become owners of capital rather than relying solely on their labor as a source of income and security, the Committee recommends the adoption of a national policy to foster the goal of broadened ownership. . . Whatever the means used, a basic objective should be to distribute newly created capital broadly among the population. Such a policy would redress a major imbalance in our society and has the potential for strengthening future business growth."*
>
> (1976 Annual Report of the Joint Economic Committee of the U.S. Congress)

The Carter administration has announced its intention to submit to Congress a package of comprehensive reforms to the U. S. tax system. No one knows exactly what that package will contain and whether it will represent some fundamentally new directions in U. S. tax policy. But if there is to be a new world economic order, as President Carter has promised, no stone should remain unturned in the debate that will shape the tax philosophy of the President. It is in that spirit that this article is written.

The monumental task of reforming the U. S. tax system requires willingness to go back to the beginning, to reexamine fundamental principles and ideals from which this unique nation was born, and to question any assumptions in current economic and tax philosophy that may be inconsistent with those fundamentals. The forthcoming debate will certainly center around issues of *justice, equality, tax expenditures or subsidies* and *loopholes*, terms bound to produce confusion and divisions among Americans if their thinking remains shackled along present ideological lines. This article will suggest a philosophical framework that offers new definitions for these vague expressions and an alternate perspective for understanding basic issues of tax reform. It attempts to shed more light on the philosophy behind the creeping movement on Capitol Hill to foster a new national goal of broadened capital ownership. And it attempts to explain the broader context surrounding employee stock ownership plans (ESOPs) and how the ESOP fits into a more comprehensive national ownership strategy, within which a totally new approach to taxation is a prerequisite. Finally, this article offers new guideline suggestions to unite opposing forces on some of the most controversial issues facing tax reformers. At the very least, the writer hopes to provoke thinking people, persons who recognize their responsibility for making today the decisions that will determine the way of life twenty or thirty years from now, to think again.

MARX AND ENGELS OR KELSO AND ADLER?

Since the goal of equality has a certain universal moral ring to it, as we boldly approach the tax system as an instrument for achieving greater equality for Americans, we should be reminded of de Tocqueville's final warning to us after observing American democracy in action:

> The nations of our time cannot prevent the conditions of men
> from becoming equal, but it depends upon themselves whether
> the principle of equality is to lead them to servitude or freedom,
> to knowledge or barbarism, to prosperity or wretchedness
> (Alexis de Tocqueville, *Democracy in America*, 1840).

Let us start with a simple thesis. Political democracy cannot preserve the institutions of a free society unless everyone can participate on an equal basis. An economically free and classless society—another way of describing economic democracy—is therefore both a goal and a means for supporting political democracy. Where opportunities to accumulate wealth are grossly unequal, great inequalities in the distribution of wealth are readily seen as flagrant contradictions to the goal of a free, just and economically classless society. Therefore, attacking the problem of inequality of wealth is a legitimate concern of a democratic government. How to build an economically free and just social order, however, forces us to think about what we mean by economic justice.

A thorough search through the literature of Western civilization for a pathway to a just economic order, will eventually lead the serious scholar to two seminal philosophical works, each diametrically opposed to the other, not in their quest for an economically free and classless society, but rather in the moral and political principles and the institutional framework each considered necessary for achieving economic democracy.

That the first one, written in 1848, has had a profound and growing influence on tax philosophy and tax reforms around the world, is hardly debatable. In the second chapter of *The Communist Manifesto*, Karl Marx and Friedrich Engels presented a list of ten measures "which appear economically insufficient and untenable, but which in the course of the [communist] movement, outstrip themselves, necessitate further inroads upon the old social order, and are unavoidable as means of revolutionizing the mode of production." Marx and Engels described these ten measures as "despotic inroads on the rights of property" which the propertyless masses will use to "wrest, by degrees, all capital from the bourgeoisie [and] to centralize all instruments of production in the hands of the State." Besides calling for abolition of property in land, the extension of factories and instruments of production owned by the State, and the centralization of the means of communication and transport in the hands of the State, among other things, the second and third items on the list were:

(2) A heavy progressive or graduated income tax.
(3) Abolition of all rights of inheritance.

If Marx and Engels have correctly predicted that the ultimate conclusion of their pathway to economic justice is a society where everyone is equally propertyless, equally liable to labor for a single employer, the State, and equally dependent for their subsistence on wealth redistributed by the State ("the dictatorship of the proletariat"), do the roots of

America offer a better road to a free and classless economic order?

Directly challenging Marx and Engels, Louis O. Kelso and the eminent American philosopher Mortimer J. Adler reasoned in *The Capitalist Manifesto* (1958) that, while concentrated capital owner-ship was manifestly unjust and destructive of a free and democratic order, a higher order of economic justice should be built upon the propo-sition that everyone, as a fundamental human right, must have equal opportunity to become an owner of capital. Property as an institution was not the fundamental flaw of nineteenth century capitalism, as Marx and Engels asserted. And the redistribution of income is not necessarily just and orderly. Rather, countered Kelso and Adler, an industrial society could achieve a more just and orderly distribution of wealth by preserving the institution of private property and redis-tributing future ownership opportunities. Thus, as new and more advanced technology is added, more and more and gradually all per-sons would gain direct property stakes in productive resources. Fol-lowing the wisdom of America's founding fathers and some of history's greatest political philosophers since Aristotle, Kelso and Adler made a logical and socially compelling case (to which no article as brief as this can do justice) that the institution of property is a prerequisite for preserving a free society and the foundation upon which all other human rights must be grounded.

Since, in the words of Daniel Webster, "power naturally and in-evitably follows the ownership of property," a society where all power is supposed to rest in its citizens, must necessarily develop means to keep property broadly diffused.

The worldwide moral appeal of this fundamental right is recog-nized by Article 17 of the UN's Universal Declaration of Human Rights, which reads: "Everyone has the right to own property, alone as well as in association with others."

Moreover, argued Kelso and Adler, welfare and charity, while jus-tified as humane, short-term expedients for coping with severe cases of economic deprivation, offer no lasting politically realistic solutions to economically unjust situations. As expedients, however, they can be carried on simultaneously with a comprehensive long-range pro-gram for restructuring the future ownership patterns of a society.

The Kelso-Adler version of a just society rests upon three basic principles of economic justice:

The Participation or Input Principle
(Equal Opportunity to be Productive)

Since everyone has the right to life, everyone must be provided, as a fundamental human right, the right to produce a self-sufficient income. In other words, one can legitimately participate as a pro-ducer of marketable goods and services, either as a worker or as an owner of capital instruments, or both. In terms of a high technology society, Kelso and Adler would redefine the term equality of economic opportunity to require government to lift all barriers and take affirmative action to promote more equal access to the future ownership opportunities. Where new capital formation is added through such a uniquely "social good" as expanded bank credit, for example, this means that everyone should be provided equal access to society's capital credit system.

The Distribution or Outtake Principle *(Private Property)*

Reward should be based, not on one's clout or on charity, but on the value of one's input to production, whether through one's human efforts or through one's ownership of productive capital, or both. If a person wants to consume more, it follows that he must produce more; otherwise he must become dependent on the wealth produced by someone else's labor or someone else's property. However, just as the denial of one's entitlement to the fruits of his hands or mind is a denial of his property rights in his own body, taking away anyone's property income is a direct erosion of his property rights in the means of production.

Under the private property principle of wealth distribution, how would prices, wages and profits be determined? Following Aristotle, Kelso and Adler would allow the free and competitive marketplace to determine what is a just wage, a just price, and a just profit. Neither coercion on the buyer or on the seller of any goods or services would be allowed. In the freely competitive marketplace, the laws of supply and demand, not special privilege or superior clout, control economic values. In this democracy of the marketplace, consumer sovereignty reigns and everyone's vote counts.

The Feedback or Limitation Principle *(Anti-Monopoly)*[1]

Where a few own too much of the means of production and most of society owns too little property or none at all, justice is automatically denied. No one is born with property in the means of production. In a free society everyone is born with property in their own bodies. The ownership of capital is wholly determined by society's institutions, which in turn are products of society's laws. Hence, no monopoly can exist without the approval or tolerance of government. Since most technological gains are produced by improved tools (i.e., machines, techniques, structures, organizations), an economy is inherently unjust if government permits a monopoly over the ownership of its instruments of production. Such a monopoly is a systematic denial of equal economic opportunity because it denies others the right to produce enough to support themselves by owning the tools that produce wealth. Since tools continue to produce more with less and less human efforts, concentrated capital ownership, if left uncorrected, leads inevitably to redistribution and the eventual breakdown of the other two principles of economic justice. By allowing a few to produce radically more that they and their families can consume, others are forced into conditions of dependency. One man's surplus is another man's poverty.

If Kelso and Adler's version of economic justice is more sound than that of Marx and Engels, then we can well understand why tax reform during the last sixty years has failed so miserably. What becomes almost self-evident is that tax reformers in general have put the cart before the horse. By discouraging new capital formation through discriminatory taxes on property and property incomes and emphasizing redistributive goals of taxation instead of encouraging broadened ownership opportunities, tax reformers have elevated the tax system and government stimulated demand to a position higher than the nation's wealth production system, upon which all tax revenues and everyone's ultimate standard of living depends.

Sound Tax Policy Follows Sound National Economic Policy

A sound tax policy cannot be constructed upon confused or unsound political or economic principles. The Kelso-Adler concept of economic justice offers a solid foundation upon which business, labor, and government can forge a new consensus and new common strategy to enable our Nation to cope more realistically with today's industrial world, with our capital and other shortages, and with the challenges we can expect from accelerating technological change.

Sound tax policy is based upon a reassertion that once made America the last best hope of mankind. *It would recognize that government does not produce wealth and that every subsidy must originate with those individuals whose productive toil and productive capital actually produce society's marketable goods and services, including those diverted through taxation.* It would also recognize that wealth is produced most efficiently within competing privately owned enterprises vying to satisfy private consumer demand, with every buyer voting with his own dollars to reflect his choices among available goods and services.

Government, through its taxing and spending powers, has the power to redistribute wealth, in addition to carrying on its originally conceived and more normal functions of enforcing contracts, protecting property, suppressing violence and otherwise maintaining a just and peaceful society. And to the extent it can create legal tools like the business corporations to meet the needs of society, it can regulate them. On the other hand, when business corporations, voluntary associations, or any other specialized social inventions become socially dysfunctional and create, rather than solve, problems for society, government is the instrument through which we overcome the problem, directly or through a restructuring of our institutions and laws. It is not in the nature of government to leave social vacuums unfilled.

As a result of defects in our economic institutions, wealth patterns in America have become grossly distorted and plutocratic. The gap between the very rich and the very poor continues to widen. Class divisions between propertied and non-propertied Americans produce a never-ending political battle. This is reflected in the 1976 Annual Report of the Joint Economic Committee, which found that the richest 1% of Americans own over 50% of all individually owned corporate equity and receive about 46% of all corporate dividends, and that concentrated ownership patterns will only worsen in the years ahead because of traditional methods used by U.S. corporations for financing their new capital formation.

Today, as a result of the maldistribution of ownership and income, we have reached a point where government itself is suffering from an acute case of functional overload. Public redistribution and efforts to control the economy have placed responsibilities on government that are contrary to its very nature. The mere shifting of centralized governmental activities to state and local levels totally ignores this problem. Reorganization of the federal bureaucracy is similarly futile.

The State—civilization's most important social invention—can no longer effectively carry on the highly specialized and limited functions for which it was originally designed. The State, in the view of many, is mankind's only legitimate monopoly, our social contrivance for monopolizing coercion and violence. As such, however, it is a highly dangerous and unnatural tool when it tries to assume powers best left to private individuals and their associations, especially where market disciplines are present to govern economic decision-making.

Next to the State itself, the modern corporation is our most important social tool. It is an excellent vehicle for absorbing technology, harnessing together talent and capital, and marketing on a global basis. Since industrial capital produces an increasing share of society's wealth, a sound and just governmental policy would remove roadblocks to broader participation in corporate equity ownership for all households, so that the need for governmental intervention and income redistribution would gradually and systematically be reduced to tolerable levels. The corporation is, after all, a mere creature of the law and to the extent it does not serve the ends of justice, our system of justice is necessarily deficient.

Encouraging growth of the corporation while broadening the base of its future stockholder constituency means that the necessary costs of government can then be shared by a constantly growing base of citizens with private incomes distributed directly in the form of paychecks and dividend checks from our corporate sector as a whole.

From a political standpoint, a corporate stockholder constituency consisting of a more representative base of American households would also automatically make management of our largest and most powerful corporations less vulnerable to self-proclaimed consumer advocates and overregulation by government. As it becomes more directly people-connected and people-empowering, the corporation will become more popular as an instrument of society. Corporate profit would soon lose its social and political attackers as companies provided second incomes to the broadest possible consumer base. Making its future growth opportunities accessible to every citizen would enable the corporation, in my opinion, to make a quantum advance in its own evolutionary development as a major component of a democratic society. (In terms of its presently narrow constituency base and its efficiency as a direct distributor of mass buying power, the mass production corporation is still remarkably primitive, about comparable in historical terms to the democratic form of government over a thousand years ago.)

The new approach recommended in this article would reconstruct the economic system, along the lines of the four pillars illustrated in the following figure.

What is an ESOP and How Does it Help Advance the Kelso-Adler Principles of Economic Justice?

Congress has acted five times since late December 1973 to promote the ESOP.[2] What has surfaced thus far is only the tip of the proverbial iceberg. Below that surface lies the revolutionary private property philosophy and comprehensive ownership strategy first articulated by Kelso and Adler. Too scholarly in its tone to inspire a new political movement and too revolutionary in its ideas to gain the support of economists and academics wedded to orthodox ideologies and the economic status quo, this blueprint for an advanced socioeconomic order seldom is associated with the history of ESOP, although both were inspired by the same person, San Francisco lawyer and investment banker Louis O. Kelso.

When this writer first became associated with Kelso in 1965, to most politicians, businessmen, and labor leaders, ESOP sounded like the author of ancient parables and Kelso was a famous winning race horse. By 1972 several dozen ESOPs were established. Since Congress legitimated the ESOP in 1974, an estimated 200 or more classical ESOPs have been launched.[3] The mass media and professional

The Four Pillars for Building a More Just Economy

Pillar 1
Expanded Capital Ownership

Goal   Promote widespread citizen access to capital ownership

Means   Democratization of productive credit

Result   Decentralizes economic power and profit sharing to each citizen

Pillar 2
Limited Economic Power for the State

Goal   Shift ownership and control over production and income distribution to the private sector

Means   Limit government power over economy

Result   Promotes economic justice for all and increases revenue for public sector programs

Pillar 3
Free and Open Markets

Goal   Restore free and open markets

Means   Gradually eliminate all non-voluntary methods of determining prices, wages, and profits

Result   Decentralizes economic choice and empowers each person as a consumer, a worker and an owner

Pillar 4
Private Property

Goal   Restore personal rights of property in the means of production, particularly in corporate equity

Means   Reform laws which deny shareholders the original rights of property

Result   Secures personal choices and economic self-determination

journals have begun to take serious notice of the ESOP and since 1974 articles on the ESOP have appeared in *Time, Newsweek, Fortune, Business Week, The Wall Street Journal, The American Bar Association Journal, Harvard Business Review, The Tax Executive, Barron's* and even *The Village Voice.* Many criticisms have surfaced regarding the ESOP, some valid and constructive, some simply nit-picking and totally negative, some based upon fear and ignorance. Few recognized that the ESOP, even in its primitive form, is only a small part, a single instrumentality, of a much bigger picture. The most comprehensive compilation of the pros and cons of ESOP were covered in two days of congressional hearings in late December 1975 before the Joint Economic Committee. Without attempting to address these problems here, let us examine the nature and purpose of this controversial tool.

Here is how the Senate Finance Committee, chaired by the ESOP's most ardent champion on Capital Hill, Senator Russell B. Long, describes the ESOP:

> Employee stock ownership plans make it possible for workers in the private sector of our economy to share in the ownership of corporate capital without redistributing the property or profits from existing assets belonging to existing owners. Since its first application as a financing tool in 1957, [ESOPs] have been implemented by a growing number of successful U.S. corporations. Through the vehicle of a specially designed tax-exempt trust, this method of finance offers corporations certain tax incentives and cost-reductions not available under conventional methods of finance. The [ESOP] also allows workers to accumulate significant holdings of capital in a tax-free manner during their working careers, while being taxed only on second incomes received in the form of dividend checks or on their assets when removed from their trust accounts [Sen. Report 93-1298, *Trade Reform Act of 1974* (Nov. 26, 1974) 158-9].

From this description it seems clear that the classical ESOP is not a mere stock bonus plan, although its legal basis can be traced to the same provisions of the U. S. tax laws which deal with stock bonus plans, profit sharing plans, pension plans, thrift plans and other IRS-qualified employee benefit plans. Like the stock bonus plans and the relatively few profit sharing plans that invest heavily in company stock, it is not basically a retirement vehicle, but is designed to link all employees of a company to the full status of stockholders, up to 100% of the company's equity ownership.

The ESOP is an ownership creating tool, plus. Unlike profit-sharing and conventional stock bonus plans, the ESOP, if properly designed, adheres rigidly to protecting the private property rights of other shareholders, as mandated by Kelso-Adler principles of economic justice. It does not share their profits with nonowners. It does not dilute their ownership rights by simply issuing new stock without a corresponding increase in productive capacity or in disposable cash available to the corporation for corporate investment purposes. It merely makes capital growth and growth profits accessible to new ownership. Unlike thrift plans, stock purchase plans and stock option plans, the ESOP is a credit device and requires no cash outlay whatsoever from those to whom new equity opportunities are to be extended. Instead, it makes the magic of nonrecourse corporate financing work for new owners, based on credit designed to be amortized with expanded future corporate profits. It should not be adopted by a management unwilling to be accountable to its employees in their newly acquired status as stockholders. And the ESOP should not be adopted for financing growth, unless the expansion capital is expected to pay for itself. Then, as long as a baseline after-tax cash flow per share held by present shareholders is maintained in the future, all projected increases in after-tax cash flow can legitimately be applied for building ownership of newly issued equity into employees, without violating the property rights of existing shareholders.

Here's how the classical ESOP works for financing corporate growth: Suppose a $10 million company with 10 owners and 100 workers needs to double its plant capacity and having paid out dividends in the past, finds itself with little or no retained earnings. With solid contracts on hand to justify the expansion program, the company turns to a syndicate of lenders who are willing to lend the necessary ten million dollars for the second plant, repayable with future after-tax dollars. Management hears about the ESOP and sets one up to cover all 200 employees (including the new 100 employees to be hired when the second plant becomes operational). The ESOP borrows the $10 million, the company gets its cash by selling $10 million in new shares to the ESOP at the current market value, the company guarantees the ESOP's credit by agreeing to pay out of projected future profits enough cash to the ESOP to service the ESOP's debt. If the stock is not pledged as collateral, it is held in an unallocated account. As installments of the ESOP's debt are paid, blocks of stock, once paid for, are divided up according to payroll and placed in each of 200 individual trust accounts. At the end of the financing period on this single transaction, therefore, the average employee will have gained $50,000 in new equity and the right to future dividend checks to supplement his payroll and retirement checks. The original 10 owners will not have lost any of their original equity or dividend rights from their $10 million investment. Even better, the company, through the unique privileges Congress has extended to ESOP financing, is permitted to service the debt for its expansion capital with pre-tax, rather than post-tax corporate dollars, a tax advantage that increases the company's cash flow by roughly 50¢ on every dollar borrowed by the ESOP. This is so because Congress has specially recognized the ESOP, both as a socially improved technique of corporate finance and as a new form of employee benefit. The ESOP must be approved by the Internal Revenue Service (IRS) and is policed by the IRS and the Department of Labor. Up to 15% of covered payroll,[4] the cash for servicing the ESOP's stock acquisition debt is treated as a tax-deductible contribution. Although dividends may currently be used to accelerate repayment of the ESOP's debt, under present tax laws stock dividends are discouraged. In the future, Congress may allow corporations to take tax deductions for dividends paid out, perhaps initially only for ESOP acquired stock. (See proposals below.)[5] Then ESOP financing would be designed to be repayable primarily with projected pre-tax dividend payouts rather than employee benefit dollars, which under today's accounting procedures create an illusion of reducing corporate net earnings.

The Investment Tax Credit ESOP

In contrast to the classical ESOP, the investment tax credit ESOP can be justifiably labeled as a giveaway, not from present shareholders but from the federal treasury. Nevertheless, unlike other tax subsidies, this bonus to companies adopting an ESOP contain the seeds of the quiet and creative revolution launched by Kelso and Adler. It points to a new direction for business, labor and government and to a gradual overhaul of the tax system itself, along lines suggested in this paper.[6]

Tax Philosophy Behind the Classical ESOP

As noted earlier, the classical ESOP involves no giveaway from present owners. And, unlike the normal 10% investment tax credit, tax deductible payments to a classical ESOP are wholly distinguishable from tax subsidies and should no more be considered a taxpayer gift than that which permits corporations to deduct wages and salaries from gross earnings. While many tax deductions are hardly distinct from direct government expenditures, and thus can appropriately be labeled subsidies or "tax expenditures" under today's unjust tax system, this is not the case for deduction of debt service contributions to an ESOP. Rather, from a standpoint of the philosophy of economic justice upon which the ESOP is based, the double tax penalty on corporate profits is a direct violation of the private property rights of a corporate equity owner. *The corporation income tax is therefore inherently an unjust tax under any so-*

cial system which is based upon the institution of private property. If all corporate net earnings were deductible to the corporation to the extent they were paid out directly to the equity owners as dividends and taxable as personal incomes, the double tax problem would vanish. (See proposal below.) It is in this light that the nature of the ESOP can be properly understood.

Behind the ESOP is a philosophy of taxation and a carefully conceived strategy to remove gradually the tax system's present bias against property and property accumulations, on the one hand, and, at some point, to reduce the government's use of the tax system as an income redistribution mechanism, on the other. The 48%[7] corporate income tax involves pure redistribution. Instead of treating all incomes the same, whether they are derived from capital or labor, the tax on corporate profits dilutes by half the property incomes (and thus the property rights) of present shareholders. Then when that income becomes available to owners in the form of dividends or capital gains, the government takes a second and third bite out of the remainder. Where the corporation tax is a direct frontal attack on the institution of private property, the ESOP offers a powerful means for counterattacking in a manner that will simultaneously serve other desirable social goals: it can help overcome shortages in private sector capital formation; it fosters more equity financing; it can help foster more private sector jobs in the fabricating and operations of newly added plant and equipment; it can help expand the federal revenue base from expanded private payrolls and dividend rolls; and it can help create a broader base of stockholder constituents to help corporations surmount unreasonable and unwarranted political attacks. In contrast to true tax subsidies, the ESOP is a solution, not an excuse for perpetuating or ignoring structural flaws in our major economic institutions.

Under a comprehensive national plan for stimulating and redistributing future growth opportunities directly among Americans who have no capital, three basic ownership diffusing mechanisms[8] would be employed to link capital to individuals: employee stock ownership plans (ESOP), to cover employees of viable enterprises; consumer stock ownership plans (CSOP), to cover all regular customers of regulated public utilities and mass transit systems; and individual stock ownership plans (ISOP), to provide people who do not work for viable corporations in the competitive sector of the economy with the means to gain a diversified holding of newly issued stock reflecting growth of the competitive corporate sector. Each of these tools is structured to reduce drastically the cost of new capital formation and to overcome present tax and credit barriers to a more equitable sharing of future ownership opportunities.

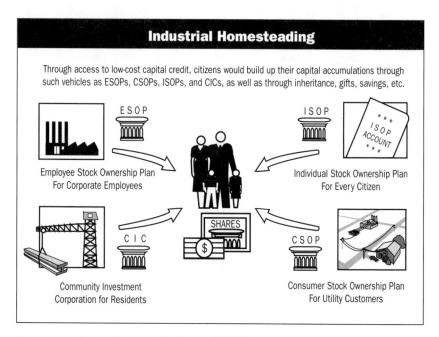

Industrial Homesteading

Through access to low-cost capital credit, citizens would build up their capital accumulations through such vehicles as ESOPs, CSOPs, ISOPs, and CICs, as well as through inheritance, gifts, savings, etc.

ESOP
Employee Stock Ownership Plan
For Corporate Employees

ISOP
ISOP ACCOUNT
Individual Stock Ownership Plan
For Every Citizen

CIC
Community Investment
Corporation for Residents

SHARES
$

CSOP
Consumer Stock Ownership Plan
For Utility Customers

Employee Stock Ownership Plans (ESOP)

As noted previously, present laws already provide for the establishment of ESOPs, although even existing ESOP law could be improved considerably to make the ESOP more attractive to corporate management, labor unions, existing stockholders, and to the employees themselves. Acceleration of private sector investment rates, virtually everyone would agree, is the best means for overcoming economic scarcity and for absorbing into productive jobs close to ten million people whose talents are now being wasted in unemployment lines and in nonproductive and wasteful jobs on public and private payrolls. Hence, the highest priority in channeling new capital financing in both the competitive and noncompetitive public utility sectors of the private economy should be placed on the use of ESOPs. It offers new efficiencies and cost savings for capital creation and it offers a meaningful trade-off for inflationary increases in wage and fringe benefit levels. A share in the capital growth pie and in corporate profits offers a far more significant economic benefit than has ever been demanded through collective bargaining for working Americans. Slicing up among workers the $3 to $5 trillion capital pie that the economy expects to be adding in the decade ahead could average as much as $50,000 each for 100 million workers, assuming (without expecting) that all new capital will be financed through ownership diffusing mechanisms.[9]

In the competitive sector, at least one third to one half of a company's annual capital expansion budget should be reserved for financing through an ESOP covering all its employees. Another portion might be reserved for the ESOPs covering employees of outside suppliers and construction firms that help fabricate that company's new plant and equipment. And the remaining portion of its expansion capital, especially for Fortune 500 companies, should be financed through the sale of new equity to ISOPs.

Individual Stock Ownership Plans (ISOP)

The ISOP should be considered alongside the pay-as-you-go Social Security System, which places a heavier and heavier redistributive burden to meet its costs on the young and on future generations. The ISOP would, in contrast, provide directly income-producing private sector assets to meeting the growing needs of America's retirees, including the military, teachers and public servants.

Within the non-regulated competitive sector of the economy, all future growth (not replacement capital) of SEC-qualified firms, which is not financed through ESOPs would be financed through ISOPs, established for individuals at their local banks as a supplement to each American's participation in the Social Security system. For example, a company like AT&T might voluntarily decide to sell new equity shares representing, say, one-half of this year's AT&T expansion needs. Based upon their present overall wealth accumulations and projected new ownership opportunities each year from all sources, plus some other relevant factors, each adult American under one version of an "Industrial Homestead Act" (see "Low-interest Bank Credit" below) would be allocated a quota of credit to buy a diversified block of the AT&T and other newly issued qualified equity shares. The ISOP, like the ESOP, would be qualified by the Internal Revenue Service to permit tax-free accumulations. Low interest bank loans to the ISOP would provide the funds to buy newly issued equity directly from corporations "qualified" by the Securities and Exchange Commission. The loans would be nonrecourse to the ISOP participant and would be structured to be repaid wholly with projected tax-deductible dividends paid out by each of the corporations selling their new equity on the new ISOP market. Stockmarket speculators and other secondary market sources would not be allowed to sell to ISOPs. Once shares of stock are paid for, the owners would receive the dividends as taxable second incomes.

Consumer Stock Ownership Plans (CSOP)

Corporations with a fixed base of customers in the regulated segment of the U.S. economy (e.g., telephone companies, electric and gas production and distribution utilities, mass transit, cablevision systems) would gain opportunities to fund their expansion through new equity issuances sold to CSOPs and ESOPs, again, with low-interest credit provided from commercial lenders and re-payable with future pre-tax profits. A new mass transit system, for example, might have 25% of its total construction costs funded by an issuance of equity shares through an ESOP covering all those involved in constructing the system, another 25% through an ESOP covering its operating and maintenance employees, and the remaining 50% financed through a CSOP designed to build equity shares into each of its future regular customers. Like the ESOP and ISOP, the CSOP would be a tax-free equity accumulator and an account would be set up for each regular transit rider, tied into his monthly billing account. Rates would be set so that, after taking into account any real estate profits earned by the mass transit system, mass transit riders would cover the full capital costs and operational costs of the system, without government subsidies. But as a patronage rebate, the regular rider would get back a piece of the action, represented by shares released to his CSOP account as the CSOP's debt is repaid with pre-tax dollars paid in the form of tax-deductible dividends on CSOP-held shares. Released shares would be allocated among users according to their relative patronage of the system. Future dividends on CSOP stock would be used to offset each user's monthly bill.

Essential Non-Tax Policies for Encouraging the Democratization of Future Capital

(1) *Low-Interest Bank Credit*

Under an "Industrial Homestead Act" strategy, the Federal Reserve system, using its present powers to expand bank credit through the discounting of eligible paper,[10] would reduce effective commercial bank interest rates to 2% to 3% for banks making loans to IRS-qualified ESOPs, ISOPs, and CSOPs to enable mature, well-managed corporations to sell newly issued equity to their workers and other Americans. All loans would be self-liquidating and nonrecourse to the individual and would be repayable with projected pre-tax profits. The low-interest rates and the use of pre-tax dollars for servicing capital formation debt would, of course, lower the cost of capital expansion within the private sector at least when compared to the use of after-tax dollars and today's high interest rates. This would lower costs on all U.S. goods and services, improving U.S. trade balances. Only when all wasted and nonproductive human talent gained work opportunities in the growing private sector and all other resources became fully employed, would the Federal Reserve clamp down on the supply of low interest credit. Any further expansion would not increase production and would therefore be inflationary. A sound national ownership program would aim at a target of zero rate of inflation and a maximum rate of production.

(2) *The Capital Diffusion Insurance Corporation (CDIC)*

One major barrier to broadened ownership is the requirement by lenders that borrowers have collateral before they can receive credit to own new capital. The purpose of such collateral is to cover the risk of default. But most nonowners have no assets to pledge to lenders. To overcome the collateralization barriers, Kelso turned to principles of insurance as a substitute way of collateralizing credit for spreading future ownership opportunities among people without assets.

A Capital Diffusion Insurance Corporation would be established to operate with functions similar to those of the Federal Government's home mortgage insurance agency (FHA) and the Pension Guarantee Insurance Corporation(PBGC).[11] Part of the interest payment on loans to ESOPs, CSOPs, and ISOPs, perhaps 0.5% to 5%, would be used to pay an annual premium to protect the lending institutions against the full losses in the event of loan default, to cover the eventuality that the companies issuing the stock against which the loans were made, would no longer be capable of generating profits. Naturally, the safer the companies whose debt-repayment ability is insured by the CDIC, the lower the premium charges necessary to spread the risk of loan default over the overall economy. Differential risk categories, with adjustable premium rates, could be set up for grouping participating corporations, based upon their maturity, earnings history, the quality of their management, the nature and special risks of their industry, somewhat along the lines of Moody's and Standard & Poor bond ratings.

Similar to the pension insurance now being offered by the PGIC, the CDIC could also offer portfolio insurance for an additional premium for employee accounts within ESOPs, which normally lack the kind of diversification that would be found in ISOPs. It would insure workers against the downside risk, so that, upon retirement, a worker would be guaranteed a high percentage of the initial values for all company stock purchased in his behalf through his ESOP account. Then, even if the company failed, he would not lose all his retirement assets before he had a chance to diversify. Premiums could be kept relatively low if CDIC portfolio insurance for ESOPs were limited to companies that had been in operation on a profitable basis for at least three years. The premium costs to cover the high risk, start up companies would be astronomical, compared to those for mature companies with a solid track record of earnings.

Where Do We Go for Tax Justice?

On the Purpose of Taxation

If tax reformers become persuaded that redistributive taxation is morally wrong and contrary to the basic values and objectives of a free and democratic society, that redistribution keeps the rich rich and shackles the average taxpayer to wage serfdom, that redistribution leads to unnecessary shortages and bureaucratic wastes, that it perpetuates mass propertylessness, then it may be possible to make a new beginning in rebuilding today's overly complex, inherently unjust tax system. Until someone offers a more definitive overview of what constitutes tax justice, let us take advantage of the guiding principles and general strategy conceived by Kelso and Adler, at least to analyze some of the central issues all tax reformers must face. Any new beginning must start with the simple question, "Why do we have a tax system?" If we reject Marx and accept Kelso, the answer is also simple: to yield the revenue to pay the costs of a limited government, without damaging the incentives to the maximum production of wealth and the broadest distribution of capital ownership. From this point, a whole new set of conclusions follow:

The bias in the present tax laws against property accumulations and property incomes should be removed. The bias in favor of redistribution, as a practical matter, must be more gradually phased out, as redistribution of income is supplanted with an effective program of redistributing future ownership opportunities. The tax system and federal laws generally should be restructured to encourage the creation, accumulation and the maintenance of property, its widespread distribution among all households, and the maximum generation of new wealth and improved technology within the free enterprise system.

Government should announce a target goal for the economy of *a minimum floor of capital self-sufficiency* for every household to achieve within the next thirty years. A national ownership plan, including new tax laws, would be launched to reach that goal, similar to the manner in which government assisted Americans in the building of our agricultural base through the Homestead Act of 1862. Although the 160 acre ceiling made sense in distributing shares of our necessarily finite land frontier, the amounts that could be accumulated under the proposed "Industrial Homestead Act" program is limited only by our talent, our know-how, our technological potential, and our ability to mobilize all our resources in building a new and more productive industrial frontier during the next several decades. Hence, in today's world, a target floor is more appropriate than a ceiling as the focus of government initiatives under a national ownership program. Where most government initiatives in the last century have tended to centralize economic power, these initiatives would aim at widely diffusing economic power, while keeping it in the hands of individual citizens.

An effective tax system would offer incentives for the enterprise system itself, as the principal source of wealth production, to become a more direct and efficient distributor of mass purchasing power for all consumers in the economy.

As the need for income redistribution and governmental intervention within the private sector lessens to an irreducible minimum, the functions and costs of government should drop progressively, eventually to the tolerable levels projected by the founding fathers. Instead of constricting private initiatives and production, as under today's tax laws, government under a soundly conceived national ownership strategy, would become the catalyst for stimulating expanded production of a more competitive free enterprise system.

Since government, by its nature and highly specialized social functions, is a monopoly, it is not inherently an efficient producer of wealth, as the followers of Marx are beginning to discover. And, with a few rather unfortunate exceptions, government in the United States does not engage directly in the production of real wealth. Although some redistribution advocates seem to assume that all wealth is produced by government, taxpayers know otherwise. Since the wealth necessary to cover the costs of government are products of private labor and private capital, *taxes should be viewed as charges to consumers for essential services not available through the private sector*. Unlike other services, however, the buyer of public services is compelled to buy and the government will remain the sole seller, at least until these same services can be satisfactorily provided through the competitive enterprise system. This seemingly minor change in emphasis could open up some new ideas for privatizing (democratizing) government services and new opportunities for creative businessmen.

Direct or Indirect Taxation

Any tax blunts incentives, but a direct income tax on individuals is the least damaging, and, at the same time, places before the electorate the cost of government. User fees for government services, like camping fees and grazing fees, are also legitimate direct taxes. But sales taxes, value added taxes, payroll taxes, most excise taxes, and other indirect taxes are not just or economically sound methods for covering government spending, since they mask the spending patterns of public servants and elected officials from close taxpayer scrutiny and direct accountability. Indirect taxes (including Social Security and unemployment taxes) also add to the costs of goods, thus shifting taxes to the consumer, reducing the competitiveness of U. S. enterprises and also our growth within the global marketplace. Taxes on property discourage new construction, improvements, and maintenance. But taxes on corporations are the most counterproductive of all forms of indirect taxes. The corporation income tax damages the corporation, an invention of man that is indispensable to the maximum production of wealth. To the extent return on investment is reduced, growth is stifled and the investment will go elsewhere.

But there is a more serious adverse and unjust effect of present corporation income tax laws flowing from the wide array of incentives the tax system now offers to the financing of industrial growth without the issuance of new equity instruments. The nondeductibility of dividends encourage the use of retained earnings or conventional borrowings for financial growth. (This is reinforced by tax subsidies, investment tax credits, tax exclusions and other loopholes to encourage investments in ways which make the rich richer.) By perpetuating exclusionary patterns of corporate finance, the corporation tax minimizes opportunities for all households to share in the growth opportunities of the economy.

Rates of Taxation

A growing number of tax scholars have argued that the case for progressive or graduated rates of taxation is uneasy at best.[12] If redistribution of income (in contrast to a redistribution of future ownership opportunities) is a form of direct discrimination against property, a progressive income tax is inherently an unjust tax, assuming one accepts the Kelso-Adler, rather than the Marx-Engels, version of economic justice.

But what about the poor? No more effective aid can be provided the poor than allowing them to share in the new job and ownership opportunities within a healthy and growing private economy. The problem of those still too poor to share in the cost of government can be handled through tax exemptions or tax credits, and perhaps even the kind of negative income tax advocated by Nobel prize winner Milton Friedman.

Yet responsible citizenship is best served when everyone pays some direct tax. In an economy productive enough to provide a high standard of living for all households, which would be the long-range goal of economic decision makers, the cost of government would be minimal. Since government benefits should be equally accessible to each member of society, absolute justice would demand an equal per capita charge on all individuals, without regard to their income levels. But this, of course, is impractical at this stage of our economic history.

A more realistic and just tax today would be *a flat or proportionate rate* imposed on all direct earned and unearned incomes above a poverty-level income for all taxpayers. A single tax rate would be administratively more efficient than a progressive or graduated tax. Ideally, the flat tax on individuals would cover all government expenditures each year, including welfare, defense, interest on the Federal debt, social security obligations, unemployment and all other current spending not covered by user fees. It could also cover the cost of health insurance premiums under universal minimum coverage, including subsidies for the poor. This will allow for the gradual or immediate elimination of regressive payroll taxes on workers and companies, making the economy more competitive. And it would help make government vastly more accountable to the electorate. If tied into a vigorous national growth and expanded ownership strategy, one could easily imagine future candidates for public office actually competing for votes on the basis of who could offer the best government services at the lowest flat rate. *Each year's single direct tax rate could be adjusted up or down to provide sufficient revenues to avoid budget deficits.*

Under a progressive or graduated tax, on the other hand, political irresponsibility and waste is more easily tolerated. Many voters believe that the heaviest costs are borne by a tiny fraction of high-income individuals or by fat cat corporations, or they fail to appreciate the dangers of printing press money where there are sizable budget deficits. A flat tax would help raise the levels of economic sophistication of the taxpayers. Another shortcoming of a progressive or graduated tax is that tax evasion and the search for tax loopholes by wealthy taxpayers increase as tax rates increase. And when inflation forces workers into higher tax brackets, pressures for additional pay increases add more fuel to the inflationary fires.

Resources tend to be misallocated under a progressive or graduated tax. Economic decisions become increasingly made, not on their economic merit, but on tax considerations. Thus, high tax brackets stifle growth and incentives to innovate and increase production, making all of society the poorer and less competitive.

Earned or Unearned Income

Under the Kelso-Adler theory of economic justice, the earnings from one's property in the means of production are morally indistinguishable from the earnings produced by one's skill or brainpower. Since they are both rewards directly related to production, they should be taxed alike. And discrimination against property discourages investment and reduces society's overall productive capacity.

Karl Marx considered profits as income stolen from labor. Our tax laws that discriminate against property incomes reflect the same bias. But if capital is recognized as a producer of wealth, then capital incomes (whether distributed or undistributed) are legitimately earned by those who share property rights in that capital, the same as those paid for their skills and ingenuity. The most serious problem with laws that discriminate against property incomes is that they hurt the poor more than they do the rich. Access to the full, undiluted stream of earnings from capital is a prerequisite for the financing on credit of broadened ownership opportunities and for more widespread distribution of second incomes among today's non-owning citizens, including civil servants, many professionals, teachers, the military and the unemployable.

The only form of income that can properly be classified as unearned is that which is truly gratuitous and wholly unrelated to the production of marketable goods and services. Examples of unearned income, which should be included for direct taxation (once poverty-level incomes are exceeded) at the same rate as earned incomes, are: welfare checks, unemployment checks, social security checks, food stamps, gifts and bequests, unclaimed valuable finding, gambling gains, and other gains not immediately converted into tax-free or tax-deferred individual capital accumulations, as described below.

Individual Capital Accumulations

As discussed previously, building capital self-sufficiency into every American household cannot take place overnight. But once we establish a specific minimal level or floor for individual asset accumulations as a ten- or twenty-year goal to strive toward, it allows everyone to focus on the importance of property and the need to remove all institutional barriers to the broader distribution of ownership opportunities as expeditiously as possible. *The floor of capital accumulations per household should represent the industrial equivalent of the 160 acres of frontier land that the federal government made available to its propertyless citizens under the Homestead Act of 1862.* Thus the tax laws should be reconstructed to encourage the tax-free (or at least tax-deferred) accumulation of an "industrial homestead" for all Americans over their working careers, consisting of a growing number of equity shares in the economy's expanding industrial frontier.

A tax-qualified ISOP could be set up in the name of each individual, from birth, at a local bank to serve as his or her tax-free accumulator of capital. Shares acquired through ESOPs and CSOPs could be rolled over into one's ISOP account tax-free,[13] as well as income-producing property acquired through tax-free gifts and bequests. Each individual's total acquisitions would continue to accumulate in a tax-free manner until the federally established capital sufficiency floor was reached. Thereafter, future accumulations would lose these tax privileges and become taxed at the current flat rate, thus discouraging grossly excessive, monopolistic accumulations of capital in the future. Upon death or when all or part of the assets are sold to increase consumption incomes, such tax-deferred assets would be taxed at the flat rate then prevailing. Fairness in the distribution of future ownership opportunities would mainly be controlled through the traditional IRS tax-qualification controls over discriminatory allocations and, more importantly, through the Federal Reserve Board's control over credit extended by commercial bank lenders to ESOPs, CSOPs, and ISOPs to foster growth of the private sector economy.

Under H.R. 462, the proposed Accelerated Capital Formation Act introduced in 1975 by Ways and Means Committee member Bill Frenzel, this tax-free floor was set at $500,000. Whatever the target amount, it should be set at a level that both fosters initiative and a desire for income independence for its owner, and it could be adjusted to rise with cost-of-living increases. To encourage the continued accumulation and retention of income-producing investments, and to discourage squandering, all tax-qualified accumulation trusts would be required to pay out all property incomes on a regular basis as second incomes to the owners, subject to direct personal income taxes.

The rationale behind permitting tax-free accumulations below excessively large wealth concentrations follows the principle that new capital formation and widespread capital accumulations should be encouraged, both for promoting economic democracy and for raising the standard of living for all citizens. Taxes on property slows down the capital creation and accumulation process. On the other hand, a direct tax on the incomes from already accumulated capital assets is simpler to understand, less harmful to investment and the care of property, and easier for tax authorities to administer.

Offsetting Revenue Losses from Reduced Corporate Tax Revenues and from the Channeling of Personal Income Into Tax-Exempt Homestead Accumulations

Presently the federal corporate income tax accounts only for 14% of total federal revenues.[14] It would shrink in relative size only gradually under even the most optimistic rate of implementing a national ownership strategy. The question is whether the benefits to be derived, from the standpoint of American business, labor, the voting public, and even the Treasury itself, is a worthy trade-off for this shrinkage of corporate tax revenues. To weigh the trade-off, one must focus on the big picture. The overall dynamics that should be expected in the proposed comprehensive national ownership strategy are two-fold: (1) to increase private production, private taxable job incomes, and private taxable property incomes; and (2) to reduce federal budgets for unemployment, job subsidies and welfare. Hence, the overall tax burden, as now-wasted manpower and other resources are absorbed within a faster growing private sector, should gradually be reduced. To argue that the trade-off is not worth it, considering

today's high unemployment rates and continuing high rates of inflation, would seem preposterous.

Government Debt and Government Deficits

Since tax policy affects the size of the government's debt and government deficits in general, a few comments on the wisdom of debt
and deficit spending policies are in order.

Under the influence of Keynesian economic concepts, the objective of many tax decisions in the past forty years was to cure inflation
and unemployment. Keynes assumed the continuance of historic patterns of extreme maldistribution of capital ownership, and sought
merely to fine-tune that malstructured economy through the bureaucratic manipulation of government tax, spending, interest, and money-
creation machinery. Structural reforms to our corporate ownership
patterns were not part of Keynes' approach to the problems of unemployment and inflation.

In the Kelso-Adler strategy, however, the structural void left by
Keynes is met head-on. Kelso and Adler would attack inflation and
unemployment at the roots. The main thrust of their approach is to
super-stimulate expanded rates of private sector capital investment,
financed so as to broaden the base of equity owners in society.

The credit financing of corporate expansion must meet rigid standards of feasibility and must be repaid as a self-liquidating investment. New dollars flow directly into new productive capacity. In
sharp contrast, government debt seldom, if ever, finances any production increases. Rather, it goes into nonproductive spending, war,
and even into wastes of human talent and natural resources. Government debt is therefore inherently inflationary. Even worse, when
government spending is not matched with current tax revenues, the
inflationary impact worsens. Funds must either be borrowed (thus
diverting those same funds from productive investment in the private sector) or simply issued as printing press money.

Today the Federal debt already exceeds one half trillion dollars or
35.5% of the GNP.[15] Annual interest charges on this debt—one of the
highest expenses in the entire budget—amounted to $34.6 billion in
1976 and are rising.[16] President Carter envisions a $68 billion deficit
for the current fiscal year (widened from President Ford's $57.2 bil-
lion) and projects at least a $57.7 billion budget deficit for fiscal 1978.[17]

From a standpoint of economic justice, government deficits make
no sense at all. They cause inflation and are therefore a pernicious
form of hidden tax on the public, most painful to the poorest members
of society. A just tax system would work toward the elimination of
future inflationary budget deficits and to curb further increases in
the already bloated government debt. Better yet, a concerted effort
should be made to begin to repay this debt.

Inheritance Policy

Under a national ownership strategy, inheritance policy should be restructured to discourage excessive concentrations of wealth and, in order to promote individual initiative and capital self-sufficiency, to encourage the broadest possible distribution of income-producing assets. Gift and estate taxes therefore should not be imposed on the donor or his estate (including that accumulated within proposed "industrial homestead" vehicles). Rather, taxation should be based on the size of the recipient's total accumulations after receiving the gift or bequest. If the value of the recipient's asset accumulations remain below the floor mentioned above, no tax would be imposed on the newly acquired assets. Above that floor, a reasonable asset transfer tax (or a flat rate tax on "excess" industrial homestead accumulations) would be paid.

Asset Transfer Tax

Above the targeted homestead accumulation floor, an asset transfer tax or the flat rate tax would be imposed on each new owner to discourage future excess concentrations of wealth and economic power when assets transfer from one generation to the next. This would replace the existing estate and gift tax systems. The asset transfer tax and flat rate tax could be avoided by distributing excess accumulations to others, including family members, friends, and employees, as long as their personal accumulations remain below the floor.

Integration of Personal and Corporate Income Taxes

The double tax penalty now imposed on corporate profits is becoming widely accepted as an unjust form of tax discrimination that should be eliminated. Some reformers are proposing to mitigate this problem through a highly complicated and arbitrary compromise that not only avoids the problem but worsens it. Instead of eliminating the double tax directly at the corporate level, they would permit a partial deduction for dividend payouts to the corporation and a redistribution oriented partial tax credit for shareholders. Hence, it neither restores private property in corporate equity nor does it promote expanded distribution of equity issuances. It merely makes the top 1% who own the majority of directly-owned outstanding corporate shares even richer.

The Kelso-Adler theory of tax justice would attack this problem directly with elegant simplicity. It would recognize that property and profits are inseparable and therefore *all corporate net earnings, whether distributed or retained by the corporation, would be treated as earned by its owners and therefore should be taxable at the personal level, on the same basis as any other direct income.* Under this alternative, *the corporation would be treated for tax purposes like a partnership*, with its business expenses (including depreciation and research and development) attributed and deductible at the enterprise level and all capital incomes attributed individually according to each owner's proprietary stake in the business. To encourage more equity financing of corporate growth, higher dividend payouts must be encouraged and alternative low-cost sources for financing must be made available to expanding and viable new enterprises.

Dividend Deductions at the Corporate Level[18]

Corporations should be allowed a dollar-for-dollar tax deduction for any dividends they distribute either (1) directly to their shareholders (including beneficial owners, such as employees under tax-qualified ESOPs, profits sharing plans, pension plans, etc.) to the extent such earnings become currently taxable at the individual level or (2) to repay stock acquisition indebtedness on any new equity issuances through tax-qualified financing mechanisms that further the goals of a national planned ownership program.

Capital Gains Taxation

How to tax capital gains is a continuing source of much of the complexity and confusion that now plague our tax laws. How would a property-oriented theory of tax justice handle this problem?

First, it would restructure the tax laws to encourage investment and discourage speculation. It would add disincentives to gambling in high-risk securities and the commodities market, at least for non-wealthy individuals. Tax laws would be designed to facilitate the acquisition, accumulation and retention by today's capital-deficient Americans of long term investments, held mainly for their potential of yielding high, steady, and relatively secure second incomes to supplement their paychecks and retirement checks in the future.

To the extent capital gains income results from short term purchases and sales of commodities and securities, as under present law it should be treated like any other kind of direct personal income. Such capital gains are no different than the purchase and sale of any other goods for a profit, or for that matter, gambling gains.

Capital gains from long term holdings deserve different treatment, however, under a national strategy to broaden the base of capital ownership. As recommended above, to the extent that investments are accumulated within a tax-qualified vehicle, the gains should be permitted to increase tax-free or tax-deferred, until the individual affected reaches a targeted floor of capital self-sufficiency. Above that level capital gains would be subject to normal taxation after indexing for inflation.

If all of the proposals recommended in this article were adopted, the capital gains problem would gradually disappear. Much of the appreciation in the values of corporate common stock can be traced to the retention by management of earnings for meeting their capital requirements. As dividend payouts increase (encouraged by tax-deductibility of dividends at the corporate level) and as new sources of equity financing become readily available through the discount mechanism of the Federal Reserve System, the value of individual shares would tend to stabilize over time and be based on current and projected dividend yields per share. Hence, long term capital gains would be less a source of future government revenues.

To some extent, long term capital gains result, not from the increased productive value of the underling assets, but from a gradual debasement of the American currency. Only inflation-inducing government economic policies can be blamed for these increases in profits and capital values. Hence, except where prices increase from natural shortages, government should assume total responsibility for inflationary increases in the value of investments. Therefore *capital gains taxation should always be inflation indexed to see if any gains in value actually exist.*

State and Local Tax Systems

Today, a heavy portion of local revenues come from the taxation of property, thus discouraging investment and improvement of industry and residential property in their areas. Sales taxes also increase price levels, encourage tax evasion by local merchants, discourage trade, and generally can cause one area to become less attractive than another. Since high production, high incomes, and a higher quality of life rests on the quality of the structures, industrial equipment and facilities, and technology available to the residents of an area, it should be obvious that *taxes on local property are counter productive and should be gradually supplanted with a universal system of state and local taxation based upon the direct incomes of its residents from whatever sources.* Thus federal tax policy should create additional incentives for state and local taxing authorities to gradually shift to direct flat rate income taxes at the individual level, for the same reasons outlined above. To simplify tax collections, the state and local rates could be set at a percentage of the federal tax imposed on residents of the area. Another advantage of this approach is that all areas of the country would become tax-neutral for investment purposes, thus increasing the nation's overall efficiency in the allocation of our manpower and other resources.

Tax Simplification

Although corporate income tax returns would still be important for disclosure purposes and for corporations unwilling to pay out their earnings fully to their stockholders, most of the tax revenues would flow from the expanded personal tax base. The personal income tax

return and the tax system itself would, as result, be enormously simplified and easier to understand. A simple one-page personal income
tax return would be well-received by the American taxpayer.

Most personal deductions and tax credits could be eliminated
under a flat-rate tax system, restoring the neutrality of the tax system over people's consumption choices. Personal exemptions, however, could be raised to the poverty level, so that the poorest families
only would pay no taxes, including payroll taxes. But by filling-in a
simple annual income tax return, a poor family could qualify for a
negative or reverse income tax (or refund) as proposed by the conservative economist Milton Friedman.

A Quadrennial Census of Wealth

Through assets accumulated with ESOPs, CSOPs and ISOPs,
within one generation, the nation would gain a useful profile of total
property accumulations and its wealth distribution patterns. It would
also be a way of meeting the recommendation of the Joint Economic
Committee in its 1976 Annual Report calling for:

> a quadrennial report on the ownership of wealth in this coun-
> try which would assist in evaluating how successfully the
> base of wealth was being broadened over time (p. 100).

In the final analysis, a wealth census is no more onerous or an
invasion of privacy than an annual income tax return. And since
under a national ownership strategy at least 95% of American households would be classified as capital deficient and therefore beneficiaries of a planned ownership program, one could reasonably anticipate
little taxpayer resistance to a quadrennial wealth census, if it was
carefully designed and communicated to the American people. Even
the wealthiest families would gain by a reduction of the confiscatory
bias of the present tax system and the promotion of private property
industrial homesteads based, not on a redistribution of present wealth,
but a redistribution of future growth opportunities.

A Challenge and a Tool

The main purpose of this article is not to offer definitive answers
but to suggest some new questions that tax professionals might pose
in evaluating tax reform proposals in the future. It is not intended to
leave the reader feeling comfortable, because the history of tax reform leaves little room for optimism about the future of the privately
owned corporation and the free enterprise system in general. But, it
might aid the social-minded business statesman to gain some deeper

philosophical insights into the history and trends of tax reform over the last century. Whether Karl Marx' tax strategy will succeed in finally destroying the privately owned corporation and converting it into one owned and controlled by a dictatorship of the proletariat, remains an open question.

Some in the business world seem unconcerned as to who signs their salary check. They seem to have thrown in the towel to Marx. Others seem prepared to take a new stand against further erosion of our private property system. It is the latter to whom this discussion is primarily addressed.

The author rejects the piecemeal and narrowly partisan approach to tax reform. This is a call for a new tax philosophy that will transcend the interests of special power blocs and interest groups. The tax system affects each of us, and will certainly affect the kind of society we will bequeath to future generations of Americans. Armed with a set of principles that are totally consistent with the revolutionary philosophy that fathered our nation, each of us can better judge tax reform proposals as they are presented to the American people.

When proposals are delivered to Congress, we need to judge whether those proposals will move us toward tax justice or toward further tax injustice, whether they support property or are further despotic inroads on the rights to property, whether Karl Marx has won another victory or whether we have turned in a genuinely new direction.

Senator Russell Long, when in 1973 he urged his Senate colleagues to consider converting the failing northeast rail system (Conrail) into a 100% employee owned private corporation, said:

> [T]here are but three political-economic roads from which we can choose. . . .
>
> We could take the first course and further exacerbate the already intensely concentrated ownership of productive capital in the American economy.
>
> Or we could join the rest of the world by taking the second path, that of nationalization.
>
> Or we can take the third road,[19] establishing policies to diffuse capital ownership broadly, so that many individuals, particularly productive workers, can participate as owners of industrial capital.
>
> [T]he choice is ours. There is no way to avoid this decision. Non-action is a political decision in favor of continued, and indeed increased, concentrated ownership of productive capital.

Notes:

[1]The labeling of this third principle has been criticized by some Kelsonians as negative and too confining, considering the synergism of Kelso's economic growth strategies. Hence, the "Principle of Harmony" has been offered as more appropriate as a guide for just social action when either participative justice or distributive justice is violated by society's laws or institutions. See "Economic Justice in the Age of the Robot," and also the discussion of Say's Law in "The Binary Economics of Louis Kelso" in this book.

[2]By 1993, Congress has passed 20 laws affecting ESOPs.

[3]By 1993, the National Center for Employee Ownership reported the existence of between 9,000 to 10,000 U. S. ESOP companies with about 11 million U. S. workers with over $60 billion in assets. Several other countries, including the United Kingdom, Egypt, Hungary and Argentina have enacted laws to encourage ESOPs.

[4]Since this article was written, the tax reforms of 1984 have raised the ceiling on tax-deductible contributions to 25% for the repayment of principal and an unlimited amount to cover the repayment of interest on ESOP debt.

[5]Congress adopted this proposal in 1986.

[6]The investment tax credit ESOP was eliminated by Congress in 1986. It accomplished its original objective of seeding the idea of ESOP within America's largest corporations and most powerful unions. It also led to other more fundamental improvements in ESOP laws.

[7]In 1993, this tax is 34%, but may be increased again to 38% or higher by the Clinton Administration.

[8]Proposals to include the Community Investment Corporation (CIC) as a fourth vehicle were recommended first by Senator Gary Hart and Cong. Parren Mitchell in connection with their enterprise zone proposals in 1981. The Clinton Administration has included the CIC as an asset democratization vehicle in background papers supporting its Economic Empowerment Zone legislation presented to Congress in May 1993. CICs would enable residents in urban and rural zones to acquire shares in and receive dividend incomes from local real estate planning and development corporations in a manner similar to ESOPs.

[9]In 1992, according to the *1993 Economic Report of the President*, America adds about $1 trillion annually in public and private sector capital, infrastructure, and residential and nonresidential structures, all or most of which could be financed through "Industrial Homesteading" vehicles. This amounts to about $4,000 annually for every man, woman and child in America, or $240,000 in assets for a family of three over a period of 20 years. In contrast, most Americans in 1992 owe more than they own. The average American today is obligated with a $43,000 slice of America's total debt of over $11 trillion, most of which represents consumer debt and nonproductive borrowing by government for wars, expanded public bureaucracies, subsidized jobs and welfare.

[10]Under Section 13 of the Federal Reserve Act of 1913, the Fed was empowered to discount "eligible" agricultural, commercial and industrial paper. It also has the power to set a special discount rate of 1% or less to cover service costs. If activated, this mechanism would provide a nonsubsidized, off-budget substitute for all current tax subsidies for encouraging investment, including the 50% exclusion of interest earnings for lenders to ESOPs, which was added in 1984 to encourage banks, insurance companies and mutual funds to make loans at lower rates to ESOPs.

[11]In his writings in the 1980's, Kelso modified his CDIC proposal, substituting a national reinsurance system to further spread the risk of loan defaults and to support a network of private sector insurers of bank lenders to expand capital ownership. This system, unlike most government-supported credit insurance schemes, however, should be structured to limit the liability of taxpayers to the government's actual investment in the reinsurance fund.

[12]Walter Blum and Harry Kalven, *The Uneasy Case for Progressive Income Taxation.*, University of Chicago, 1953.

[13]In 1984, Congress allowed for an analogous tax-deferred rollover of ESOP assets into an Individual Retirement Account or other qualified deferred compensation plan which a participant received in one lump-sum. This was liberalized in 1992 to include incremental distributions rolled over into another qualified plan.

[14]By 1992, corporate income taxes had shrunk to 9% of total Federal revenues.

[15]By 1993, the Federal debt had increased eightfold to over $4 trillion.

[16]By 1993, Federal taxpayers paid over $200 billion annually in interest charges alone. This payment to America's creditors is more than one-half the cost of World War II, and exceeds the cost of all other wars in America's history combined, including Korea and Vietnam.

[17]In his 1993 budget, President Clinton projected a fiscal deficit of over $300 billion.

[18]This reform was adopted for shares held by ESOPs in 1984. It should be extended to all shareholders.

[19]With the collapse of communism in the Soviet Bloc starting in the late 1980's, the pendulum for those countries seems to have swung from the second to the first alternative, albeit at great pain to most citizens. Despite the remarkable advances resulting from ESOP initiatives around the world, the third road is yet to be implemented as the main path of national economic policy by any country in the world, including the United States.

IV

Practical Applications

Practical
Applications

It is easy to dismiss discussion of esoteric economic concepts as the modern equivalent of debating how many angels can dance on the head of a pin. The ideas and programs for dealing with the problem of poverty detailed in previous sections of this book may seem to be unrelated to the "real world," and impracticable in the everyday world of business, politics and government. Academic theories for the cure of poverty can sound nice but and have little or no practical application. Yet the difference between most cures for poverty espoused by academia and government, and those in this book is that not only are these ideas and programs grounded on solid moral principles, they have been applied—and have been proved to work.

"Value-Based Management: A Framework for Analysis and Action" outlines a concept which aims at transforming the business corporation as well as the labor union as basic social institutions. Value-Based Management is based solidly on the principles of shared moral values, maximization of customer satisfaction, and a just compensation system. Thus, the authors apply the principles of economic and social justice at the level of the enterprise. Value-Based Management provides a framework which empowers the individual worker, through the restructuring of the corporate environment, to realize his potential and enhance his own dignity and sovereignty in concert with others in the workplace.

The next five articles in this section, "Ownership Starts at the Crack of Dawn For Allied Plywood Corporation Employees/Shareholders;" "How the Workers Run Avis Better;" "Taming of the Screw: How Fastener Industries Figured out the Nuts and Bolts of Running an ESOP Company;" "Peasants Fight and Buy Stock to Save Beleaguered Plantation;" and "The Great Game of Business (Or, How I Learned to Stop Worrying and Teach People How to Make Money)," relate how businesses have adopted some of these principles and programs, and raised their levels of productivity and profitability. These cases demonstrate that justice and business success can go hand-in-hand.

Conformance with moral principles is, in the long run, the most practical way a business can be run: "Good ethics is good business." Yet, while this is true, it is not always easy to convince people. Adoption of Employee Stock Ownership Plans (ESOPs) in over 10,000 companies in the United States of America covering over 11 million workers, and the evolution of the expanded ownership culture in those corporations demonstrates most graphically the soundness of the moral and ethical approach.

Granted, then, the expanded capital ownership model can work for individual businesses. But what about an entire economy? The remaining three articles in this section, "Beyond Privatization: An Egyptian Model for Democratizing Capital Credit for Workers;" "The Abraham Federation: A Framework for Peace in the Middle East;" and "The Third Way: America's True Legacy to the New Republics," demonstrate that the principles laid out in this book can be applied on the macro- as well as the micro-economic scale.

In "Beyond Privatization: An Egyptian Model for Democratizing Capital Credit for Workers" Norman Kurland and Dawn Brohawn address the problem facing many countries today: how to deal with the difficulties of transforming into a market economy from a state-dominated socialist economy. Using the term "democratization" instead of "privatization," to highlight the necessity for creating a broad base of capital ownership, the authors outline a detailed program by which governments can both divest themselves of State Owned Enterprises (SOEs) in a just and equitable fashion, and create first-class enterprises capable of competing in world markets and of employing workers whose jobs are threatened by the transition from socialism. They give a concrete example of how such a project has been carried out in the case of the Alexandria Tire Company, of Alexandria, Egypt.

"The Abraham Federation: A Framework for Peace in the Middle East" addresses a political problem with economic overtones, rather than an economic problem with political elements, as is the case with divestiture of SOEs. What do you do when two or more different cultural groups have what each considers a just claim to possession of the same territory? The amount of land is relatively fixed, so it is impossible to create more of it to satisfy competing claims. Traditionally, the solution has been to fight, with the territory awarded to the victor. Norman Kurland proposes that the high-technology frontier— new tools, new structures, and new machines that can be fabricated upon the land— be substituted for finite land and natural resources as the source for the democratization of future wealth opportunities. Since man's capacity to build and rebuild tools is virtually limitless, the source of the problem—increasing claims on static wealth—is removed. Such a solution—especially if given special barrier-free trade status by the United States and other countries—could be applied not only to highlighted trouble spots like the West Bank and Gaza, but also to the situations in South Africa, Sri Lanka, Cyprus, the Balkans, and Northern Ireland.

Having addressed economic problems with political elements, and political problems with economic factors, the final article in this section, "The Third Way: America's True Legacy to the New Republics," proposes a solution in the case where a society is faced with both political and economic ruin: the political dissolution of the former Soviet Union, and its inextricably linked economic collapse. The programs outlined give a blueprint for rebuilding a nation's economic and social structures from the ground up, not by copying the capitalist model or tinkering with the socialist model, but by transcending both of them.

The programs outlined in the articles are not meant to be taken as applying only in cases where the national economy or government is on the verge of collapse. Throughout most, if not all, of the developed world, the wage system relied on by capitalism, socialism and all variations between the two extremes, has created a system of economic injustice destructive of the family. It has become the norm in industrialized economies that the wage income of a single worker is insufficient to meet the material needs of a family. This is the result of the human worker having to compete with increasingly productive technology for his job.

Combined with this is the growing private and public dependence on consumer (i.e., nonproductive) credit. Not only do governments habitually spend far more than they realize in tax revenues and make up the difference with borrowed funds that are not spent on productive projects, but the private citizen in many countries is often deep in debt. Many people are forced to borrow money to pay for the basic necessities of life as the result of inadequate personal income. Others, who might have had sufficient income to meet their needs and even live in relative comfort, deliberately assume a burden of debt in order to acquire the luxury goods and ephemeral status symbols so much a part of a consumerist and materialist society. As a result, the husband and the wife are forced to work outside the home in competition with increasingly productive technology in order to bring home wages sufficient to make ends meet. With both the mother and the father away from home, the children must also go outside the home and family in order to receive care.

This is a complete reversal of the traditional family structure prior to the Industrial Revolution, where both the husband and wife worked at home, and care of the children was part of the function of the family. Under a national or universal program of expanded capital ownership, as outlined in the article on the Third Way, a wage income could be supplemented or replaced completely with earnings from the family's capital assets, allowing one or both parents to resume the critical place in the home and still derive a living income. This would be the obvious solution to such problems as the living (or minimum) wage and government control of day care. Government intervention in either area has failed to bring about any real or lasting improvement in the quality of family and community life, as has been amply demonstrated in the Scandinavian versions of the Welfare State, and the United States of America's high-wage and decreasingly competitive economy.

It becomes ever more clear that a true Third Way based on expanded capital ownership is not just a way to go, it is the moral way, the only way to go.

— 9 —

Value-Based Management[1]: A Framework for Equity and Efficiency in the Workplace

by Dawn K. Brohawn

In collaboration with

Stephen F. Hardiman, Norman G. Kurland and Thomas J. Simon

As the world prepares to enter a new millennium, change has become the rule of the day. From the macro to the micro level, from the global marketplace to the individual enterprise, long-sacred ideas underpinning the economic status quo are being challenged.

Leaders in business and labor, spurred by competition or sheer survival, are reexamining such basic questions as how people participate in production and how they earn an income. Inexorable forces—advancing technology, expanding worldwide communications and information networks, the increasing mobility of capital and labor (particularly technical know-how), unpredictable geopolitical conditions, rising populations, and the opening of global markets—are shaking the foundations of "business as usual."

Consequently, institutions such as the corporation and the labor union are being impelled into an intense period of reformulation. Shareholders, infuriated by soaring executive pay in the face of plummeting corporate profits, are organizing to demand their property rights.[2] Workers, lulled by annual cost-of-living increases and promises of job security, are now desperate merely to have a job, any job. Management, seeking a magic bullet to raise corporate productivity, is shifting from autocratic (Theory X) to participatory (Theory Y) to empowerment (Theory Z) approaches.

Profound changes are taking place in the labor movement as well. From a peak of 35 percent of the American nonagricultural work force in 1954, union membership fell to 15.8 percent of employed wage and salaried workers in 1992, according to the U.S. Department of Labor. Evidencing an even more dramatic decline, just 11.5 percent of all U.S. private sector employees today belong to a union, compared with 36.7 percent of federal, state and local government workers.[3]

Some within the labor movement are therefore questioning whether the old modes of thinking are sufficient or even viable. Irving Bluestone, former Vice President of the United Auto Workers, and his son and professor of political economy, Barry Bluestone, note in their recent book *Negotiating the Future: A Labor Perspective on American Business*:

> [I]n recognition of the requirements of the global market-place, we believe that labor and management have more in common than in conflict. Finding a new structure for labor-management relations that rests on common interests and mutual concerns is, we argue, a *sine qua non* for economic prosperity if not outright survival.[4]

Long-accepted assumptions and theories which have patterned our economies and workplaces are proving themselves inadequate for reconciling the common man and woman with the coming Age of the Robot. It is not just a matter of retooling our industries or retraining our workforces. We are being forced back to the drawing board, to reconstruct the institutions and systems which sustain us.

A House Divided

While frequently maligned as a tool for exploiting human beings, the corporation is, notwithstanding, a remarkable social invention for increasing business efficiency. Its main functions are to: (1) aggregate, organize and maximize the efficiency of labor and capital for the production and distribution of goods and services; (2) maximize financial return to shareholders; and (3) insulate from the risks of the business the personal (non-corporate) assets of the owners. The corporation has thus become the most significant organizational form for facilitating the production, marketing and distribution of goods and services on a global scale.

When we look at most business corporations, however, we generally see a disharmony of interests. Owners and management seek higher profits, lower costs (particularly labor costs) and greater efficiency. Workers and unions, meanwhile, seek higher fixed wages/benefits and job security. Customers desire higher quality goods and services at a lower price. Governments, of course, want a stable economy and a bigger tax base.

From the standpoint of the corporation, the divergence of interests between owners, workers, unions, the government, and other "stakeholders" can only weaken its competitiveness within a global marketplace. With pandemic recessions threatening the survival of small and giant companies alike, we can only wonder how long a house so divided can stand.

In the long run, the critical question for every enterprise is whether there are universal principles and a practical framework of action which can unite these divergent interests, so that the enterprise can work for everyone's benefit.

Assessing the Structural Flaws

Business organizations reflect their external as well as internal institutional environments. A truism, perhaps, but we often overlook the degree to which laws, policies, procedures, and rules shape the creation, operation and development of a company. Significantly, as nations and businesses enter the Age of the Robot, we find that their economic environments are manifestations of the anachronistic, nineteenth century-style "wage system."

All wage systems—whether capitalist, socialist or mixed—share some basic assumptions. They presuppose that a small number of people, or the State (run in the name of "the people," of course), will own the means of production. They also presume that everyone else

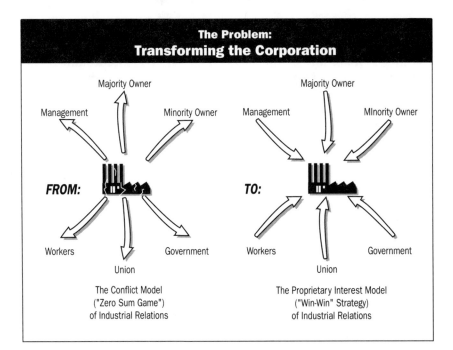

The Problem:
Transforming the Corporation

FROM:

Majority Owner
Management   Minority Owner

Workers   Government
Union

The Conflict Model
("Zero Sum Game")
of Industrial Relations

TO:

Majority Owner
Management   MInority Owner

Workers   Government
Union

The Proprietary Interest Model
("Win-Win" Strategy)
of Industrial Relations

must therefore be workers-for-hire or welfare recipients.

Consequently, most people are led to believe that the only legitimate way they can raise their standard of living is to receive higher and higher wages, salaries and other fixed benefits. The resultant ratcheting up of costs (primarily through rising fixed labor rates) naturally works against a business' ability to operate effectively in the competitive marketplace.

But as the wage system grows, working people lose their means to acquire economic self-sufficiency. They end up dependent on a job or welfare. Management and labor, buying into the wage system's zero-sum, conflict model of industrial relations, pit themselves against each other. Meanwhile, businesses go under, workers walk the unemployment lines, and ownership and economic power grow more concentrated in fewer and fewer hands.

If the conflict-producing wage system is destroying our economies and workplaces, what is our alternative? Starting within the corporation, how can we introduce a "win-win" system for running business that creates broadly enjoyed prosperity and empowerment? As we "re-engineer" the corporation to fulfill these objectives, what would its management system look like?

Management's Dilemma:
Sorting out the Buzzwords from the Basics

Another consulting industry has recently emerged: repairing the damage in companies which have installed "Total Quality Management" ("TQM"), one of the newer and highly touted additions to management's "tool kit." A 1991 survey of 300 electronics companies by the American Electronics Association found in fact that "73 percent had quality programs in place, but of these, 63 percent said they had failed to improve quality by even as much as 10 percent."[5]

Few would argue that approaches such as "Total Quality Management," "quality circles," and "Management by Objective" articulate good principles (e.g., improving communications between managers and workers, and encouraging greater worker commitment to quality and customer service) and promote useful practices (statistical quality control, gain sharing linked to increased productivity, etc.). So what accounts for the dubious success rate of many of today's management theories and techniques?

Some of the blame can be laid at the feet of those selling (or buying) a quick, slick cure for slumping corporate competitiveness and profitability. And uncontrollable forces in the business environment—such as market downturns, the sudden obsolescence of a key technology, and hostile credit policies and tax laws—can buffet the strongest of companies.

But the main problem with all these approaches is not what they offer. It is what they leave out. Because they omit key building blocks, they inevitably fail over the long-term to *systematize and institutionalize* high involvement and true empowerment of working people.

Searching for the Missing Pieces

Today's management theories and techniques tend to fixate on *how* people do things—on "process" for its own sake. While new and improved processes may facilitate better interactions between individuals or may temporarily spark motivation, these approaches are often piecemeal, superficial and short-term in their means and objectives.

Furthermore, many new management techniques ignore the importance of creating a regular, understandable, and fair system of economic feedback (both short-term and long-term) linking workers' compensation and rewards to their increased contributions to the bottom-line. A recent survey of 100 top managers from Fortune 500 companies by Rath & Strong management consultants showed that 87 percent believed that "delivering value to customers was critical." Yet "80 percent of the same companies did not tie compensation for all employees to customer satisfaction."

A senior engineer and founder of IBM's Activity Based Management Competency Center, observed: "TQM or any of the other alphabet soup programs really are not cost-effective until every individual employee can see some benefit to them personally."[6]

Process-focused approaches also tend to ignore the management structures within the enterprise which confer real power—the ability to influence, direct, hold accountable, act upon, or achieve an objective. These structures (whether they be a company's bylaws, governance and shareholder representation structures, production and distribution methods, compensation systems, or policies and procedures) embody organizational values and habit patterns built up over time. For good or bad, such institutional structures guide and reinforce the actions of human beings within the organization. They are the "system software" that drives the company's ongoing operation.

Process vs. Structure: A False Dichotomy

We should not, however, trivialize the importance of sound process. After all, participation (a key principle of economic justice) is an ongoing process. But without *structure*, you have process which goes nowhere and leaves nothing behind. A company which ignores the impact of the institutional environment on human behavior cannot adequately address such long-term challenges as: (1) how to make participation a permanent part of the company; and (2) how to ensure that participation is not leader-manipulated.

Clearly, a participatory corporate culture also needs to establish new organizational structures, or redesign existing structures, to systematically diffuse power down to every individual. This will best ensure that participation does not become something which can be terminated at the whim of the leader.

In this respect, "structure" refers to a framework of powers, like a constitution, which defines a person's rights, responsibilities and duties. Such structures of a business organization include its written core values and code of ethics, its bylaws, policies, rules and organizational systems. These set the parameters for the processes which emerge. They also govern the power and control relationships between owners, management and employees.

History has shown that participation without the structure for channelling power down to each individual is tenuous and short-lived. On the other hand, structure without human participation is like a house without people living in it. A structure becomes static and obsolete without human interaction and organized process. It soon becomes disconnected from the real-life needs of human beings. It loses its soul.

Thus, good structure (reflecting good values and design principles) cannot be separated from good process, or vice versa.

Ownership: The Missing Keystone

A common objective of every business approach and management theory is to formulate those factors which will actually improve a company's productiveness and profitability. One thing is clear—a motivated workforce, all other things being equal, is a more productive workforce than one which is not.

Many experts in personal and organizational development have observed that a basic key to motivation derives from the human need to feel a sense of control and responsibility over one's own life and work. Thus, management jargon of the moment speaks of "empowering" workers," letting them "participate," and making them "feel like owners."

All too often, unfortunately, the rhetoric of *psychological* ownership obscures the fact that *property* ownership is integral to full empowerment. Why is direct ownership, or private property, so critical? The answer is that property confers "inalienable" (or permanent) rights to profits, to information, and to governing power, that cannot be taken away from an owner within a legal system that protects property.

Without full rights of property, "participation" and "involvement" become mere manipulation by those who hold real power over the livelihoods of others.

Because power is inextricably linked to property, the process of participation without the substance of property (where people have something tangible they can lose) eventually becomes meaningless.

While there is a valid distinction in the modern corporation between management and ownership, as pointed out by Berle and Means,[7] the property nexus gives the owner, through his representatives on the corporate board of directors, the ultimate control over the affairs of the corporation. For the efficient operation of the enterprise, professional managers must have effective day-to-day control over corporate decisions. But by law, managers are supposed to be accountable to all the owners, and can be removed by the elected board of directors if they fail to perform effectively for the benefit of the shareholders.

What a voter represents to the machinery of governance in a political republic, a shareholder represents in a corporation's governance: the ultimate holder of power, who can delegate his power to representatives to whom managers must report. The voting power of a single shareholder of a large corporation may seem insignificant. But when combined with the power of other shareholders, his power is the most effective check against non-accountable or corrupt management, and is the key to effective representational democracy in the corporation.

There is another reason why "worker empowerment and participation" without real ownership will not stick. Psychological rewards such as praise and recognition are important to human beings. But a management approach which does not tie economic rewards to improved performance and results will in the long-run generate apathy, if not resentment on the part of workers. They eventually realize that they are working to create profits for someone else.

But does significant ownership participation really help a company compete and succeed? Growing evidence indicates that the most healthy, productive and profitable companies are those which share ownership, profits, information, and power with all workers so that each can become more fully involved and actively connected to the organization's performance.[8] Going beyond the rhetoric of empowerment and participation, these organizations consistently and systematically demonstrate respect for the dignity and rights of the individual worker. These rights notably include the right to share as an owner in the increased productiveness and profits of the company.

Jack Stack, President of Springfield Remanufacturing Corporation (SRC) in Springfield, Missouri, explains in his book *The Great Game of Business* how sharing information ("open book management"), ownership and power with all the employees made his company so successful. In 1983, in a management-led buyout of a failing division of International Harvester, 119 SRC employees purchased their company through an employee stock ownership plan (ESOP). Four years later, from a first year's loss of $60,488, pre-tax earnings had risen to $2.7 million. Nine years after the buyout, the SRC workforce had increased from the original 119 employees to 650, and the value of SRC's stock had increased from 10 cents per share to $18.30, an increase of *18,200%.*[9]

As Jack Stack puts it, "You can accumulate more wealth by sharing equity than by keeping it all yourself." Why is this? One reason, Stack observes, is that "a company of owners will outperform a company of employees any day of the week."

Value-Based Management: A System for Rebuilding the Corporation

A commitment to fostering true participation and empowerment in the corporation, however, necessitates an ongoing system which purposefully promotes the dignity and development of every person affected. Such a system would provide all workers access to the means and opportunities to maximize the value of their contribution to the organization. It would structure the company as a whole to deliver maximum value to the customer. In return, that system would also reward every worker for the value of his contributions, linking him to the organization's performance in the marketplace.

Such a comprehensive framework is called *Value-Based Management (VBM).*[10] As both a business philosophy and management system, Value-Based Management is organized in accordance with universal principles of economic and social justice.[11] The objective of VBM is to increase long-term corporate profitability by providing value to the customer. Its ultimate purpose is to economically empower each person as a worker and an owner.

VBM embodies two precepts of *equity*: (1) that people are entitled to a proportionate share of what they helped to produce with both their labor and their productive assets; and (2) that all people are entitled to live in a culture that offers them equal dignity and opportunity.

As an interlocking philosophy and problem-solving framework, VBM recognizes the interdependency between moral values and material value. It holds that maximizing justice and maximizing productiveness and profits within a free market system can and should be mutually reinforcing. What Value-Based Management uniquely offers is a moral framework for succeeding in the global marketplace.

The central value of Value-Based Management is the *value of every person*—each worker, each customer, each supplier. VBM empowers people and raises their human dignity and quality of life by enabling them to enjoy goods and services of the highest value. Its principal means for achieving this end is expanded capital ownership.

Building a Lasting Ownership Culture

Management science, in its deepest human sense, is a branch of social morality which guides the continual creation and perfecting of those invisible structures called "institutions." Management systems largely determine the degree to which institutions, such as the corporation, can be structured to promote the dignity and empowerment of each person affected by those "going concerns."

In transforming the workplace, Value-Based Management seeks to provide every worker with the most effective means to become a co-owner of the place where he works. VBM's primary means for turning workers into corporate shareholders is the Employee Stock Ownership Plan (ESOP). This powerful tool was uniquely designed to restructure corporate finance—which historically has been the taproot of ownership concentration. The ESOP provides workers with access to capital credit to pay for their shares out of future corporate profits which they help the company to earn.

A well-designed and empowering ESOP is a flexible legal structure which can also help solve the problem of how to build and sustain a participatory ownership culture beyond the lives of its founders. The ESOP offers a framework for establishing management systems that can survive poor managers or managers unable to accept a corporate philosophy based on the dignity and empowerment of workers.

The ESOP alone, however, is insufficient for building a value-based corporate culture. The ESOP has in a few cases been used as a tool to exploit workers.[12] Or the ESOP can be designed in such a way as to deprive workers of their full rights as first-class shareholders, thus violating the fundamental principles of private property and economic justice underlying Value-Based Management.[13]

How a particular ESOP is designed reflects both the company's external (legal) environment as well as its internal culture and values. Within a corporate culture moving toward participatory ownership, ESOP is merely one component, albeit a vital component and powerful tool of the overall system called Value-Based Management.

The Three Components of a Value-Based Management System

What does a Value-Based Management system look like? A birds-eye view of VBM reveals three interconnected components reflecting both ethical and material aspects of "value":

(1) **Value-Based Operational and Governance Structures**. A social structure, such as a business corporation, should be engineered to achieve a specific function, according to sound principles and *universal moral values* which enable people to interact more effectively together. The sharper its organizational focus and better its structural design, the more likely the company will succeed and prosper.

    The overall structure or "invisible environment" of a particular company consists of such institutional elements as: a company's statement of core values, code of ethics, and mission statement; its strategic, operational, financial and marketing plans; its organizational charts, bylaws, etc. These substructures largely affect the quality of the interactions among people, as well as those between people, their physical environment and tools. In VBM terms, these interactions of people with their physical and institutional environments make up the overall "culture" of the company.

(2) **A Value-Based Focus on the Customer.** VBM's focus on serving the customer derives from a belief in the value of each customer as a human being, who as such deserves to be treated with dignity and fairness.

    VBM also recognizes that it is ultimately the customer who signs the paycheck of everyone in the company. In terms of the main social purpose of a business—namely, delivering goods and services of the highest *value to the customer*—Value-Based Management follows a simple formula:

$$V = \frac{Q}{P}$$

where V=Value, Q=Quality, and P=Price

In other words, value will rise as quality of goods or services increases and/or price decreases. The "V=Q/P" formula offers a key to long-term success in the competitive marketplace.

(3) **A Value-Based Pay and Reward System.** Assuming that the company's structure is based on sound ethical principles and its central focus is on delivering maximum value to the customer, then the reward system should also be structured to reflect these principles. Under VBM, every person in the company is compensated for the *value of their contributions or inputs* to the company, both as workers and as owners. This component of VBM (which is measured by a company's quality and cost control systems, and is reflected in the company's "bottom line"), reflects the "private property" principle of distributive justice.[14] It represents pay based on performance and contribution, not charity.

Initiating a VBM System

While Value-Based Management is based on universal moral principles which relate to human nature and the basic needs of human beings, *how* these principles are implemented will be different in each company. This is because every company, like every person, is unique. Each will be shaped by such factors as size, industry, location, demographics, marketing strategy and leadership style; each will reflect its own corporate "personality" with its own history, cultural values and traditions.

In structuring a new company or reengineering an existing company to improve its performance, a corporate leader who wants to institute the Value-Based Management system should start the process by developing a written set of:

(a) company *core values* (commonly shared ethical principles which define what the company stands for and which guide how the organization operates and grows); and

(b) a *code of ethics* (a set of habits for guiding individual behavior toward strengthening the company's culture and interpersonal harmony).

Ideally these core values and code of ethics are (i) agreed upon by consensus by every person in the company, (ii) reflected in the company's organizational structure and bylaws, and (iii) subject to periodic review and improvement (as with the "renewal process" practiced at Herman Miller, Inc. of Zeeland, Michigan[15]). These principles serve as the "compass" for guiding a company's operations and governance, as well as the daily interactions of its members.[16]

Building upon the foundation of a written set of core values and code of ethics, the organization should then design or reengineer its internal structures in accordance with the three main components of the VBM system. Among the most vital VBM structures and processes are:

- VBM education programs for corporate prime movers and key executives
- The training of an in-house VBM technical team with primary responsibility for introducing, improving and sustaining the VBM process at all levels of the company
- Customer-focused quality improvement systems
- Equity-linked compensation systems, including team and individual cash incentives and entrepreneurial rewards (i.e. dividends) which are regular, frequent and formula-based (linked to unit and company-wide profits)
- Statistical quality control systems tied to participatory problem-solving and cost saving
- Two-way (upward and downward) accountability systems
- Participatory conflict resolution systems
- Corporate ownership and governance systems (legal structures), including:

  — An "empowerment ESOP" and other ownership-expanding corporate finance strategies, where individual workers share as first-class shareholders in the equity growth, voting power, and profits of their company.
  — Participatory corporate governance structures with appropriate checks-and-balances, allowing employee-shareholders to select their own representatives.[17]
  — An ownership-linked model of labor-management relations.

- Technical training linked to customer service and cost savings
- Open book management (financial and shareholder education and information sharing with built-in confidentiality safeguards).[18]

Value-Based Management recognizes that changing a corporate culture does not happen overnight. The habits of people and institutions were ingrained over time; only through constant reinforcement over time will the new habits of ownership take root.[19]

Leadership in a Value-Based Management System

High involvement management systems such as Value-Based Management are leader-guided, but not leader-dependent. They derive their energy and creativity from "below," but their direction and goals from "the top"—specifically from the values and vision of the leader, as they are manifested in the workplace. For this reason, Max DePree, Chairman of the Board of Herman Miller notes: "The first responsibility of a leader is to define reality."[20]

Genuine leadership values are universal, absolute values such as Truth, Love and Justice. These values (ideals which are never perfectly comprehended or attained) complement yet transcend purely personal and subjective values. They help to unify people's divergent self-interests toward a common set of objectives. No matter the context—whether it be business, politics, or sports—the vital role of the leader is to guide and *empower others* with a shared set of principles, a shared vision and shared goals. A leader must also recognize his or her own human imperfection and accountability under those higher universal values to other people.

VBM defines a genuine leader as the ultimate servant and teacher, one who empowers others to realize their hidden potential, not one who rules by coercion or is accountable only to himself. Leadership within a culture based on universal values is reflected in a commitment to the value *of each person*, and to delivering value *to each person*. Max DePree observes:

> In addition to all of the ratios and goals and parameters and bottom lines, it is fundamental that leaders endorse a concept of persons. This begins with an understanding of the diversity of people's gifts and talents and skills.[21]

True leaders promote working environments that surface, encourage and develop leadership in others.

If the leader is doing his job right—is articulating and teaching universal values, and is inspiring a long-term vision—he will encourage others to buy into those values and that vision. The successful leader knows that once those guiding principles have been internalized by others in the company, he can trust them to make intelligent decisions. This requires, of course, that people be given the necessary education, tools and information for making those decisions.

Institutionalizing leadership values serves the organization and its constituencies in another way: If the wrong person steps into the leadership position, the system will generate its own pressures to remove that person as the leader, because that person's values will clash with the values of the organization.

Once established, a successful value-based system will not easily disappear just because an authoritarian leader comes into the organization or if a good leader becomes a bad leader. This is because a value-based system is one where the system itself has built in a safeguard against monopolized or non-accountable power. The structured decentralization of ownership, power and accountability down to every person in the company offers the ultimate in checks-and-balances, and the most practical way to minimize abuses of concentrated power.

Value-Based Management and the Labor Movement

Value-Based Management seeks to transform the corporation into a more inclusive and just mechanism for delivering value to the customer and generating broadly owned wealth for workers and shareholders. It is also designed to transform the labor union into a social institution for delivering economic justice through expanded capital ownership.

For the small business owner of a nonunion company, Value-Based Management's concern with the union's transformation may seem irrelevant. However, in the global picture, particularly with respect to major industrial and service corporations, the labor union is a fact of life.

A developed economy cannot remain strong without a strong industrial base. And the competitiveness of large unionized corporations within the global marketplace will affect growth in the national economy, and thereby affect the growth and profitability of smaller, nonunion companies which serve and supply the major corporations. Thus a new and more collaborative "social contract" between management and labor unions within companies affected by global competition from lower-wage foreign competitors, is in the long-run critical to every company's success.

Why is Value-Based Management important for the labor unions? The drastic decline in the number of union members in the private sector indicates a major shift in the economic structure of the U.S. It also raises the question of whether the labor movement will continue to be relevant in the productive/private sector. This decline of the labor movement in the U.S. industrial sector can be attributed to the shrinking global competitiveness of U.S. corporations, brought on by the failure, on the part of both management and labor, to abandon the antiquated and conflict-ridden wage system.

Unions are considered by most business executives to be the "kiss of death." Small businesses in particular fear unions as an outside force antagonistic to the interests of the company. Given the proclaimed allegiance of union leaders to the "conflict/adversarial labor-management relationship"[22] —a blatantly anti-business, anti-profit, and anti-ownership by-product of the zero-sum "wage system"—it is not surprising that many business executives (who may themselves reflect the autocratic or paternalistic orientation of the wage system) would rather see unions go down the drain.

However, the union was democratic society's original answer for addressing injustices at the workplace which attended the birth of the Industrial Revolution. In fact, unionism was born to bring social and economic justice for working people, particularly nonmanagement workers. This is still a valid social need. The problem with the labor movement, from the standpoint of Value-Based Management, is that it became transformed into an instrument for accommodating to the wage system, and thus not for achieving justice. And in some cases, it can be fairly said, unions have empowered their leaders, not their members.

Rather than seeking direct ownership and empowerment for its members (which necessitates a thriving private sector and profitable companies), unions have sought to raise fixed labor wages and benefits. This strategy, in the long-run, will make businesses noncompetitive. And it ultimately defeats the union's social purpose of protecting the rights and long-term welfare of workers.

How Henry Ford Fathered
The Modern Wage System

To understand how the labor movement became locked into the wage system, one need only look at the story of Henry Ford, the father of modern wage feudalism. From the vantage point of Value-Based Management, we can see where Ford went right and where he went wrong.

Following sound VBM principles, Henry Ford launched the modern industrial era in America by reducing in stages the price of the basic automobile from over $900 a car to $330 a car, thus delivering more value to the customer. (The phenomenal growth of the personal computer industry can be attributed to the same formula for success.)

Ford was wrong, however, when he excluded his workers from direct ownership and profit sharing opportunities as a means of supplementing their market wages. He chose instead to raise artificially the purchasing power of his workers by increasing the market wage rate to $5.00 a day from $2.50 a day. Having locked out the workers from the opportunity to share in the gains and capital expansion of the Ford Motor Company, Ford let the genie out of the bottle. He established a precedent and unleashed social and political forces which disconnected wages from productiveness, and inevitably, in the face of rising global competition, propelled American labor costs to over $20 an hour.

It is hardly surprising that in the 1960's lower-wage Japanese auto workers were able to out-compete their American counterparts in terms of price and quality. The unit labor costs of the Japanese wage system were a fraction of those in the U.S. wage system. And what happened to the American worker is now happening to Japanese workers, as manufacturing in Japan shifts to low-wage countries. According to the *Wall Street Journal*, "the average Malaysian worker earns in a month what a Japanese or German worker earns in two days."[23] To understand the strident opposition of American workers to the NAFTA agreement with Mexico, one need only recognize that average manufacturing compensation (wages plus benefits) in Mexico is only 15% of manufacturing compensation in the U.S.[24]

In hindsight, it is unfortunate for today's high-wage American workers that Ford did not offer his workers an alternative where their gains would be linked directly to productivity and bottom-line profits. For example, in employee ownership companies like Allied Plywood Corporation of Alexandria, Virginia[25] and Lincoln Electric Company of Cleveland, Ohio,[26] workers have received in some years as much as two to three times more from profits than they have from wages. By sharing in monthly cash bonuses, annual bonuses, ESOP shares and dividends, workers at these companies have increased their job security and total cash compensation without increasing fixed labor costs.

Clearly we cannot turn back American wage rates to levels of the early 1900's. But management, workers and unions in Japan, the U.S. and other high wage countries now have the opportunity to rewrite their "social contract" and begin to serve the customer through the V=Q/P formula of Value-Based Management. So does the rest of the industrializing world which today looks to Japan and the U.S. for answers which can be found only in companies which have adopted the principles of Value-Based Management.[27]

Operating under wage system patterns, labor unions can only exacerbate the competitive problems of industry. For its own long-term survival and revitalization, as well as the good of society in general, the labor movement needs to reevaluate its attachment to wage system incentives. It needs to become a more positive force for business competitiveness, growth and economic justice through expanded capital ownership.

Under Value-Based Management, the labor union and other democratic forms of worker associations can play a vital role within the corporation and society, raising the living standards of their members by enabling non-owning workers to share in equity growth and profits.

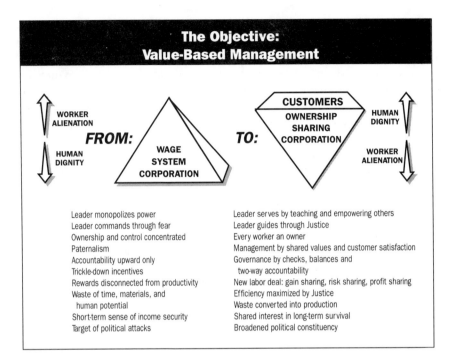

The Objective: Value-Based Management

FROM: WAGE SYSTEM CORPORATION
WORKER ALIENATION
HUMAN DIGNITY

TO: CUSTOMERS / OWNERSHIP SHARING CORPORATION
HUMAN DIGNITY
WORKER ALIENATION

Leader monopolizes power	Leader serves by teaching and empowering others
Leader commands through fear	Leader guides through Justice
Ownership and control concentrated	Every worker an owner
Paternalism	Management by shared values and customer satisfaction
Accountability upward only	Governance by checks, balances and
Trickle-down incentives	two-way accountability
Rewards disconnected from productivity	New labor deal: gain sharing, risk sharing, profit sharing
Waste of time, materials, and	Efficiency maximized by Justice
human potential	Waste converted into production
Short-term sense of income security	Shared interest in long-term survival
Target of political attacks	Broadened political constituency

Redefining the Roles of Management and the Union

Under Value-Based Management, an essential role of the union (or other democratically elected body representing nonmanagement employees) is to provide an institutional counterbalance to the role of a company's management. While VBM seeks to unite all workers as owners, it is clear that management and nonmanagement workers reflect distinct interests. Furthermore, in well-functioning companies with unions, professional managers and the union have clearly defined roles and functions.

Management, which must have the ultimate responsibility and authority for making daily operational decisions, should be mainly concerned with satisfying customer demand by offering higher quality goods and services at lower prices than its competitors. Management's effectiveness can then be measured by the company's ability to generate profits on invested capital, subject to the normal external constraints of reasonable regulatory, union, and market forces. Management's focus in a participatory ownership company, therefore, must continue to be on efficiency, productivity, and profits. Otherwise, the workers, in their role as owners, will suffer the consequences.[28] Management must also be held accountable for its decisions; when managers do not do their job, they can be replaced.

The role of the union under Value-Based Management, on the other hand, should be exclusively concerned with issues of economic justice for nonmanagement employees, from individual grievances to bargaining with management over compensation, safety, ownership rights and other issues affecting nonmanagement employees. In sizeable enterprises, the union or similar body should also organize non-worker stockholders for asserting their ownership rights and prerogatives vis-à-vis management and the board of directors.[29]

No matter how benevolent or participatory a company's management, there is always a human tendency at some point to withhold power from others. (This stems from the underlying fear of those who hold power that others may use that power unwisely or against them.) Whether the institution is a worker-shareholders' association formed voluntarily within the company or whether it is a body organized by a union, nonmanagement worker-owners need some form of democratic organization which has the internal solidarity of the workers. This would give workers the status, access to information and power necessary to bargain effectively and settle grievances with management when they arise.

What would be the new role of the labor movement under Value-Based Management?[30] Simply, unions should become facilitators of Value-Based Management, collaborating with management on ways to increase productiveness and profitability, helping their members negotiate for larger ownership stakes, profit sharing and full shareholder rights, and for using their considerable political influence for promoting expanded capital ownership opportunities for all citizens. Under Value-Based Management, unions will recognize that by promoting the long-term good of the corporation, they can bring long-term good for working people.

Conclusion

In the final analysis, Value-Based Management redefines traditional power relations within the enterprise and other economic institutions. VBM cannot take root where management wants to remain accountable only to itself, or where ownership power is structured to remain concentrated at the top. It also cannot exist where nonmanagement workers (or their representatives) and management cling to the conflict-ridden wage system.

Leadership in a value-based management company requires a long-range vision, patience, persistence, and the willingness to share power with employees. For many owners, managers and executives, the idea of sharing equity with workers will be impossible to accept. But for those who seek a new management system based on the sharing of equity and power, there will be many rewards. As Jack Stack notes:

Equity is the basis for all long-term thinking. It is the best reason for staying the course, for sacrificing instant gratification and going after the big payoff down the road. If you have equity and understand it, you know why it's important to build for the future. You can make long-term decisions. You still pay attention to the day-to-day details, but you're doing it for the right reason: because it's the best way to achieve *lasting* success.[31]

Value-Based Management recognizes that each person's identity and development flows from his or her work, both economic and non-economic. In this sense, every person is a worker, of one kind or another. Where people work together for serving others in the economic marketplace, Value-Based Management offers a new moral framework for raising their dignity and quality of life, while building efficiency and justice at the workplace.

Notes:

1 *"Value-Based Management" and "VBM,"* are service marks of Equity Expansion International, Inc. (Washington, D.C.), which has granted permission for use in this article.

The author wishes to acknowledge the important contributions to this article by Stephen F. Hardiman, Norman G. Kurland and Thomas J. Simon. Together with the author, these members of Equity Expansion International's Value-Based Management project team have been refining VBM's conceptual framework into an applied management technology.

2 One such organization promoting shareholder rights is United Shareholders of America, 1667 K Street, N.W., Suite 770, Washington, D.C. 20006.

3 "Unions, After the Fall," *The Washington Times* (May 2, 1993) A14.

4 Barry Bluestone and Irving Bluestone, *Negotiating the Future: A Labor Perspective on American Business* (New York: HarperCollins Publishers, Inc., 1992) xiv.

5 "Totaled Quality Management," *Washington Post* (June 6, 1993) H1.

6 Ibid.

7 Adolph A. Berle, Jr. and Gardiner C. Means, The Modern Corporation and Private Property (New York: Commerce Clearing House, 1932).

8 See "The Performance Effects of Employee Ownership Plans," a study by Michael A. Conte and Jan Svejnar, which appears in *Paying for Productivity: A Look at the Evidence*, Alan S. Blinder, ed. (Washington, D.C.: The Brookings Institution, 1990).

9 John P. (Jack) Stack, *The Great Game of Business* (New York: Doubleday, 1992) 3-4.

10 The term "Value-Based Management" ("VBM) was first coined in the mid-1980's by lawyer-economist Norman Kurland, an internationally recognized pioneer in Employee Stock Ownership Plans (ESOPs) and expanded capital ownership methodologies. VBM, as first formulated by Mr. Kurland and the author, offers a practical application within the workplace of Louis Kelso's binary economic theory and moral principles of participatory ownership.

11 Value-Based Management follows the theory of economic justice first advanced by the ESOP inventor Louis Kelso and the philosopher Mortimer Adler in their book, under the controversial title of *The Capitalist Manifesto* (New York: Random House, 1958; reprinted by Greenwood Press, Westport, Connecticut). The three principles of the Kelso-Adler system were later refined by the Center for Economic and Social Jus-

tice. VBM's core philosophy of economic justice is comprised of:

1) an "input" or *participation* principle of justice (how people in a modern economy can contribute legitimately through their labor *and* capital);

2) an "outtake" or *distribution* principle (how people receive a just return for their labor or capital contributions, with the value of those contributions being determined in the competitive free marketplace; and

3) a "feedback" or *harmony* principle (which monitors whether or not the system is maintaining balance between the participation and distribution principles; Kelso and Adler referred to this as the "anti-monopoly" principle).

For a more in-depth discussion of this theory of economic justice, see "Toward Economic and Social Justice" (Arlington, Virginia: Center for Economic and Social Justice, 1986).

[12] See *Business Week* cover story "ESOPs: Revolution or Ripoff?" (April 15, 1985) 94-108, 174. Another source on ESOP abuses is Joseph R. Blasi's book, *Employee Ownership: Revolution or Ripoff?* (Cambridge, Massachusetts: Ballinger Publishing Company, 1988).

[13] Over the last decade, the blossoming of the shareholders' rights movement and employee share ownership plans in America are among the phenomena representing a growing force to restore property rights and economic justice for corporate shareowners.

It should also be pointed out that for almost two decades, the ESOP community in the U.S. has been split on the issue of voting rights of employee-shareholders with respect to their ESOP-held stock. The ESOP under U.S. law has been criticized by many people around the world for allowing closely held companies with ESOPs to dilute the property rights of employee-shareholders by withholding the right to vote their shares in the manner of an ordinary shareholder (except, as required by U.S. law, on major issues such as a merger or the sale of the company). Thus most ESOP companies in the U.S. do not allow their employee-shareholders to elect a representative to their company's board of directors.

ESOP advocates such as Senator Russell Long have argued (*Business Week*, September 12, 1988, page 6) that making the "voting passthrough" mandatory would halt the adoption of ESOPs, thus sabotaging the long-term goal of broadening the citizen base of corporate share owners. Even supporters of democratic or participatory ESOPs, such as Corey Rosen of the National Center for Employee Ownership (ibid.), have acknowledged that in terms of the measurable impact on employee motivation and productivity, participation at the job level has a much greater effect than giving workers the right to vote their shares.

While both these arguments may be true and pragmatic from the standpoint of encouraging more ESOPs, they ignore the moral issue regarding the property rights of an owner. It can be said quite fairly that most ESOP participants have been relegated to the status of second-class shareholders.

In order to reconcile the pragmatic and moral demands of the "ESOP voting issue," ESOP proponents such as Norman Kurland have suggested that all present ESOP incentives be left untouched, with no legal requirements for voting passthrough. However, Kurland argues, any significant improvements in incentives for ESOPs (e.g., access to low-interest bank loans through the discount window of the Federal Reserve) should be conditioned on full ownership rights for employee-shareholders.

[14] See endnote 11.

[15] Max DePree, *Leadership is an Art*, (East Lansing, Michigan: Michigan State University Press, 1987) 85.

[16] In his best-selling book *The Seven Habits of Highly Effective People* (New York: Simon and Schuster, 1989), Stephen R. Covey mentions the importance of company mission statements and other organizational expressions of core principles. In developing these statements, Covey emphasizes, "Everyone should participate in a meaningful way—not just the top strategy planners. . . . [T]he involvement process is as important as the written product and is the key to its use" (page 139).

[17] The National Labor Relations Board (NLRB) in recent decisions has been critical of worker-management participation groups, TQM and quality circles. A central issue seems to be on how the worker representatives are selected. To the extent that people are selected on a top-down basis to represent the viewpoint of nonmanagement employees, the NLRB has frowned upon this practice. A solution to this problem is to ensure that all, or a significant percentage, of those selected as "representatives of the workers" be selected democratically by the workers themselves in order to ensure that the representative enjoys the confidence and support of workers, and not simply be symbolic leaders. Certainly where a union selects the worker representatives, this question should never arise.

[18] Stack, op. cit., Chapter 5.

[19] In addition to *The Great Game of Business* and *The Seven Habits of Highly Effective People* cited above, there are other good sources providing case studies and practical methodologies for building an effective participatory ownership culture. While some of these sources are not completely consistent with all of the principles of VBM/Kelsonian theory, they contain useful how-to material.

Frank T. Adams and Gary B. Hansen, *Putting Democracy to Work: A Practical Guide for Starting and Managing Worker-Owned Businesses*, (San Francisco: Berrett-Koehler Publishers, 1992).

Robert Levering, Milton Moskowitz, and Michael Katz, *The One Hundred Best Companies to Work for in America,* (New York: Signet, 1985).

Tom Peters and Nancy Austin, *A Passion for Excellence: The Leadership Difference*, (New York: Warner Books, 1985).

John Simmons and William Mares, *Working Together*, (New York: Knopf, 1983).

William F. Whyte and K.K. Whyte, *Making Mondragon: The Growth and Dynamics of the Worker Cooperative Complex*, 2nd edition, (Ithaca: ILR Press, 1991).

Other useful materials can be obtained from:

National Center for Employee Ownership at 2201 Broadway, Suite 807, Oakland, California 94612

Northeast Ohio Employee Ownership Center, Department of Political Science, Kent State University, Kent, Ohio 44242

[20] DePree, op.cit. 11.

[21] DePree, op.cit. 9.

[22] In his presentation at the University of Notre Dame on May 3-4, 1982, Secretary-Treasurer of the AFL-CIO, Thomas R. Donahue stated: "We believe in a conflict theory of collective bargaining as the soundest basis for worker representation, worker participation and worker gains, in the current labor-management climate. . . ." ("A Trade Union Perspective of Laborem Exercens," 14).

[23] Karen Elliott House, "Malaysian Premier Says U.S. Policies Hurt Chance for Global Growth, Stability," *Wall Street Journal* (March 29, 1993) A8.

[24] For the main thrust of the opposition in the U.S. Congress to a free trade agreement with Mexico, see article on the editorial page of the *Washington Post* (September 17, 1993, A21), entitled "NAFTA: Exporting U.S. Jobs," by Representative David E. Bonior, Democratic House Majority Whip.

[25] See article on Allied Plywood Corporation by Tom Peters in Section 4 of *Curing World Poverty: The New Role of Poverty.* Also see article by Norman G. Kurland, "Practical Guidelines for Building Justice at the Workplace," *Every Worker an Owner*, (Arlington, Virginia: Center for Economic and Social Justice, 1987).

[26] Maryann Mrowca, "Ohio Firm Relies on Incentive-Pay System to Motivate Workers and Maintain Profits," *Wall Street Journal* (August 12, 1983) 23.

[27] See articles on Avis Rent-a-Car, Fastener Industries, Allied Plywood, La Perla and Springfield Remanufacturing in Section 4 of *Curing World Poverty*.

[28] Letter of CESJ President Norman G. Kurland to Dr. David Ellerman, Industrial Cooperative Association, September 4, 1980.

[29] Ibid.

[30] For an in-depth discussion of the new role of the union under Value-Based Management and participatory ownership, as well as a worker ownership-linked "new labor deal" and safeguards to safeguard the specialized institutional roles of management and the union, see Kurland article in endnote 25.

[31] Stack, op.cit., p. 210.

— 10 —

Model ESOP Companies

After all the theory has been aired, the question foremost in the mind of any rational person is, "How do these ideas, fine as they are, fit in with the real world?" In answer to this legitimate question, the following articles on model ESOP companies are presented to show that good theory does indeed work. Although none of the companies profiled reflects perfectly the entire expanded ownership economic model, each one demonstrates how far these theories can be implemented in a typical work place, even in today's generally unfriendly and restrictive legal and business environment. Further, they demonstrate the practicality and economic feasibility of these concepts when pitted against more traditional methods of running a business.

So successful are these principles that some of the most widely-known companies in the world have adopted total or partial worker ownership as an employee incentive and benefit.

"The Employee Ownership 100," prepared by the National Center for Employee Ownership (Oakland, California), is the latest available list of the largest U. S. companies that have implemented at least 30 percent ownership sharing as part of their corporate culture.

The Employee Ownership 100

Reprinted from the National Center for Employee Ownership newsletter, July/August 1993

This list includes the largest 100 firms (by number of employees) that, as of May 1993, were at least 33% owned by their employees. The list is based on NCEO data. For an updated list, the reader may want to contact the National Center for Employee Ownership, 2201 Broadway, Suite 807, Oakland, CA 94612.

Company	City	ST	Business	Empl	Ownership
Kroger Co.	Cincinnati	OH	Supermarkets	170,000	Nonmajority
McDonnell Douglas Corp.	St. Louis	MO	Aerospace	128,000	Nonmajority
Rockwell International	El Segundo	CA	Conglomerate	109,000	Nonmajority
Publix Supermarkets	Lakeland	FL	Supermarkets	65,000	Majority
Tandy Corp.	Ft. Worth	TX	Electronics	41,000	Nonmajority
TWA*	St. Louis	MO	Airline	28,000	Nonmajority
Coldwell Banker	Chicago	IL	Real Estate	24,000	Nonmajority
Grumman Corp.	Bethpage	NY	Aerospace	24,000	Nonmajority
Figgie International Inc.	Willoughby	OH	Fire Protection	16,000	Nonmajority
EPIC Healthcare	Irving	TX	Hospitals	14,000	Majority
Avis Inc.	Westbury	NY	Car Rental	13,500	Majority
Ruddick Corporation	Charlotte	NC	Holding Company	13,100	Nonmajority
Science Applications Intl.	San Diego	CA	R&D & Computers	13,000	Majority
Hallmark Cards, Inc.	Kansas City	MO	Greeting Cards	12,000	Nonmajority
Price Chopper	Schenectady	NY	Supermarkets	11,800	Nonmajority
Stone and Webster	New York	NY	Engineering	9,000	Nonmajority
The Parsons Corp.	Pasadena	CA	Engineering, mining	8,000	Majority
Amsted Industries	Chicago	IL	Industrial Products	7,600	Majority
Avondale Shipyards	New Orleans	LA	Shipbuilding	7,500	Majority
Weirton Steel Corp.	Weirton	WV	Steel Manufacturer	6,900	Majority
The Journal Company	Milwaukee	WI	Newspapers/Comm	6,800	Majority
Morgan Stanley	New York	NY	Securities	6,700	Majority
Lincoln Electric	Cleveland	OH	Arc Welding	6,600	Nonmajority
Austin Industries	Dallas	TX	Construction	6,500	Majority
Wheeling Pittsburgh Steel	Wheeling	WV	Steel Manufacturer	6,330	Nonmajority
Quad/Graphics	Pewaukee	WI	Printing	5,400	Nonmajority
Herman Miller Inc.	Zeeland	MI	Office Furniture	5,400	Nonmajority
W. L. Gore Associates	Newark	DE	High-Tech Mfr	5,000	Majority
Republic Engineered Steel	Massillon	OH	Steel Manufacturer	4,900	Majority
Graybar Electric	St. Louis	MO	Electrical Equipment	4,800	Majority
Davey Tree Expert Company	Kent	OH	Tree Service	4,600	Majority
Wyatt Cafeterias, Inc.	Dallas	TX	Cafeterias	4,500	Nonmajority
King Kullen	Westbury	NY	Grocery Retail	4,200	Nonmajority
Fiesta Mart	Houston	TX	Grocery Chain	4,000	Nonmajority
Treasure Chest Advertising	Glendora	CA	Printing	4,000	Majority
CH2M Hill, Inc.	Corvallis	OR	Engineering, Arch	4,000	Majority
American Business Products, Inc.	Atlanta	GA	Paper Products	3,894	Nonmajority
Dentsply International	York	PA	Dental Supplies	3,500	Majority
Herbereger's	St. Cloud	MN	Retail	3,500	Majority
Tyler Corporation	Dallas	TX	Diversified Holdings	3,400	Nonmajority
Lifetouch	Minneapolis	MN	Photography Studios	3,000	Majority
Nationwise Auto Parts	Columbus	OH	Auto Supply Chain	3,000	Nonmajority
Arthur D. Little	Cambridge	MA	Consulting	2,600	Majority
American Cast Iron Pipe	Birmingham	AL	Iron Pipes, Fittings	2,600	Majority
National Steel and Shipbuilding	San Diego	CA	Shipbuilding	2,600	Majority
U. S. Sugar	Clewiston	FL	Sugar Processor	2,550	Nonmajority

*Pending

The Employee Ownership 100

Company	City	ST	Business	Empl	Ownership
Imperial Holly Corporation	Sugarland	TX	Cane Sugar	2,500	Nonmajority
Crucible Specialty Steel	Syracuse	NY	Specialty Steel	2,500	Majority
Inter-Regional Financial Group	Minneapolis	MN	Brokers	2,500	Nonmajority
Applied Power Inc.	Butler	WI	Auto Equipment	2,400	Nonmajority
Phelps Inc.	Greeley	CO	Construction	2,300	Majority
Swank Inc.	Attleboro	MA	Leather Goods	2,300	Majority
Tandycrafts	Ft. Worth	TX	Crafts	2,300	Majority
Norcal Solid Waste Systems	San Francisco	CA	Waste Disposal	2,200	Majority
Reliable Stores	Columbia	MD	Department Stores	2,100	Majority
Century Telephone Enterprise	Monroe	LA	Telecommunications	2,020	Nonmajority
Houchens Food Store	BowlingGreen	KY	Supermarkets	2,000	Majority
Granite Construction Company	Watsonville	CA	Hwy/Hvy Construc	2,000	Nonmajority
Allied Group	Des Moines	IA	Insurance	1,900	Nonmajority
Cranston Print Works	Cranston	RI	Textile Printing	1,800	Majority
Piper Jaffray	Minneapolis	MN	Brokerage	1,750	Nonmajority
Okonite Company	Ramsey	NJ	Wire and Cable Mfr	1,700	Majority
Alex. Brown & Sons	Baltimore	MD	Investment Bankers	1,654	Nonmajority
McLouth Steel	Trenton	MI	Steel Manufacturers	1,650	Majority
Dahl's Inc.	Des Moines	IA	Supermarkets	1,600	Majority
Rural/Metro Corporation	Scottsdale	AZ	Fire/Emergency Svcs	1,600	Majority
Waremart	Boise	ID	Supermarket Chain	1,600	Majority
Bureau of National Affairs, Inc.	Washington	DC	Bus/Info Publications	1,590	Majority
Guckenheimer	RedwoodCity	CA	Food Distributors	1,550	Majority
Michael Baker Corporation	Beaver	PA	Engineering	1,500	Majority
North American Rayon	Elizabethton	TN	Rayon Manufacturer	1,500	Majority
Angeles Corporation	Los Angeles	CA	Real Estate	1,400	Majority
Matthews International	Pittsburgh	PA	Marking Devices	1,350	Majority
Dillingham Construction	Pleasanton	CA	Construction	1,300	Majority
National Refractories	Oakland	CA	Refractory Mfr	1,300	Nonmajority
Cherokee Textile Mills	Sevierville	TN	Textiles	1,300	Majority
AECOM	Los Angeles	CA	Energy Technology	1,250	Majority
Kolbe and Kolbe	Wausau	WI	Window Mfr	1,250	Majority
Topps Co. Inc.	Brooklyn	NY	Chewing Gum	1,200	Nonmajority
National Health Corp. ESOP	Murfreesboro	TN	Long-Term Health	1,200	Majority
Burns and McDonnell Engineering	Kansas City	MO	Engineers, Arch	1,150	Majority
Sundt Corporation	Tucson	AZ	Construction	1,100	Nonmajority
BCM Engineers	PlymouthMtg	PA	Environment, Arch	1,100	Majority
Erickson's	Hudson	WI	Supermarkets	1,100	Majority
STV Engineers	Pottstown	PA	Engineers, Arch	1,070	Nonmajority
Alma Desk Co.	Highpoint	NC	Furniture Mfr	1,050	Nonmajority
Mutual Savings Life	Decatur	AL	Insurance	1,050	Majority
Halmode Apparel	Roanoke	VA	Women's Apparel	1,050	Majority
Columbia Aluminum	Goldendale	WA	Aluminum Mfr	1,035	Nonmajority
Cianbro Corporation	Pittsfield	ME	Heavy Construction	1,000	Nonmajority
Spartan Printing	Sparta	IL	Printing	1,000	Majority
Rosauer's	Spokane	WA	Supermarket	1,000	Majority
Ecker Enterprises	Chicago	IL	Printing	1,000	Majority
Crystal Thermal Products	Cumberland	RI	Plastics	1,000	Nonmajority
Owen Healthcare	Houston	TX	Healthcare	1,000	Nonmajority
Prime Source	Irvine	CA	Hardware Retail	1,000	Majority
Houston NW Medical Center	Houston	TX	Hospital	1,000	Majority
Jerrell Inc.	Dallas	TX	Apparel	1,000	Nonmajority
Rockford Products Corporation	Rockford	IL	Threaded Fasteners	1,000	Majority
Justin Industries	Ft. Worth	TX	Boot Manufacturers	1,000	Nonmajority

Allied Plywood Corporation:
Ownership Starts at the Crack of Dawn for
Allied Plywood Corporation Employees/Shareholders

*(Reprinted from Tom Peters' **On Achieving Excellence** [August 1988]*
Vol. 3, No. 8. © 1988 TPG Communications.
Reprinted with permission. All rights reserved.)[1]

Dedication to service is more than a tradition at Allied Plywood Corporation, the dominant supplier of building materials in its Washington, D.C., metro area. It is ingrained from the very top level of management, through the ranks to warehousemen and delivery truck drivers. The tone and the pace are set by President/CEO Bob Shaw's attention to customer service and his example of long hours on the job.

Shaw's roots at the company grow deep, starting 33 years ago at age 16 when he delivered newspapers to Allied founder Ed Sanders, who hired the youngster to unload rail boxcars at Allied. The work ethic learned then persists at Allied, where employees on their own often work more than 12 hours. As full owners of the company through an ESOP, or Employee Stock Ownership Plan, employees are keen on everybody pulling their share of the load and providing first-name attention to customer service.

On some days, Allied Plywood Corporation warehousemen and truck drivers voluntarily work from 4 a.m. until well into the evening loading and unloading tractor trailers and freight cars at the company's Alexandria, Va., central distribution center.

"They're that motivated," says Bob Shaw, president and chief executive of Allied, a lumber and building materials wholesaler with five locations in the Washington, D.C. metro area. But it's much more than overtime pay that sparks such dedication.

Allied employees own the company through an ESOP by which an employer either contributes company shares to the ESOP trust or turns over cash to buy company stock. At Allied, however, employees already own 100 percent of the company and, through an unusual profit-sharing plan, don't have to wait until they retire to cash in on accrued benefits of the ESOP started in 1978.

An Immediate Reward

"With an ESOP, there's no immediate reward," says Shaw. "So we devised a plan whereby employees receive a percentage of gross profits each month. We call it a monthly profit-sharing plan."

In place since shortly after the company started in 1951, the plan is based on $500 increments called "goals." When the break-even point after expenses is reached, up to 33 percent of Allied's monthly gross profit is distributed among those employees who choose to participate in the plan. One year that amounted to about $10,000 per employee, according to Secretary-Treasurer Gene Scales.

Depending upon the gross profit results and number of employees on the plan, there may be as many as 300 to 400 incremental goals per month. Additionally, when the company's books are closed at year-end, what remains from gross profit, after payment of monthly goals and allowance for retained earnings, is distributed as bonuses.

Since Allied's founding family sold the company to its ESOP in 1982, sales have grown from $6 million to about $41 million in the fiscal year ending September 1993 and the payroll from 22 to 122 employees.

Plan Improves Absence Record and Productivity

The profit-sharing program is credited with improving an historically low rate of absenteeism—"so low, it's hard to measure, it averages less than two-tenths of one percent, or about fifty or sixty days a year for the more than 120 employees," says Scales. While there are no precise measures of increased productivity, Scales compares Allied's performance with competitor companies doing approximately the same yearly sales volume, but with 150 to 200 employees.

Allied's monthly profit-sharing also works in the customer's favor, says Shaw, "because the employee knows where his or her paycheck comes from—that it starts with the customer. We get frequent calls from our customers complimenting our employees." Customers say they deal with Allied because "our people are friendly and warm," comments Scales. "The know customers on a first-name basis and take care of them right away. They don't treat customers like a number."

Supervising Each Other Pays Off

Shaw says Allied's profit-sharing package also helps reduce the number of supervisors. "These people supervise themselves and each other. They don't have to have a supervisor standing over them to make sure they work. They'll go right over to a company truck driver and tell him, 'Hey, Joe, you're driving this truck a little too fast or cutting these corners a little too short. That's costing me money because you're raising our expenses'."

Because each new employee hired is another person with whom the monthly profit-sharing and year-end bonus must be split, Allied workers are "very conscious of making sure we really do need a new person, and that that new person is going to contribute to the overall profit of the company," says Shaw. At most companies, management decides if and when to hire additional help. "They spread the work load around," notes Shaw. "But here, we're spreading the profits, and the employees worry about that."

Employees also participate directly in compensation and other corporate decisions through representation on the board of directors. The board includes three hourly and three management-level employees, plus an outside attorney. Board meetings are held quarterly, but employee meetings are called when necessary.

"We found that in the past, if we had a meeting just to have a meeting, it wasn't effective," Shaw says. "But if there's an issue, some rumblings, or something in the system that's going wrong, we have a meeting then and there. All employees attend." Additionally, Shaw's door is "always open, from 6 in the morning to when I leave, sometimes at 7 at night," he says.

Could a monthly profit-sharing plan similar to Allied's work for companies of all sizes? Shaw believes it could, if management is willing. "Do the managers want to share the profits? That's the biggest thing," he says. "Management today has to make that adjustment. Do we share profits with employees now or when?" As Allied's experience shows, sharing with them now has many payoffs.

Translating the Lessons to Your Organization

(1) *An ESOP is important, but it doesn't go the distance.*
The Allied Plywood case argues forcefully that the long-term gains that should accrue from an ESOP are not motivating enough, because the benefits of stock ownership aren't tangible until a much later date. The ESOP, they believe, is a significant step, but the productivity gain-sharing is of equal importance because it is money in the employee's pocket today—immediate feedback.

(2) *The stakes are high.*
First, as noted, Allied's program consists of both an ESOP and a productivity gain-sharing arrangement. More significantly, that gain-sharing amounts to fully one-third of profitability. (That's noticeable, to put it mildly.)

(3) *Customer satisfaction increases, even if the program is based on increases in productivity.*
It boils down to a process of wholesale involvement. Almost every indicator improves as a result. The improvements are not in any way limited to the particular basis for which the additional pay is granted.

(4) *The process is self-policing.*

As noted, Allied's employees are tough as nails on hiring any additional people. Throughout my experience with wholesale involvement, I have always found that the standards set by employees (despite management's preliminary fears) are much more stringent than anything that management would ever dare impose.

Note:

[1]Statistics regarding sales, number of employees and absenteeism have been updated to reflect activity through the fiscal year ending September 30, 1993.

Avis:
How the Workers Run Avis Better

by David Kirkpatrick
*Reprinted from **Fortune Magazine**, December 5, 1988*

Employee ownership is the best thing to happen to the No. 2 car renter in a long time. For a lot of companies it could be the key to better performance in the Nineties.

A year has passed since the employees bought Avis, and when Chairman Joe Vittoria isn't out pumping the troops for ideas to help improve customer service he is often fielding inquisitive calls from executives of major corporations. With 12,500 employees, Avis is the best-known company in America fully owned by an employee stock ownership plan, or ESOP. Vittoria, 53, says Avis's success with the plan has executives from "much bigger" corporations thinking seriously about creating one themselves.

It's easy to see why. As America moves toward a more service-oriented and highly leveraged economy, ESOPs seem made to order. Employee ownership has proven particularly effective in motivating workers to provide extra effort in customer service. Provisions in the tax code render debt a lighter burden on ESOP-owned companies than on conventional competitors.[1] ESOPs have been around a long time, and most own only a small percentage of a company's stock. But 1,500 companies, with 1.5 million employees, were majority-owned by ESOPs at the end of last year, and the number is growing.

Those curious corporate callers hear nothing but encouraging words from an enthusiastic Vittoria. "Believe me, the ESOP works, and it works very well," he exults, sitting in his large but spartan office at headquarters near New York's Kennedy Airport. In typically frugal Avis style, the room appears not to have been redecorated since Avis moved in 21 years ago. The tall, folksy CEO proudly reports that operating profit for the first six months of 1988 rose 35% over the same period in 1987, when Avis was owned by Wesray Capital, an investment firm that purchased it in 1986. (Operating earnings for 1987 totaled $177 million on revenues of $971 million.) By year-end Avis will have repaid about $90 million of the $650 million the ESOP buyout added to the company's debt obligation—more than double the projected repayment.

"Right now Avis is on a roll," says Charles Finnie, an analyst at the Baltimore brokerage Alex. Brown & Sons, who is widely considered the country's most knowledgeable observer of the rental-car industry. "The ESOP has really improved their morale and productivity and service." Avis's share of the brutally competitive airport market, where 70% of all car rentals take place, is up a point to about 27%, and all internal measures of service quality are setting records. On-time arrivals of airport buses have risen from 93% to 96%, for example. Service-related customer complaints were rising at the time of the employee buyout but have subsequently dropped 35%, from 1,918 in the 12 months ended in August 1987 to 1,238 a year later.

The lesson from Avis is not that an ESOP is a quick fix. Says Vittoria: "Just creating an ESOP isn't going to make you a better company. It's how you involve the employees, it's how you maintain a dialogue, listen to their input, and use it." Since the buyout, Avis has organized employee participation groups as a conduit for ideas, and everything from billing to bathrooms to baby seats is changing as a result. Corey Rosen, executive director of the National Center for Employee Ownership, a nonprofit research group in Oakland, California, applauds Avis's effort to increase employee involvement. But he is frustrated that it is still unusual. Most ESOP executives mistakenly believe employee ownership alone will boost productivity, and shun participative programs.

The center's research has found that if an ESOP-owned company allows workers to participate in decisions about their jobs, it will grow an average of 11% faster than if it doesn't. Says Rosen: "An employee comes to work and is motivated as an owner, but that motivation is useless unless there's a structure to use the ideas, experience, and knowledge he or she has. And Avis has taken all this to heart." Rosen believes employee involvement programs can be helpful in any company but are more likely to succeed with employee ownership.

Wesray Capital and senior Avis managers had bought the company, then part of Beatrice Cos., from Kohlberg Kravis Roberts & Co., the leveraged-buyout firm that controlled Beatrice. Led by Wesray Chairman Ray Chambers, the group paid $1.6 billion in July 1986 and after selling off some assets sold Avis to the ESOP for a stunning $740 million profit just over a year later. (Former Treasury Secretary William E. Simon, the WES of Wesray, withdrew from active involvement before the Avis purchase.)

In this type of leveraged deal, an ESOP borrows the money to buy the company, or part of it, in the name of the employees. A trustee holds the shares and is mandated to represent the interests of the eventual shareholders. As the company pays off the debt, shares are allocated to employees in proportion to their pay. Managers receive shares in the same proportion as car cleaners, but federal law restricts anyone from receiving an allocation of more than $30,000 of ESOP stock in any given year. By the end of this year, employees at Avis will own about ten shares per $1,000 of annual compensation.

Vittoria predicts that within 15 to 18 years all 24 million shares will be held by employees, who must remain at least five years for their shares to be vested. An outside appraiser appointed by the trustee values the shares annually. The current value is $5.22, which will certainly rise this year to reflect the company's impressive performance. Even after shares are awarded to an employee, the trustee holds them. When a vested employee leaves the company for any reason, the trust buys out the shares at the most recently assessed price (with the full value of the payout as taxable income to the employee).

"We're going to give a lot of people an opportunity to build a nest egg here that they would never have been able to build in their lives," says Vittoria. That's just what Louis Kelso had in mind. As the inventor of the ESOP and its indefatigable advocate, he passionately believes that capitalism will not survive unless capital ownership is more evenly distributed across the economy. He declares: "For employees of service enterprises not to have a piece of the action is almost another form of slavery."

Kelso, 74, finds it inexcusable that all leveraged buyout don't have at least an ESOP component. He says that the first ESOP buyout he orchestrated—at Palo Alto's Peninsula Newspapers in 1956—was the first LBO. He also claims that in about 1964 he introduced LBOs to George Roberts, who was courting the niece of one of Kelso's law partners, and to Roberts's friend Jerome Kohlberg. "I taught them the art of the leveraged buyout. Now they're just using it for the wrong purposes, to make themselves and a few people richer," laments Kelso. Kohlberg and Roberts have no comment.

Despite Avis's success at rousing employees with the plan, they would never have become owners were it not for the generous tax benefits Kelso has won for ESOPs over the years. In the early Seventies he convinced Russell Long, then the potent chairman of the Senate Finance Committee, that employee ownership was good for the economy. Long helped write a succession of bills that aided ESOPs. Lenders to an ESOP pay taxes on only half the interest they receive and can thus charge lower rates. Avis routinely carries a huge debt in connection with its fleet of vehicles—about $1 billion at the time of the deal. The management figured a way to include that sum in the tax-favored ESOP debt. Result: The company significantly lowered its cost of doing business.

Another major concern for Vittoria was to get Avis off what he and everyone else there call its "merry-go-round" of owners, ten since it was founded in 1946 and five (Norton Simon, Esmark, Beatrice, KKR, and Wesray) in the five years before the employee buyout. Vittoria, who had been CEO of Hertz, arrived at Avis in 1982. Managing for a different owner each year had been enormously frustrating. One solution would have been taking the company public, but Vittoria worried that public ownership could have left the company vulnerable to another takeover. The first time he ever heard the term ESOP was in a meeting with Wesray investors. Other Avis executives remembered considering an ESOP back in 1977, before Norton Simon bought the company. Once it became clear that the fleet debt would qualify for the ESOP tax advantages, Wesray's partners at Avis began pushing for employee ownership.

Avis already had a fine reputation for service, and its share of the crucial on-airport market was edging up, while Hertz's dropped from 37% to 32% between 1982 and 1987, according to Finnie of Alex. Brown. He adds that Avis also had the best operating margins among the largest rental companies. Since all of Avis's major competitors have changed hands recently and as a result increased the debt loads, that extra ESOP debt was not much of a competitive disadvantage.

The biggest surprise about employee ownership at Avis is how effective is has proven as a marketing tool. Even before the deal was complete, James Collins, Avis's vice president for sales and marketing, suggested to ad agency Backer Spielvogel Bates that the ESOP might be a good advertising hook. Backer's staff was skeptical. But when the agency commissioned a study of 1,000 typical car-rental customers it found an astonishing 77% believed that employee ownership would mean better service. Says Collins: "The number knocked our socks off."

"Employee ownership translates into an amazing halo," says Randy Hackett, Avis's account manager at Backer. The agency produced a series of television commercials and print ads showing eager workers and announcing, "Avis is the only major rent-a-car company owned by its corporate employees." A new version of the company's famous tag line announces, "We're trying harder than ever." Independent tests found the copy more effective at swaying consumers than any Avis ad Backer had ever produced. Follow-up studies conducted after the commercials began airing this spring showed a dramatic increase in favorable perceptions of Avis. Even Craig Koch, president of Hertz's North American division, a man singularly unimpressed by the new Avis, concedes, "The only advantage I see to the ESOP is that it gives them a good advertising campaign. It's something consumers will listen to."

Some large corporate customers are listening. Says Robert W. Anderson, director of corporate travel for Unisys, which splits its $15 million in annual car rentals between Avis and Hertz: "Employee ownership has got to be a winner. Avis is absolutely superior in customer service, though they were pretty good to begin with." When Westinghouse named Avis its primary car-rental supplier in April, every Avis employee in Pittsburgh, where Westinghouse is based, signed a letter to travel managers there pledging to provide the best possible service. "We were really impressed," says Betty Lou Luketich, manager of business travel. "When employees own a company there is a definite difference in their attitude. Our travelers say they have noticed."

Avis employees show a palpable enthusiasm for the changes that have come since the ESOP. Fears of pay cuts and layoffs have proven groundless, and managers no longer worry that the new owners beneath them might prove unruly and unmanageable. Though employees still hold little stock, most are impressed with the company's more open management style. Many refer with satisfaction to the advertising campaign, and a striking number tell inquiring visitors, "We're trying harder than ever."

"We feel we have closer contact with management," says Roberta Beckelman, a telecommunications specialist at Avis's Worldwide Reservations Center in Tulsa. "We're ready to voice our opinions and we know we will be heard if we do." John Sellers, director of reservations at the Tulsa center, concurs. "In the past, people felt management couldn't really listen to their ideas because we weren't in control of our own destiny," he says. It's easier to manage now: "We've seen a reduction of lost time, and we've actually had employees coming to us asking us to tighten some of our performance standards. That would never have happened prior to the ESOP."

Even employees with gripes give the company a break. Mike Trissel, an Avis bus driver at Fort Lauderdale International Airport, is unhappy that the company insisted on bonuses rather than wage increases in recent local union negotiations. "I feel we should have at least gotten a cost-of-living raise," he says, "but I can see they have a large debt now, and they want to pay it off as soon as they can." And Trissel adds: "Everything else here is 100% positive."

Though some ESOPs exclude union members, Avis decided to make its 2,800 unionized employees owners too. "We wanted to have everybody on the same team and not create two classes of people," says human resources vice president Donald Korn. Negotiations have been a bit more cordial since the buyout. Union officials seem generally pleased with the plan, since it required no explicit concessions on their part, but several worry that Avis, like many ESOP-owned companies, may eventually try too substitute the ESOP for pension benefits. Avis says it retains the option to change pensions. The union officials say they would fight to prevent that.

Employee participation groups comprising representatives from each job category now meet at least monthly at each of Avis's company-owned locations in the U.S. (employees at the many smaller franchise locations are not included in the ESOP). Scores of valuable ideas have surfaced. A sales staffer suggested that the Avis sales force could use an internal charge card instead of American Express when renting Avis cars on the road. The switch saved the transaction fee paid to American Express as well as the concession fee Avis pays to the airport for every paid rental. Says field operations vice president Robert Salerno: "That's maybe another $30,000 or $40,000 that just went to the bottom line."

Employees don't just make suggestions—they follow up. Says Avis Fort Lauderdale district manager Dan Falvey: "In many cases people will go out on their own time and get prices on materials for some idea they've had and come back to the committee and say, 'Hey, should we do it?' And we make the decision as a group. We're not sitting there as managers and employees. We're sitting there as a group of employees in Fort Lauderdale, asking how can we provide better service." They must be coming up with good answers. Since the ESOP purchase Avis has beaten Hertz in Fort Lauderdale market share for the first time ever.

Falvey has to watch himself, though: "If I as the district manager decide to get a new carpet for the office, employees will now come up to me and say, 'Wait a minute, how much is this costing us?' They're half kidding, but the whole message of the ESOP is that you are an owner. We pay off the debt—we own a piece of this company."

Operations chief Salerno says the manager's role is changing. "This whole participation process has put a lot of burden on management to get the people involved and interact with them," he says. "So we're starting a new program for managers on how to deal with people. It takes a lot of work and pressure to instill this thing in the whole company. We don't want people to think it's today's fad, and in a month it'll be gone."

Vittoria, Salerno, and others criss-crossed the country after the ESOP buyout, meeting face-to-face with about 7,000 employees. Top executives still meet regularly with representatives of the participation groups and circulate among employees at all levels. Vittoria says he has respected the knowledge of front-line employees ever since he started in the business in 1960, as a rental agent for Hertz in New York City. "I've always been a believer in visible management, but now I'm doing it more because it has greater value," he says. "This is not the time for management to start taking vacations. I've worked harder since this ESOP was formed than I have in many years." So have a lot of other Avis employees, it appears. They may not have imagined that this would be part of becoming capitalists, but the results are hard to argue with.

Note:

[1]**How the Tax Code Encourages ESOPs**

• When an ESOP borrows to buy stock, not only are the interest payments tax deductible—so are repayments of principal.

• A commercial lender may exclude from taxable income 50% of the interest earned from loans to an ESOP. Most lenders pass part of this saving on to the ESOP.

• Dividends paid on stock that is held by an ESOP can be deducted from corporate taxable income.

• Owners of privately held corporations who sell their shares to an ESOP can defer the capital gains tax if they reinvest the gains in the stock of a U.S. corporation within a year.

Fastener Industries:
Taming of the Screw: How Fastener Industries Figured Out the Nuts and Bolts of Running an ESOP Company.

*Reprinted from **Bank Notes Magazine**, National Cooperative Bank, October-November 1986*

Welds apart

A 100 percent employee-owned company, Fastener Industries has secured its market niche by manufacturing and stocking over 1,200 types of specialized weld nuts, weld screws and adjusting levelers.

Here's a blue-chip list of customers any company would be proud to call its own: Black and Decker, Ingersoll Rand, Robertshaw Controls, Hewlett-Packard, Burroughs, Amana, Trane, Steelcase, Lennox, Coleman, and General Electric.

But impressive as they sound, names like these are just an average day's destination for the shipping department at Fastener Industries. They're among the 5,500 or so original equipment manufacturers throughout the United States that rely on the specialized weld nuts and weld screws that Fastener Industries' two factories turn out five days a week.

"Give me five minutes in your home or office," says Rich Biernacki, president and CEO of Fastener industries," and I'll find some of our nuts and bolts. Just about anyone who puts things together with metal could be an account of ours."

In the generally bleak landscape of American basic industry, Fastener Industries is a standout success story. The manufacturer of over 1,200 different types of weld nuts and weld screws, Fastener Industries has secured its market niche as a low-volume specialty producer of precision weld fasteners, a market that inexpensive Asian manufacturers have not entered. The company has about 120 employees, and annual sales of around $11 million.

Based in Berea, Ohio, Fastener Industries is a 100 percent employee-owned ESOP company, and as such, is an eligible borrower of the National Cooperative Bank. NCB provides Fastener with long-term financing and a short-term revolving line of credit.

"From the Bank's point of view, Fastener is a model credit," says Jack Lyman, NCB senior loan officer for commercial lending. "As a democratically organized company, it's precisely the kind of business NCB was chartered to serve. And as an example of a small company sold to its employees by retiring owners, it's a model of the kind of ESOP our Bank is ideally suited to handle."

Incorporated in 1905 as the Ohio Nut and Bolt Company, Fastener Industries (which still trades under the Ohio brand name) has long been a successful manufacturing concern. Owned by the Whelan family for more than 50 years, the company was always considered a good place to work. It was a consistently profitable outfit, and offered employees above-average wages, bonuses, and benefits, including a 35 hour week for production workers with pay higher than that received by 40 hour workers in other plants.

In 1979-80, when the family decided to sell its interest in Fastener, Biernacki, who was then treasurer, approached the Whelans with the idea of selling the firm to its employees. "It made sense to me that ownership should be shared," says Biernacki. "After all, it was the productivity of the employees that was responsible for our profits. And by sharing ownership democratically, I figured the company could improve on its already successful track record. And in fact, it has."

When the idea was presented to Fastener's employees, the vast majority greeted the concept enthusiastically. They voted to utilize their profit-sharing monies for the purchase of the company's stock, and combined with other financing arrangements, gained full control of the company in 1980.

Since the conversion to employee ownership, many outside observers have called Fastener "a model ESOP." The Fastener By-Laws provide full voting rights to the employee-owners, who elect the company's five-member Board of Directors. In turn, the directors name a five-member committee to administer the ESOP. Employees are eligible participants after one month's work at the company and are immediately 100% vested. Voting is done on a one-share/one-vote basis, and ownership of the company is widely diffused—Biernacki owns the largest piece of the company, yet has less than four percent of the outstanding shares.

Upon termination or retirement, Fastener's employees may take cash or stock. Most distributions have been lump sums, with the average pay-out in the $90,000-$100,000 range. In order for the employees to make the best financial decisions upon receiving the ESOP distribution, the company provides up to four hours of free consultation with financial consultants.

Employees are kept informed about the business side of the company through a series of regular meetings and one-on-one discussions with managers, board members, corporate officers, and Biernacki himself. "They work for me," says Biernacki of Fastener's employees, "but I work for them too. The only way all of us are going to know what's going on is through continual communication."

Both of Fastener's plants have plant managers, but other supervisors are few. Each employee is responsible for his own machines or area, and most seem to take their duties seriously. Fastener Industries has no labor unions and all employees are salaried.

"The important thing to remember," reminds Biernacki, "is that this company has always been profitable. And because it had a solid profit-sharing plan in effect for many years, the employees were able to buy a strong, going concern without putting any cash on the table." The employees did, of course, have to turn their profit-sharing funds into Fastener stock, but by betting on themselves, their gamble has paid off handsomely. According to the company's figures, each employee's stock has more than tripled in value since the ESOP conversion six years ago.

And how do Fastener's employees feel about being the owners of their company? The National Center for Employee Ownership surveyed the company's employee-owners recently, and concluded that Fastener's workforce scored extremely high on work motivation and job satisfaction.

A walk through one of Fastener's plant floors confirms the Center's findings. "For me, it's basically like having my own business," says Jim Carroll, the manager of the plant. "Not only do we all work harder, we've seen our workmates retire with sizeable sums of money, and that's a tremendous incentive." "With the ESOP, just about everybody has the opportunity to grow to their full potential," adds Tom Kwiatkowski, tool and die maker and ESOP Committee Member. "Apart from the financial rewards, we now feel that our advancement is based on our achievement, not just the whim of an owner or supervisor."

And because it's a worker-owned company, Fastener imparts a cooperative mentality not often found in conventionally-owned for-profit corporations. "We're all in this together and we're all accountable to each other," says Paul Lake, Traffic manager. "It's our money we're spending, and our investment we have to protect. When something doesn't work, we're all involved in fixing it, because if the problem isn't solved, we're the ones losing money."

Concludes Biernacki, "when people work for somebody else, the natural tendency is to center on one's self interest. That used to be the case at Fastener. But now I think, that is superseded by concern for the welfare of the ESOP. We're all in this together, and together we have to make it work."

Update:
Ohio's Fastener Industries Acquires New Subsidiary

Reprinted from **Bank Notes Magazine**, *December 1987*

Fastener Industries, Inc., an Employee Stock Ownership Plan (ESOP) company that manufactures over 1,200 types of specialized weld screws, nuts, and adjusting levelers for a variety of industrial users completed the acquisition of Joseph Industries, Inc., a distributor of fork lift replacement parts, on October 1, 1987.

Based in Berea, Ohio, Fastener Industries is a member-borrower of the National Cooperative Bank, and was profiled in the October/November 1986 issue of Banknotes. NCB provided financing to assist Fastener in the purchase of Joseph Industries.

According to Rich Biernacki, Fastener's president and chief executive officer, Joseph Industries will be operated as a wholly owned subsidiary, and its 50 employees will be included in the ESOP maintained by Fastener.

"This acquisition gives us the diversification that we recognized we needed," says Biernacki, "and with it, we're happy to make 50 more workers into employee-owners." Adds Jack Lyman, NCB vice president for commercial lending who assisted Fastener in the Joseph transaction, "Not only does this make excellent sense for Fastener's long term business objectives, it brings another small, well-managed industrial company into the ranks of employee ownership."

Fastener is a 100 percent employee-owner company. It was founded in 1905 and became an ESOP in 1980. Joseph Industries was founded in 1969 by Harold Joseph who owned the company until it was purchased by Fastener. For fiscal year 1987, Fastener expects gross sales of approximately $12 million, while Joseph Industries experienced gross sales of over $5 million. For fiscal year 1988, the combined company is projecting sales of $18 million.

La Perla (Guatemala)
Peasants Fight and Buy Stock to Save Beleaguered Plantation

by Robert England
*Reprinted from **Insight Magazine**, June 16, 1986*

(**Summary:** *After Marxist guerrillas killed the patriarch of a plantation, his sons struck back, selling stock to their workers and giving them a stake in the plantation's future. Now the Reagan administration wants to see if the rest of Latin America can profit from the idea.*)

In Guatemala, in the remote Ixil Triangle region of the nation's high lands, an 11,000-acre coffee bean plantation called La Perla (The Pearl) seems to be winning an economic, military and ideological war with Marxist guerrillas.

The idea that drives La Perla, the only plantation left in the Ixil area, is worker stock ownership. Since December 1984 the plantation has been 40 percent owned by its 500 mostly Ixchel Indian laborers.

It is no less than a competing model of economic and social justice for the region. It promotes the redistribution of wealth without seizing the property of the rich and without destroying the notion of private property. It is a vision in direct competition with the collectivist promises of the Marxists of Central America.

Social justice with private property rights intact? "Yes, yes, yes," says the head of La Perla, 37-year-old Enrique Arenas Menes. He has struggled since 1975 to save his family's plantation from being overrun by the Guerilla Force of the Poor, Guatemala's largest antigovernment guerrilla army. According to Arenas, the peasant owners have kept the plantation going even though 25 to 30 of them have died in battles with the guerrillas since 1975.

President Reagan is one of the staunchest supporters of expanding workers' ownership of the firms that employ them. An owner, in the view of Reagan and others, has a sense of commitment that someone who is only an employee may lack. In impoverished areas of Central America, worker ownership may draw peasants away from subsistence farming into more economically productive ventures—and provide them with a stake in the economic system that will diminish the appeal of Marxist rhetoric.

A commission Reagan appointed a year ago to examine the potential of the idea for Central America, the Presidential Task Force on Project Economic Justice, will make its recommendations next month.[1] No less an unyielding critic of the administration's Central American policy than Rep. Michael D. Barnes, a Maryland Democrat, says that the "La Perla project could produce a peaceful answer to the agrarian problems of Guatemala, and do so in a swift fashion."

For La Perla, the road to worker ownership has not been an easy one. Grave doubts about the future of the plantation began to emerge in 1975. A heavily armed band from the Guerrilla Force of the Poor came to La Perla and assassinated Enrique Arenas's father, Jose Luis Arenas Barrera, a Ladino from Guatemala City who first opened the fertile jungles of Ixil to coffee bean cultivation in 1941. According to Enrique Arenas, the guerrillas, who had operated in the area since about 1970 without violence, were seeking to spark a peasant revolt. Guerrilla attacks on neighboring plantations increased thereafter.

Besides the violence, the guerrillas waged a war of promises. Arenas says they told the campesinos they could own the land and become rich. "Campesinos who joined the guerrilla forces were promised Mercedes," says Jose Orive, a spokesman for the Guatemalan government who has visited the plantation. The violence and promises had their effect. By 1980 La Perla, still in the hands of six Arenas brothers, was the only plantation operating in the area. It was also increasingly vulnerable.

From 1981 to 1983 guerrilla activity increased dramatically in the nation. The strength of the Marxist forces, supplied by Cuba and Nicaragua, peaked at 6,000 to 10,000. Why did the peasants of La Perla ignore the call to join the Marxist cause and stay at La Perla in the face of guerrilla attacks? "Because of the Arenas family's long history of good relations with the workers," says Orive. The assassination of the elder Arenas shocked and horrified the workers as well as the family. It provided an emotional bond that has driven Enrique and the peasants to keep La Perla open.

In 1982, La Perla decided it would have to close down if it did not begin to fight back—literally—against the guerrillas. The guerrillas had occupied parts of the plantation—including its two landing strips—burned a Cessna 185 aircraft and stolen the payroll for 300 workers. They had already blocked the primitive roads to the nearest villages, Nebaj, 25 miles away, and Chajul, 20 miles away, making air travel the only way in and out of the plantation. That led Arenas to ask the army's chief commander, Benedicto Lucas, for permission to form a civil defense militia.

An integral part of government counterinsurgency efforts, which often were brutal in their own right, had been the establishment of civil patrols. Since they first began under the junta led by Efrain Rios Montt, they have grown into a force of 800,000 out of a population of 8 million. The democratically elected, civilian government of Vinicio Cerezo, which took office in January, still supports them.

At first the army feared La Perla's peasants might join the guerrillas, but Arenas assured Lucas the "La Perla people were faithful to the government—if they had arms they would protect themselves without the army." The army reluctantly agreed.

Virtually shut off from the world, La Perla's workers bought their own weapons, which were delivered by air in December 1982. Arenas says they had only 18 guns the day the militia was formed. The very next day they were attacked; the civil defense militia drove the guerrillas back. "They have been very, very successful," says Arenas. The civil patrol has not lost a battle with guerrillas since its formation, he claims. Today the civil patrol has 97 M-1 rifles and an assortment of 35 to 40 other guns. Two hundred La Perla workers are now members of the patrol.

Bringing a shaky peace and security to La Perla came too late, however, for a $2 million loan that the brothers Arenas had sought from the Central American Bank for Economic Integration, a bank set up by the Organization of American States with U. S. support. The loan had been approved in 1983, but the bank was then waiting for new funding. By the time funding had arrived, the increased intensity of the communist insurgency had cooled the bank's enthusiasm. The loan was canceled.

The Arenas brothers were then in desperate need of cash to keep the plantation operating. They considered selling it to other landowners. But Guatemalan economist Joseph Recinos, who had studied in the United States in the late 1960's and had become an enthusiastic proponent of worker ownership, encouraged the owners of La Perla to try the idea themselves. The Arenas brothers agreed to sell a sizable block of stock to the workers.

The idea was one with something of a pedigree—in theory at least—in Central America. In the late 1940's in Costa Rica, Alberto Martén Chavarria started a movement to fight against the notion of class struggle through worker ownership and profit-sharing by management-labor organizations controlled by workers. They were to be called *solidaristas*. The associations, as Martén envisioned them, would elect their leaders democratically, buy stock and fund profit-sharing plans from donations from workers and management.

The idea waned in Costa Rica after Martén tried to form a political party based on it. But stripped of partisan politics, the movement was reborn in 1971, when the Rev. Claudio Solano, a young priest who became director of the (Pope) John XXIII Social Science School in Curridabat, Costa Rica, began to promote the idea vigorously. Today the country has 1,100 *solidaristas* with 130,000 worker members, says Honorato Gonzalez, president of the Solidarity Union of Costa Rica. Comprising 18 percent of the labor force, it is the largest labor organization in Costa Rica. According to Arnoldo Nieto, a movement leader, it has reduced Marxist influence, which once threatened to eclipse the free labor unions, to a mere 7 percent of the labor force.

Recinos saw in Costa Rica a model for *solidarismo* in Guatemala and elsewhere in Latin America. It was particularly important, in his view, to demonstrate that the solidarity idea could be transplanted from an educated, middle-class nation like Costa Rica to the largely illiterate peasant masses of an impoverished nation like Guatemala.

La Perla is now one of some 50 *solidaristas* formed in Guatemala since 1983. They represent 10,000 workers in such industries as bananas, cement, shoes, hotels, grocery chains and banks.

The civil patrol has provided the security and worker ownership the motivation for La Perla to struggle to rebuild. The plantation had not had a profitable harvest since the day the elder Arenas was killed. In 1984 it managed to produce a meager 500,000 pounds of coffee beans. Last year, the first since employees gained their shares, production nearly doubled to 970,000 pounds, according to Enrique Arenas. This year he believes the plantation can produce 1.32 million pounds "if you Americans keep drinking coffee and the price of coffee stays up." This could produce the first profits and dividends for the workers. Arenas sees next year as an even better opportunity. If the plantation reaches its full capacity, 3.3 million pounds, it could be highly profitable.

Plantation workers earn slightly more than the average $1,200 per capita income in Guatemala. In addition, Guatemalan law requires plantation owners to provide housing and small plots for the workers to grow their own food. Some peasants earn more money by selling food from their plots.

At La Perla, the *solidarista*, headed by Avelino Soto, owns outright a general store that sells food and clothes on the plantation. The association also has exclusive rights over about one-tenth of the plantation, where its members can grow whatever crops they wish and pocket the profits. The workers are paying for their shares in La Perla S.A. over a 10-year period through payroll deductions. They enjoy full voting rights and occupy nine of the 10 seats on the board that manages the plantation.

While the economic and military successes against the guerrillas have so far been considerable, the struggle is by no means over. Although the Guerrilla Force of the Poor's numbers have dropped below 2,000, according to the U.S. State Department, a powerful contingent remains camped across the Xacibal River from La Perla. They have stepped up the frequency and strength of attacks on La Perla for more than a year.

With so much of the area in ruins, the guerrillas have focused more and more on attacking the comparative prosperity of La Perla. On Feb. 20, after the civil patrol burned the corn of the guerrillas in retaliation for an attack on coffee bean stores at the plantation, the guerrillas mounted what Arenas calls their biggest assault to date. In a half-day gun battle that began at 6 a.m., the civil patrol pushed back and defeated some 120 guerrillas who had surrounded them. Six of the workers in the militia and about 20 guerrillas died, according to the civil patrol.

Arenas expects another attack soon. The plantation is expanding the area it has under cultivation—planting corn in a far reach of its property—and the guerrillas will perceive that as a threat. "We're developing areas that used to be occupied by guerrillas," says Arenas. "They won't like it. They will attack."

The corn is being planted to feed 5,000 refugees who have flooded into the plantation over the past few years. Arenas says more than 600 former guerrillas and another 900 guerrilla sympathizers, along with their families, have taken up residence at La Perla. On May 24 a band of 83 refugees from guerrilla-held areas asked for refuge, the largest number in a single day.

As news of the struggle at La Perla has spread, support for the embattled worker-capitalists has begun to pour in. The Guatemalan government and a U.S. Christian organization, the Acts of Faith, are assisting in building a hospital there—the first in the zone's history. Payments made by the workers for their stock are helping to build the plantation's infrastructure. A road now connects two ends of the plantation, and two pickup trucks and a jeep have improved communications and defense.

Other landowners in Guatemala say they are watching La Perla closely. But they are unlikely to try worker ownership until they see favorable financial results. Says government spokesman Orive: "They have unpleasant memories of radical land reform" that was tried in the early 1950's.

Do the workers fully understand the nature of their ownership? "About two-thirds of the 500 worker-owners really realize that one day their participation will give them enough money to change their lives completely," Arenas says. "With the first profits all the people will finally be totally convinced of the goodness of this plan."

Enthusiastic supporters of the worker ownership movement plan to export the idea to Mexico and the rest of Central America, then to all of Latin America. The former U.S. ambassador to Costa Rica, Curtin Winsor, Jr., says, "It may be the single most original and significant ideological contribution from Latin America" to the world.

Arenas, too, is hopeful about the future but realistic. "We have some hard years ahead. We are willing. We are not alone. The workers are with us."

Notes:

[1]Innovative Plan to Spread Wealth

The La Perla plantation, a showcase for worker stock ownership in Central America, served as a catalyst in the creation of the Presidential Task Force on Project Economic Justice. Headed by J. William Middendorf II, the group will present recommendations to President Reagan next month for spreading the wealth in Central America and the Caribbean.

According to an advance copy of the report obtained by *Insight*, the recommendations will include some sweeping and innovative approaches to the region's economies—changes Middendorf calls "the second revolution of the Americas."

The most daring proposal is to establish a "free market of the Americas"—the United States, Central America and the Caribbean, for the moment. Those countries that drop all trade barriers would have unimpeded access to U.S. markets. So would all employee-owned companies based in the region (excluding those in Cuba and Nicaragua), regardless of trade barriers their countries impose. The hope is that this would lure outside investment into these troubled economies.

The region's heavily nationalized economies will be encouraged to privatize through the sale of state-owned companies to their employees. State companies that are substantially employee-owned would also gain free access to U.S. markets.

In a two-edged stab at Latin-American debts and what it sees as bloated state enterprises, the task force proposes that loans be swapped for equity in state-owned businesses, in two steps: A bank holding debts in Mexico, Central America and the Caribbean would trade the loan contracts for a share of the state-owned enterprises, then sell its equity to the workers via an employee stock ownership plan. Success would hinge on the ability of employee groups to make the enterprises profitable.

Employee stock ownership would be promoted vigorously in all the countries of the region. Each would set up its own Project Economic Justice. Finally, a two-tiered credit system would provide favorable lending rates for investments aimed at improving productivity.

Springfield Remanufacturing Corporation:

The Great Game of Business

or

How I Learned to Stop Worrying and Teach People How to Make Money

by Jack Stack
Reprinted from **Inc. Magazine**, *June 1992*

It's amazing what you can come up with when you have no money, zero outside resources, and 119 people all depending on *you* for their jobs, their homes, and their prospects of dinner for the foreseeable future.

That's pretty much the situation my 12 fellow managers and I faced in February 1983, our first month in business as an independent company. We were supervisors and managers at a little factory in Springfield, Mo., that up until then had been owned by International Harvester. At the time Harvester was in big trouble, cutting loose operations like ours in a desperate attempt to stay afloat. When the company offered to sell us the factory, we jumped at the chance to save our jobs. Our new company was loaded down with so much debt that we couldn't rely on traditional ways of managing, because they wouldn't produce the kind of results we needed in time to save us. So we grabbed for something new, based on what we thought of as the higher laws of business.

The first higher law is: *You get what you give.*

Here's the second: *It's easy to stop one guy, but it's pretty hard to stop 119.*

These laws of business are the reason we survived and have been successful ever since. It was out of these laws that we created the Great Game of Business.

The Great Game of Business is a whole different way of running a company and of thinking about how a company should be run. What lies at the heart of the Game is a very simple proposition—that the best, most efficient, most profitable way to operate a business is to give everybody in the company a voice in saying how the company is run and a stake in the financial outcome, good or bad. We turn business into a game that everybody in the company can play. It's a way of tapping into the universal desire to win, of making that desire a powerful competitive force. Winning the Great Game of Business has the greatest reward: continual improvement of your life and your livelihood. You get that reward, however, only by playing together as a team and by building a dynamic company.

That's what we did at the Springfield Remanufacturing Corp., and it worked for us in a big way. From 1983 to 1986 our sales grew by more than 30% per year, while we went from a loss of $60,488 in our first year to pretax earnings of $2.7 million (7% of sales) in our fourth. We never laid off a single person, not even when we lost a contract representing 40% of our business for a whole year. By 1991 we had annual sales of almost $70 million, and our work force had increased to about 650 people from the original 119. But perhaps the most impressive number concerned the value of SRC stock, worth 10¢ a share at the time of the buyout. By the end of January 1991 that 10¢ share had soared in value to $18.30, an increase of 18,200% in eight years. As a result, hourly workers who had been with SRC from the beginning had holdings in the employee stock ownership plan worth as much as $35,000 per person—almost the price of a home in Springfield.

We didn't do this by riding some hot technology or glamorous industry. Remanufacturing is a tough, loud, dirty business, where people work with plugs in their ears and leave the factory every day covered in grease. SRC remanufactures engines and engine components. We take worn-out engines from cars, bull-dozers, and 18-wheelers, and we rebuild them from the ground up, saving the parts that are in good shape, fixing those that are damaged, replacing the ones beyond repair. But our real business is education. We teach people about business. We give them the knowledge that allows them to go out and play the Game.

The Rules of the Game

People who run companies know there are really only two critical factors in business. One is to make money, and the other is to generate cash. As long as you do those two things, your company is going to be OK, even if you make mistakes along the way. I'm not saying safety is not a major issue, or delivery and customer service are not major issues. They are all major issues, but they are part of the process. They are not end results or even conditions of survival. In business you can have great customer service and fail. You can have a terrific safety record and fail. You can have the best quality in your industry and fail. The only way to be secure is to make money and generate cash. Everything else is a means to that end.

Those simple rules apply to every business. And yet at most companies people are never told that the survival of the company depends on doing those two things. No one ever explains how one person's actions affect another's, how each department depends on the others, what impact they all have on the company as a whole. Most important, no one tells people how to make money and generate cash. Nine times out of 10, they don't even know the difference between the two.

At SRC we teach everybody those rules, and then we build on that simple knowledge and take people all the way to the complexity of ownership. We try to take ignorance out of the workplace and force people to get involved, not with threats and intimidation but with education. In the process we are trying to close one of the biggest gaps in American business—the gap between workers and managers. To do that, you have to knock down the barriers that separate people, that keep people from coming together as a team.

The biggest barrier is a basic ignorance about business. Most people who work in companies don't understand business. They think *profit* is a dirty word. They think owners slip it into their bank accounts at night. They have no idea that more than 40% of business profits goes to taxes. They've never heard of retained earnings. They can't conceive how a company might be earning a profit and yet have no cash to pay its bills, or how it might be generating cash and yet operate at a loss.

That's the ignorance you have to eliminate if you want to get people working together as a team. But eliminating it is tough because most people find business incredibly boring. They really can't get too excited about making money for somebody else. Everything they've ever heard about business makes it seem complicated, confusing, hard to understand, abstract, maybe even a little seamy.

That's where the Game comes in. We tell people they have the wrong idea about business, that it's really a kind of game—no more complicated than baseball, golf, or bowling. The main difference is that the stakes are higher. How you play softball may determine whether or not you get a trophy, but how you play the business game has a big impact on whether or not you can support your family, put food on your table, fulfill your dreams. All you need is a willingness to learn the rules, master the fundamentals, and play together as a team.

Everything we do at SRC is geared toward getting people involved in playing the Great Game of Business. We teach people the rules. We show them how to keep score and follow the action, and then we flood them with the information they need to do both. We also give them a big stake in the outcome—in the form of equity, profits, and opportunities to move ahead as far as they want to go. We do all this, moreover, by using tools of business that have been around for a hundred years or more. The most important of those tools are the financial statements.

The Basic Tools of the Game

When people come to work at SRC, we tell them 70% of the job is disassembly—or whatever—and 30% of the job is learning. What they learn is how to make money, how to make a profit. We offer them sessions with the accounting staff, tutoring with supervisors and foremen, instructional sheets, and so on. We teach them about aftertax profits, retained earnings, equity, cash flow, everything. We want each of them to be able to read an income statement and a balance sheet.

Then we provide a lot of reinforcement. Once a week, for example, supervisors hold meetings throughout the company to go over the updated financial statements. Those numbers show how we're doing in relation to our annual goals and whether or not there will be quarterly bonuses. The more people understand, the more they want to know.

Suddenly, business makes sense to everybody. But to understand it, you have to look at the totality. You can't focus your attention on one job, one department, or one function. The Game takes down walls. It forces people to realize that they're on the same team, and they win or lose together. You know you're going to get rewarded, but so will everyone else. When you look at goals like profit and cash flow, that makes people understand how they all depend on one another.

Why We Play the Game

There are four basic reasons we play the game:

1.   We want to live up to our end of the employment bargain.

You take on a big obligation when you hire somebody. That person is bringing home money, putting food on the table, taking care of children. Of course, the individual has obligations to the company as well. But as much as possible I want it to be someone's choice whether he or she leaves the company. It bothers me to see people laid off through no fault of their own. Everything we do is based on a common understanding that job security is paramount—that we are not creating a place for people to work not just this year or 5 years from now, but for the next 50 years and beyond. We owe it to one another to keep the company alive.

One of the lessons we learned from the demise of International Harvester was that there is no security in ignorance. The only way to know if your job is safe is by looking at the financial statements. We had never dreamed our jobs at Harvester might be in danger. This was a company that went back 100 years, one of the 30 largest in the country. My dad had retired from it. I'd worked there for 14 years. I just *assumed* my job was secure, and I had no way of knowing it wasn't. Then Harvester went down the tubes.

We had no such illusions when we started SRC: we knew our jobs were in jeopardy from the start. To buy the plant, we'd had to come up with $9 million, of which we were able to scrape together $100,000 from mothers, fathers, in-laws, uncles, friends, and our own personal savings. We borrowed the rest. We had an 89-to-one debt-to-equity ratio. We couldn't afford to make a $10,000 mistake.

We realized there were two things we couldn't do. Number one, we couldn't run out of cash, because our creditors would close us down. Number two, we couldn't destroy from within, which would be a danger if morale got bad. If either happened, we'd lose the company and all 119 of us would lose our jobs. The more we thought about it, the more convinced we became that the best way to avoid both dangers was to communicate with people through the financial statements. Everybody had to know the company's situation at every point. We had to tell people where the cash was and make sure they were involved in deciding what to do with it. That's how the Game evolved.

We developed a system that delegates responsibility for job security by giving people a scorecard and a way to influence the score. The Game lets you see for yourself how safe your job is and shows what you can do to make it safer.

2. We want to do away with jobs.

Most companies tell employees: "Drill as many of these holes as possible, as fast as possible, and don't think about anything else." If you do that, you wind up with workers who think a job is just a job. I call them the living dead. You can't have high productivity with faceless people. They're not happy with themselves; they're not happy with their jobs; they bring you down. But you can't really blame them for feeling that way about their work when they're constantly being told to just do the job, nothing more. Why would anybody think a job was more than a job when that's all the company expects it to be? But if you set up the work to be a step on the path to something else, then it takes on a new meaning.

We try to show people they don't have to limit themselves and they do have choices. We try to eliminate the sense of being trapped—the sense that I-can't-go-anywhere-this-job-is-a-dead-end-it's-boring-my-whole-life-is-the-pits. We continually challenge people to tell us where they want to go, what they want to do with their lives. When you do that, you open a lot of doors. You get rid of a lot of the frustrations people have. You also take their excuses away, which is essential.

To be sure, some jobs are bad, demeaning—the kind of jobs nobody wants to do. We said, "Let's robotize the jobs people don't want; let's computerize them; let's get them out of the market." But once you've gotten rid of the worst jobs, then what? There are still a lot of jobs that involve putting washers on bolts. You can't walk away from it. The work is boring, but it has to be done.

The Game is an attempt to create an environment wherein all employees can take pleasure in their work, even the people who put washers on bolts. We try to take people beyond the job, to give them the opportunity to use their intelligence and achieve something. In effect, you steal a little bit of someone's brain while she's applying the manual effort. She may be putting washers on bolts, but at the same time she's thinking about ways of making her environment better, her position better, her life better. She's not just making a contribution to an end product. She's making a contribution to her own life. She's moving in a positive direction.

3. We want to get rid of the employee mentality.

The big payoff to us for playing the Game is that we become a more educated, more flexible organization. We can respond instantaneously to changes in the market. We can respond to problems in the length of time it takes to place a phone call.

We can do all that because we have a company filled with people who, not only *are* owners, but *think* and *act* like owners rather than employees. That's an important distinction. Getting people to think and act like owners goes far beyond giving them equity. Many companies set up ESOPs, expecting a miraculous change of attitude in the work force. Then they're shocked to find that people still think and act like employees: they won't take initiative or responsibility; they make excuses and blame other people for their own failures.

That's the antithesis of ownership. Owners, *real* owners, don't have to be told what to do—they can figure it out for themselves. They have all the knowledge, understanding, and information they need to make a decision, and the motivation and the will to act fast. Ownership is not a set of legal rights. It's a state of mind. You can't give people that state of mind in one fell swoop. You can only nurture it through education.

The whole idea behind the Game is to create an environment in which people are learning all the time. They're seeing all kinds of situations. We're showing them both sides of every story, allowing them to make decisions, to fail with the incorrect decisions they make, and to learn from their failures and try again. The numbers are an important part of that. They serve as the bond, the basis of trust. By giving people the numbers, I can say to them, "If you don't believe me, look it up. It's all there in the numbers." The nice part is that as you learn, you grow, you get more out of life, you have fun.

4. We want to create and distribute wealth.

If we can improve productivity, we can create a society that's continually getting better, a society in which people do more to help one another. As it is, we're becoming a society of haves and have-nots. What's happening is that the rich know how to play the Game, and they're playing it well. Meanwhile, the society as a whole has a declining standard of living. That standard will continue to decline unless we can figure out how to be more productive. Part of the problem is that you can't increase the standard of living without generating wealth, and we hate everybody who generates wealth—whether it's the oil companies or the doctors or the entrepreneurs. That's a big mistake. It isn't the *generation* of wealth that we should hate. What's wrong is the *distribution* of wealth. Our real problem is that we haven't taught people how to share in that distribution.

The only way to solve the problem in the long term is to make people conscious of generating and understanding profits, conscious of where profits come from and where they go. Somebody's got to teach people about wealth—about retained earnings, equity, what an earnings multiple is and how it can affect them individually. If we don't do it, we'll remain in this ignorant, dormant stage where we continually think a job is a job is a job. And the decline will continue.

You have to begin by getting people away from focusing on the specific mechanical things they do, because there's more to business than that. Business is dealing with some of our most pressing social issues these days, like health care. This is the first time I can remember when people on the floor, even those at the job-entry level, are paying attention to fringe benefits. Health insurance has always been taken for granted. Now it's moved to center stage. It's an overhead item, a hidden cost, a cost people don't necessarily see. It's important for people to pay attention to the cost. But how do you take them from focusing on washers and bolts to focusing on health care if you haven't devised some system for explaining it to them?

The Game is one way to do that. We're teaching people how to take care of themselves. In the process, we're redistributing wealth—we're redistributing the earnings of the company back to the people who created them.

How to Be an Open-Book Manager

When you use financial statements as management tools, you have to adapt them to your purposes. Don't rely on the kind of financial statements provided by certified public accountants. Those statements are designed to give outsiders the information they want about a company. Employees need something a little different. The general form is the same, and the standards of accuracy should be just as high, but the detail has to be broken out in a way that sheds more light on *what's happening inside the company*. The point is to show each person how he or she affects the income statement and the balance sheet. You want to report the numbers accordingly, emphasizing the ones over which people have control.

How you do that depends entirely on your business, but here are some general rules to follow:

(1) *Start with the income statement.* It is the best tool you have for drawing people into the action of the Game, because it is constantly changing. As a result, it lends itself to demonstrating cause and effect. You can use it both to monitor the action as it unfolds and to show people their role in determining whether or not the company makes money.

(2). *Highlight the categories in which you spend the most money.* Those are obviously the ones that are going to have the biggest impact on your company's profitability, so you want to monitor them very closely.

(3) *Break down categories into controllable elements.* If labor is a variable expense, you want people to see it vary. If you use trucks in your business, people should know how much you're spending there. In a sales organization, you'd keep a close eye on travel, entertainment, and other selling expenses; in a professional-service firm, you'd probably want to break down billable hours. The whole idea is to set up the income statement in a way that lets people observe the effects of what they do.

(4) *Use the income statement to educate people about the balance sheet.* While the action may center on the income statement, the balance sheet tells you the real score—how secure your jobs are, how much wealth you have created, where you are vulnerable. Once people get the hang of the income statement, it's a fairly simple matter to show them how the changes there produce changes in the balance sheet. Use the same principle of breaking down large balance-sheet categories to illuminate cause and effect.

At SRC, on our financial statements we break out the various costs involved in the manufacturing operation. Typically, those costs would be lumped together in the cost-of-goods-sold line on the income statement. That may be adequate for a banker, but it doesn't tell us very much about what's really going on in production, where most of our people work. We want them to see exactly what effect they are having on profits, so we break down the cost of goods sold into its basic elements—material, labor, and overhead. Every week the various departments forecast whether, and by how much, they are going to be over or under budget for the month. Then, after the month's close, we produce a 100-page set of financial statements showing exactly what happened where and how each person contributed.

Almost every element of the company is quantified, from the percentage of the budget spent on receptionists' notepads to the amount of overhead absorbed each hour that a person puts in grinding crankshafts. We constantly measure material costs, overhead, performance, hourly rates. Labor ratios are calculated on a daily basis—by supervisors, group leaders, department managers, the hourly employees themselves. There are numbers for everybody. Sales numbers are posted daily: who's buying, what they're buying, how they're buying. The numbers are broken down not just by customer but by product.

We didn't create this system overnight. It took us years to develop all the mechanisms we now have for keeping people up to date on the numbers, and we're still coming up with new ones. But we started out very simply. In the first year our chief financial officer would chicken-scratch a daily report to the bank showing where our cash was, where our inventories were, where our receivables were, what we owed, and so on. That would be passed around the company. People would ask, "What do we owe today?" From there, the reporting system just grew and grew.

It expanded because people kept asking for more information. The more information we provided, the more they wanted to know. They wanted to see exactly where they fit into the process: how much money they were saving the company, how much profit they had generated on a particular job, what their ups and downs were, how well a particular idea had worked. Their questions told us what information we should be reporting. Management's role was to instill the desire to know. We did that by a variety of methods—through the bonus system, the weekly meetings, and all the other games we developed along the way. But the process got started as simply as can be: by sitting down and explaining to people how the bank was measuring us and how we were doing.

It's Got to Be a Game

You can go too far trying to light the fire in people's eyes. If you do, you'll find people stop having fun and start getting scared. Then you have to pull back fast.

That happened to me at one point. I decided that each of the managers should have a list of 10 accountabilities he'd be expected to meet in the course of the year. I made them so specific that they overlapped and conflicted. People had to step on one another's toes to win. It might have worked out if each manager had done 80% of what I asked for. But I had two guys who strove to be the best in every category, and so they walked straight into each other's territory. They almost killed each other.

The mistake I'd made was to think people would look at those accountabilities as guidelines, as opportunities to help the company and help themselves at the same time. But people see an implicit threat in a list of individual performance criteria. The message is, "OK, management is telling me what I have to do if I want to keep my job."

So these two guys got into a confrontation. One of them walked up to the other and said, "Hey, you may be meeting your goal, but I ain't making mine. If I screw up, my family could be in jeopardy. I could lose my job." I heard them arguing. They took the accountabilities not as ideals to strive for but a minimum standards of performance. So I took the accountability sheets, went out in the backyard, put them in a metal wastepaper basket, and set them on fire.

I hadn't realized the fear I was building into the system. I learned two important lessons from that experience:

- *Give everyone the same set of goals.* Let all employees have the same objectives, and make sure they have to work together to achieve them. Turn success into a group effort. That way they can win together.
- *Don't use goals to tell people everything you want them to do.* Too many goals are useless. You should have only two, or, at most, three goals over the course of a year. What's important is to make sure each goal encompasses five or six things. In other words, choose a goal that people can meet only if they do five or six things right.

How Bonuses Can Make You an Eternal Bootstrapper

I am a strong believer in operating a company, any company, as if something could happen at any moment to threaten its survival. Most companies follow that principle when they are starting up. They know they could run out of cash next week, so they become extremely resourceful. It's known as bootstrapping, and it's how all businesses should be run, not just start-ups. Bootstrapping is a mentality, a way of operating on self-reliance, ingenuity, intelligence, and hard work. A good bonus system can help you build a bootstrapping mentality by putting a great deal of emphasis on job security—by reminding people what it takes to protect their jobs and by showing them how they can get more out of those jobs.

The truth is, there is only one sure way to protect jobs, and that is to be ruthless about costs. A bonus system like ours allows us to hold base salaries at a level that gives people a great deal of job security but shares with them, through bonuses, whatever additional money they generate. The more they generate, the bigger the bonuses.

Here's our process for choosing and checking our bonus numbers:

Set profit targets and maximum bonus payouts. First, we decide on the baseline for profits, the top target for profits, and the highest level of bonuses we will pay on both income-statement and balance-sheet goals. From that, we can figure out how much additional profit people might generate and how much the company will give back to them as bonuses if they hit all their targets.

In our case, pretax profits have to be greater than 5% of revenues before we pay any bonus on the income-statement goal. Above 5%, we start sharing the additional profits with people, as bonuses based on a percentage of their regular compensation. For simplicity's sake, we'll assume that everyone receives the same percentage and that the most people can earn is an extra 13% of their annual pay, which they get if we hit the maximum level on both goals—6.5% for hitting one, 6.5% for hitting the other. Let's say we have sales of $70 million per year, and our payroll is $10 million. The most we'd pay out would be an additional $1.3 million in one year (.13 x $10 million). We'd only pay that much, however, if we hit the maximum payout level on both goals, including the income-statement, or profitability, goal, which we usually set at 8.6%. For this example, let's call it 9%. That means the company would earn an additional pretax profit of $2.8 million (9% - 5% = 4%; .04 x $70 million = $2.8 million). So after we've paid the bonuses, we'll still have $1.5 million left for other purposes.

Notice we're assuming that we'll pay the maximum bonus on *both* goals, not just the profitability goal. A balance-sheet goal may not have any effect on your profits, but you'll have to pay the bonus on it if people hit it, so you must include it in your calculations.

Decide on a balance-sheet goal. Meanwhile, we are choosing our balance-sheet goal with an eye toward making sure we'll have the cash to pay the bonuses people earn. You run a big risk if you have an income-statement goal but not a balance-sheet goal: people may wind up making money without generating cash. Theoretically, all the money they make could go into inventory and receivables, and you wouldn't be able to pay the bonuses on time. That's one reason we like liquidity as a balance-sheet goal. It greatly increases the odds that we will have the cash we need to pay bonuses and do a lot of other things.

Set the targets on the balance-sheet goal. First, we look at what would happen to the balance sheet if we hit the maximum target on the income statement. Then we start kicking numbers around on the balance-sheet goal to come up with a top target that will make those extra profits available for our use.

Let's say our balance-sheet goal is liquidity, as measured by the current ratio, and we have $10 million in current assets and $5 million in current liabilities. So our current ratio is 2 to 1, or 2.00. We already know that if people hit the top target on the income-statement goal, they will generate an additional $2.8 million in pretax profits. If they also hit the top balance-sheet target, we will pay $1.3 million in bonuses, which leaves us with an additional pretax profit of $1.5 million. About 40% of that goes to taxes, so we could have additional aftertax profits of $900,000 (.60 x $1.5 million = $900,000).

We'd like to have all of that as cash. Let's say we use the $900,000 to reduce our current liabilities from $5 million to $4.1 million, while our current assets stay at $10 million. Now our current ratio is 2.44 ($10 million/$4.1 million = 2.44). We started out at 2.00. So if we keep all the additional aftertax profit as cash, we'd have about a 22% increase in the current ratio. That's the maximum increase in liquidity we can expect if we hit a pretax margin of 9% and pay out the full bonus, 13% of payroll. It means we've taken all the money left over after paying bonuses and taxes and used it to reduce our current liabilities. We haven't tied any of the extra cash up in illiquid assets.

Once we've done those calculations, we can set the targets on the balance-sheet goal. We put the biggest bounty, the 6.5% bonus, on that 22% increase in the current ratio, and we work backward from there. Since we want several payout levels, we decide to pay a bonus for every 5% improvement in the ratio. You might note that this gives people a strong incentive to reduce current liabilities rather than put the cash into current assets. If you increase current assets by $900,000 and leave current liabilities at $5 million, you wind up with a current ratio of 2.18 ($10.9 million/$5 million = 2.18). That brings you only up into the first level of the bonus payout.

Protect your equity. We never want people to forget the real payoff for playing the Great Game of business at SRC, namely, the generation of wealth in the form of equity. So we always go back to see what effect our goals are likely to have on the value of our stock.

If the company has a 9% pretax margin on $70 million in sales, it earns $6.3 million in pretax profits (.09 x $70 million = $6.3 million). Out of that $6.3 million, we pay $1.3 million in bonuses, which leaves us with $5 million pretax. We can use part of that money to build up the ESOP. That brings our pretax profits down to $4 million. We get to keep only about 60% of that amount, since 40% goes to taxes. So our aftertax profit comes to about $2.4 million (.60 x $4 million = $2.4 million). That's our retained earnings for the year, the money we have available to finance our growth, or pay down our long-term debt, or otherwise invest in ourselves. Let's say the company is worth about 10 times its annual aftertax earnings, which is the common rule of thumb. In that case, SRC's value would be about $24 million.

It's all very simple math. The bonus program generated $2.8 million in additional pretax profits. We gave out $1.3 million of that as bonuses. We put another $1 million into the ESOP. We paid taxes on the remaining $500,000 and had an additional $300,000 in aftertax earnings. That translates into a $3-million boost in SRC's value.

— 11 —

Beyond Privatization:
An Egyptian Model for Democratizing
Capital Credit for Workers

By Norman G. Kurland and Dawn K. Brohawn
Paper presented to American Banker Conferences on ESOPs, New York City,
June 12-13, 1989, as revised by authors, 1993

Introduction

"Privatization" has become a buzzword with many meanings. It can mean anything from restructuring basic economic institutions to foster a competitive free enterprise system (i.e. policy reform), to various methodologies for encouraging the private sector to perform services now being provided within the public sector. These methods can range from the elimination of subsidies and the lowering of trade barriers, to the shutting down of highly inefficient public-sector enterprises; from the sale of assets or shares in state-owned enterprises to private investors, to the contracting out of services now being performed by public-sector entities.

Regardless of how we define privatization, the predominant method today is to seek out existing savers, either domestic or foreign, who can purchase state-owned enterprises. Considering that most people live from hand-to-mouth and have very little savings to invest, particularly in high-risk, heavily subsidized state-owned enterprises, the concept of depending on existing savings pools automatically relegates most of the future ownership of these divested enterprises to only those with sufficient savings, i.e. those who already own and control most of today's private sector enterprises.

Furthermore, the very people who most need to be motivated to make these divested enterprises operate profitably—the employees—are viewed as outside contractors. In general, participation by workers, labor unions and citizens generally in the restructuring process and in the intended benefits, is at best an afterthought. Consequently, in many countries where privatization has been launched, there is often tremendous resistance from unions, workers and consumer groups who have learned that privatization may mean that they have to give up something, with little or nothing in exchange.

In response to this resistance to privatization, there has been a groundswell of interest in enabling employees of state-owned enterprises to own a piece of the action. However, these efforts have tended to be both superficial and limited. As advocated by the world's leading investment bankers who have become interested in privatization, "employee ownership" automatically means a 5—15% share for the employees. This "accepted" percentage of employee ownership is usually calculated by the "privatization gurus" based on what they think the employees of these enterprises can afford.

Thus, employee ownership (or broadened ownership generally) in the privatization process has often been promoted by specialists in one of two ways: 1) where the workers are thrown a few ownership crumbs to reduce their political resistance to privatization or to drive a wedge between workers and their labor unions; or 2) through public offerings where the majority of ownership and control will flow to wealthy domestic and foreign investors. We would lump together all these methods as part of the zero-sum approach to privatization, where the past controls the future and where one can gain only at someone else's loss.

The momentum for privatization is part of the pendulum swing away from socialism—which has proven to be unworkable—to something new. This "something new", however, cannot merely be a return to private sector "wage system" solutions with little or no safeguards against exploitation of workers and special privileges for the few. It cannot ask the workers to make concessions and sacrifices, and to work more efficiently, but for someone else's profits.

Privatization in the traditional way, for different reasons than with socialism, also won't work. The greatest obstacle to privatization is that privatization experts have been locked into the "past savings" paradigm.

An alternative paradigm that would make privatization practical involves synergy—creating new capital ownership opportunities for nonowners, without taking away existing wealth from present owners. And in most cases, this means maximizing participatory ownership opportunities for workers and citizens generally. Traditional approaches to privatization, because they are based on zero-sum game concepts and depend on previous savings and wealth, make it impossible to maximize ownership opportunities for ordinary workers.

Furthermore, ownership opportunities mean more than just the acquisition of shares. They also provide for the full empowerment of workers as first-class shareholders of the companies for which they work. Recent studies by the National Center for Employee Ownership (Oakland, California) offer evidence of a correlation between improved corporate performance and corporate cultures which integrate gain-sharing and participatory management with a democratically structured ESOP.

It has become a cliché among privatization professionals that "privatization is primarily a political process." This is certainly true, but the problem is in the paradigm of political economy from which they approach privatization.

To many policymakers, intellectuals, labor leaders, and workers in developing countries, the word "privatization" suggests "monopolistic capitalism" and a return to colonialism. In view of the top-down approaches to privatization that have been fostered by privatization experts and investment bankers around the world, the critics of capitalism are right: workers are unlikely to gain more than token benefits if others own and control their jobs. A new approach is needed, one that transcends traditional socialism and traditional capitalism.

Perhaps the time has come for advocates of economic justice within a free enterprise framework to abandon the word "privatization" in favor of the term "democratization" (a word which has admittedly been misused and abused by those opposed to free enterprise and private property). Words like "democracy" and "justice" are good words, however, and should not be abandoned to be monopolized by the left.

Expanded Ownership as a New Pillar of Economic Policy

Both public and private lending institutions have been prime culprits in fostering state ownership of productive enterprises. In the light of the world debt crisis, however, these financial institutions are beginning to face up to the errors of the past. As the primary U.S. federal agency charged with assisting developing countries in their economic growth strategies, the Agency for International Development is seriously examining the expanded ownership model. In its policy paper on "Private Enterprise Development" (March 1985, page 15), USAID states: "AID encourages the introduction of employee stock ownership plans (ESOPs) as a method of transferring a parastatal to private ownership."

In a cover letter sent on May 6, 1988 which distributed the book *Every Worker an Owner* (Center for Economic and Social Justice, Arlington, Virginia) to all USAID mission directors around the world, Administrator Alan Woods stated: "I'm convinced that whatever we

do to expand the number of people who have a stake in LDC economies will help to bring about sounder policies."

In 1988, two Presidential commissions have reaffirmed these principles. The Presidential Task Force on Project Economic Justice defined expanded ownership as "a new cornerstone for the future of U.S.
economic policy."

President Reagan's Commission on Privatization, which issued
its final report in April 1988, recommended that "employee stock ownership programs should be promoted by the Agency for International
Development as a method of transferring state-owned enterprises to
the private sector in developing countries."

And in January 1988, the Debt Management and Financial Advi-
sory Services Department of the World Bank released a document entitled "Market Based Menu Approach" which included the following:

> Debt conversions in employee stock ownership plans are a
> special case of debt-equity transaction. A U.S. presidential task
> force, headed by former Ambassador William Middendorf,
> proposed to encourage debt-equity swaps to privatize parastatal
> enterprises through the conversion of U.S. bank loans to equity,
> and then selling the equity to workers by means of employee
> stock ownership plans (ESOPs)...

A Case Study: The Alexandria Tire Company Employee Stock Ownership Plan

The Alexandria Tire Company (ATC) project in Egypt, supported
jointly by the Egyptian government and the USAID mission in Cairo,
represents the first practical application in the developing world of
the expanded ownership paradigm and the power of productive credit
as a catalyst for economic democratization. ATC was launched as a
joint effort of the Minister of International Cooperation of the Arab
Republic of Egypt and the Cairo Mission of the United States Agency
for International Development.

General

The project consists of the construction and operation of an all-steel
radial truck tire manufacturing plant at a site at the Ameriya Industrial
Complex near Alexandria, Egypt. The project, which will create 750
new private sector jobs, will be implemented under Egypt's Investment
Law (officially titled "Law No. 43 of 1974, Investment of Arab and Foreign Funds and the Free Zones, as amended by Law No. 32 of 1977").

Project costs, estimated at 370 million Egyptian Pounds (or over
$160 million), will create a facility capable of producing 350,000 heavy-

duty truck and bus tires annually for the domestic Egyptian market, roughly 30% of the total market demand. At present, some 70% is imported (the state-owned manufacturer TRENCO produces 280,000 units) and consumption is about 1 million a year. In addition to tire production, the project will include the manufacturing of carbon black, at an annual capacity of over 15,000 tons. By cutting foreign imports of this key ingredient, the project will generate additional annual savings in Egypt's balance of payments.

Of the project's total capitalization, 56% will be debt financing and 44% will be equity financing.

A new independent corporation will be formed, the Alexandria Tire Company (ATC), whose 56% debt financing (£E 207 million), will come from three hard currency sources:

- The Italian government has allocated a loan of $59 million (£E 136 million), half of which is at an interest rate of 1.5%. The repayment period will be 20 years, including a 10-year grace period.
- Foreign supplier credit will be $10 million (£E 23 million).
- The European Investment Bank will provide $27 million (£E 48 million) in European Currency Units, at 2% lower than prevailing interest rates. The repayment period will be 12 years, including a 4-year grace period.

ATC's founding equity investors (contributing 44% or £E 163 million of total project costs) will include:

	Equity Share
Transport and Engineering Company S.A.E. (TRENCO)	15.00%
Pirelli Tire Company of Italy	10.04%
Egyptian Export Development Bank	7.50%
Banque du Caire	6.50%
Alexandria Bank	6.50%
The National Bank of Egypt	5.96%
The Egyptian Company for Reinsurance	5.00%
New Investor (1991)[1]	4.67%
Misr Bank	3.00%
Industrial Development Bank	2.50%
Alexandria Commercial and Maritime Bank	2.50%
Egyptian Gulf Bank	2.50%
Suez Canal Bank	2.00%
Arab Investment Bank	0.50%
Total	74.17%

In addition, a Worker-Shareholders' Union (WSU)[2] is being formed, with an Employee Share Ownership Plan (ESOP) as its bylaws, to acquire 25.83%,[3] or 421,000 of the founding common shares of the new venture, 252,600 shares to be divided among the 750 newly-hired employees and 168,400 shares among the 3,500 employees of TRENCO, the "mother company" of the new venture.

The new venture will transfer to Egypt three kinds of "state-of-the-art" technology:

- World-class steel-belt radial tire technology backed by technical support by one of the world's leading multinational corporations;
- The Employee Share Ownership Plan (ESOP) to be administered by a Worker-Shareholders' Union, an advance in ESOP corporate finance technology;
- A new reservoir of low-cost capital credit for promoting worker ownership.

The ESOP

The ESOP uses self-liquidating productive credit to enable workers to become shareholders without reducing their savings or paychecks. Besides implementing the first ESOP in the Third World, the project will also launch the world's first Worker-Shareholders' Union (WSU) as a legal vehicle for implementing the ESOP, guaranteeing worker ownership participation and democratizing management accountability. The WSU, originally called an "Employee Shareholders' Association" (ESA) was invented to substitute for a legal trust, the mechanism which is used to implement ESOPs in the United States and the United Kingdom, but which does not exist under Egyptian law.

To finance the acquisition of the 25.83% of founding common shares by employees, the Egyptian Government through its Ministry of International Cooperation (MIC) has approved a loan of £E 42.1 million ($16.5 million) from funds generated by the sale of U.S. commodities under the USAID Commodity Import Program and deposited into an account termed the Special Account. Until the WSU is formed the loan will be made to the National Investment Bank of Egypt (NIB), as temporary borrower and fiduciary for the purchase of shares for the employees, and, after the first 200 employees are hired and the WSU is established, the loan from MIC will be assumed by the WSU along with legal title to these shares.

During the 3-year construction phase and another 3 years needed by the company to become fully operational, there would be a grace period for repaying the ESOP loan. The loan, on Islamic banking terms as explained below, would be repaid over the following 10 years wholly out of projected dividends. No employee payroll deductions would be required. During the 16-year loan period, the workers' shares would be pledged as the sole source of security on the loan. As the loan is repaid over years 7-16, the personal accounts of all participating employees would reflect shares which have been paid for during the current year and allocated among all employees according to the formula contained in the WSU. Terminated employees would have their shares cashed out by the WSU or the company.

Impact on Employees

How will the ESOP affect the average ATC employee? The average Egyptian tire manufacturing employee presently earns about £E 4,000 (about $1,600) annually. Assuming wage levels remain the same at the Alexandria Tire Company and share values do not increase from their original acquisition price, the average ATC worker (according to the feasibility study for the project) will accumulate through the ESOP over £E 33,000 worth of shares, more than 8 times his annual wages; in addition, by the eighth year after operations begin, the average ATC worker will receive a second income from dividends of £E 3,300, over and above the dividends used to repay the ESOP debt or set aside for repurchasing his share rights upon retirement. After the ESOP loan is repaid, the average worker's capital income will amount to about £E 11,800 per year. And through the voting of his shares in the ATC Worker-Shareholders' Union, he will have a voice in selecting 30% of the ATC board members and in other matters subject to shareholder voting.

TRENCO

ATC is the child of TRENCO, which was founded in 1946 as a general engineering company. In 1956, TRENCO began the manufacturing of tires and is today the only tire manufacturing facility in Egypt. While this 3,500 employee company is 100% owned by the Government of Egypt, TRENCO is one of the few profitable state-owned enterprises, a tribute to its superior management team. It currently produces 1.1 million tires per year, of which 280,000 are truck tires. In 1984, TRENCO entered into a licensing agreement with Dunlop Tires to produce automotive radial tires. It is now producing 150,000 automotive radials a year, but none are steel-belted radials. TRENCO will provide the plant site, the engineering and other technical inputs to construct the facilities and infrastructure, and approximately 26,500 tons of raw materials per year.

Pirelli Tire

Pirelli will supply the steel-belt radial technology needed by ATC. Pirelli was founded in 1923 and has a worldwide network of tire producing and distributing facilities, either wholly-owned or in joint ventures. The company produces tires for all automotive markets and possesses patents on special manufacturing technology for several tire production processes. The steel-belted truck tire production process for the type and size needed by Egypt is one such patent. Pirelli has entered into 37 joint ventures and has granted 51 licenses to manufacture its products. Thus, Pirelli has a proven track record of productivity and worldwide operational experience. Pirelli will provide all machines, moulding equipment, moulds and engineering to plan and install the equipment. Under a 10-year technical assistance agreement, Pirelli will train engineers and technicians and assist in the production process.

Financial Feasibility

Egypt's current demand for truck and bus tires is 1.0 million per year. From 1975 to 1985, demand grew by 20% per year and is projected to grow at approximately 8% during the decade 1985 to 1995. Approximately 40% of the demand is supplied by domestic production. TRENCO is the only domestic producer, but does not produce steel-belted radial truck tires.

Expected Outcomes

The project is expected to begin production of tires by the end of project year three.[4] By the end of project year five, ATC is expected to reach design capacity, 350,000 truck and bus tires per year. During this time, 750 new jobs with a payroll of £E 4 million will have been created in the private sector. ATC is projected to capture over 30% of the current and future domestic truck and bus tire market, producing net earnings of £E 31.1 million on net sales of £E 198.6 million by the year 1994. Overall internal rate of return for the project, from inception to 2006, is expected to be 17.7%.

Other macroeconomic effects of the project will include:

- Foreign exchange savings resulting from domestic tire production of $20-25 million annually, plus an additional savings of $10 million annually from domestic production of carbon black;
- Loss of Egyptian customs revenue on imported tires averaging $20 million annually, which would be largely offset by £E 30 million annually in corporate taxes by the year 2003, plus dividend and salary taxes;
- Dividends of £E 30 million annually, 90% to Egyptians, within 6 years from start-up;
- A model of a "new labor deal" for Egyptian workers, which

would be structured to restrain inflationary increases in fixed labor costs while enabling workers to increase their incomes significantly from productivity gains and profits;

- Structural reforms to encourage innovative corporate strategies which would provide Egypt with long-term competitive advantages in the global marketplace.

Special Credit Incentives for Leveraged ESOPs

Normally, in its worldwide private sector development strategies, USAID requires the use of an unsubsidized, market-related interest rate and a reasonable degree of assurance that the loan pool can be restored by loan repayments and made available for future private sector loans. The ATC ESOP project represents a breakthrough, both in its insistence on the democratization of access to productive credit and in its innovative use of Islamic banking practices for reducing the cost of such credit to workers and for increasing the likelihood of restoring the principal to the loan pool for future ESOP loans.

A major constraint that USAID has had to face in setting its interest rate policy is Egypt's inflation, which runs at an estimated annual rate of 20%-25% or higher and shows no signs of slowing down. An AID economist ran several scenarios to calculate the inflation-adjusted purchasing power of repayments of the £E 42.1 million ATC ESOP loan with different interest and inflation rates. These scenarios demonstrated that an interest rate of 7%-13% would recover only about 1/4 to 1/2 of the purchasing power of the loan.

Equity Expansion International's Egyptian legal advisor to this project, Mahmoud Fahmy, advised USAID that according to the Egyptian civil code (Article 227) a non-banking entity, such as MIC, is legally prohibited from charging an interest rate which exceeds 7%. With an interest rate of 7% and a 20%-25% inflation rate, only 23%-33% of the purchasing power of the loan would be recovered. On the other hand, Counsellor Fahmy stated that if ATC's obligation to repay MIC is stated as an absolute obligation to return the inflation-adjusted loan capital, without expressing it as a profit- and risk-sharing arrangement, such an arrangement would not be legal under Egyptian law since the inflation adjustment would be legally regarded as "disguised interest."

To avoid the conflict between Egyptian law and USAID's policy objectives of promoting unsubsidized interest rates and preserving the purchasing power of the ESOP loans, AID and the Egyptian government adopted an innovative credit policy based on the Islamic concept of "profit-sharing and risk-sharing". Under the proposed profit-sharing approach, in lieu of interest and principal payments, MIC will receive 50% of the ESOP dividends, which amount to 15.25% of ATC's total distributed profits over a 10-year period following the construction and start-up phase (project years 7-16). Based on the feasibility study performed by Pirelli and TRENCO, a 50% MIC participation in the ESOP's share of dividends for that 10-year period is projected to recover 116% of the purchasing power of the loan (the extra 16% being regarded as MIC's administrative fees and risk premium). It is expected that MIC's profits would also increase along with rising price levels and inflation-adjusted prices of truck tires, thus protecting the lender's capital.

The profit-sharing arrangement is conceptually compatible with the idea of employee ownership. The employees will be able to acquire ownership and pay back the loan only if the company is profitable. Thus, employee ownership as well as full recovery of the loan will depend on the performance of the employees and of the company. If there are no profits, the employees get nothing, owe nothing, and the shares reserved for them would be sold to the private sector at large. Since the employees have no attachable assets, in the absence of corporate profits it would be a practical impossibility to turn to the employees for repayment of the loan. And, like the borrower, the lender (for a predetermined period) is linked directly to the productivity and profits of the company. The profit-sharing formula thus appears to be an ideal solution which satisfies the concerns of USAID, MIC as the lender, ATC investors and management, the union likely to represent ATC workers, and the future employees.

USAID approved this new self-liquidating credit arrangement on April 4, 1989.

Reaction in Egypt to the ESOP innovations at the Alexandria Tire Company appears to be highly favorable, and even enthusiastic. As a result of the ATC model, the Egyptian Higher Policies Committee and the Committee for Economic Affairs has approved an additional £E200 million of funding from USAID's Special Account to initiate the stock sales of qualified government enterprises to their employees through ESOP financing. Already about a dozen government-owned companies are under consideration for these ESOP buyout loans.

The Egyptian press has also reacted favorably to the ATC model. A slew of articles have appeared, including a full-page piece on ESOP in the leading Egyptian paper Al Ahram (March 23, 1989, p. 9), and a 5-part series on ESOP by American University of Cairo's Professor of Management Dr. Khaled Sherif in the prestigious Al Ahram Economist weekly.

An article in *Al-Gomhouria* entitled "Word of Love" (Jan. 23, 1989) comments:

> USAID offered a present to the workers of Egypt. They offered £E 80 million...to be kept at a Special Account where workers will be able to attain loans that would enable them

to buy shares in their plants . . . Repayments will go back into the Account to provide additional loans to other workers and not to be returned to the U.S.

. . . The idea is new for us, but will convert the workers into owners and not employees of the new plant—shareholders, not bystanders. The worker's heart and soul will be directed to the success of the project. The feeling is that the worker, because of the ownership in the project, will be more loyal to the company and its success. In addition, the worker will receive incentives and dividends from the shares he owns.

Conclusion

Some advocates of privatization believe that who owns and enjoys the rights and powers that flow from private property is unimportant. This attitude, in our opinion, ignores the relationship between property and the empowerment of those who own and control modern instruments of production. It reflects the "fatal omission" in traditional approaches to economic development which has engendered the politics of nationalization in the first place. And it leads inevitably to concentrated control over production and basic economic decisions, and to the very opposite of effective economic policy for a democratic society.

We would argue that sharing ownership and control of modern productive property is a matter of justice and a fundamental human right, and that the democratization of private-sector capital ownership should be a basic pillar for the future of any nation's economy.

If greater efficiency is the goal of privatization, the question should be raised: Can a society have economic efficiency without economic justice? Without justice there can be no harmony in the workplace or in the economy. And social and economic justice is impossible without a system of decentralized participation, accountability and economic power. Since power and accountability follow control over productive property, and the ownership of productive enterprises is largely determined by who has access to capital credit, the key to genuine democratization of society lies in decentralized access to future productive credit among workers and consumers, as directly and personally as possible.

Good practice follows sound ideas, and successful privatizations will involve a delicate balancing of principles of efficiency with maximizing ownership opportunities for today's disenfranchised workers and citizens. This process will necessarily evolve gradually, as policymakers, corporate executives, labor leaders, and institutional lenders lift their minds above the zero-sum paradigm to a more synergistic framework designed to make every citizen an owner.

Notes:

[1]In 1991 additional equity investment was added in the amount of £E 24, 982,000, providing an additional 4.67% share of equity participation.

[2]The law authorizing the formation of a Worker-Shareholders' Union (WSU) was approved by the Egyptian National Assembly on June 22, 1992 as Chapter VIII of the Capital Markets Law (Law No. 95 of 1992. When ATC was first formed this entity was called an "Employee Shareholders' Association." After approval from the Capital Market Authority of Egypt, this entity will receive shares acquired on behalf of the ATC workers by the National Investment Bank of Egypt.

[3]The original equity acquired for workers gave them a 30.5% share which was reduced to a 25.83% share when new equity was raised, as described in note 1. This dilution resulted from the fact that the loan available to workers could not be increased beyond the original £E 42.1 million.

[4]According to Fathy El-Feky, Chairman of ATC, building construction began in June 1992 and completion is expected by November 1993. Actual full-time operation is expected to begin in June 1994.

— 12 —

The Abraham Federation: A New Framework for Peace in the Middle East

by Norman G. Kurland
© *1991 by Middle East Policy Council. Reprinted with permission from*
***American-Arab Affairs**, Spring 1991, Number 36.*

Author's Comment: This article was written before the Washington Peace Accord in September, 1993, signified by the historic handshake between Yitzhak Rabin, Prime Minister of Israel, and Yasser Arafat, Chairman of the Palestine Liberation Organization. While the author sincerely hopes that this will lead to peace, he predicts that the peace negotiations will not work, for reasons described in this article. Hence, this article remains as timely as ever, and should be kept ready for implementation when all else fails.

Introduction

Now that Iraq has been forced out of Kuwait and the Persian Gulf War is "over," few would dispute the need for a regional peace strategy for the Middle East. Certainly, as Saddam Hussein's supporters throughout the Arab World made clear, no such strategy would be complete without a settlement of the Palestinian-Israeli dispute.

For all the military brilliance, technological superiority, and moral weight behind the victory of the U.S. and coalition forces, we seem no closer to solving this conundrum. How can "self-determination" and justice be achieved for both Palestinian Arabs and Jews wanting to occupy the same land? How can this be done without Israel's jeopardizing its own security during the transition toward a comprehensive peace settlement?

There is a way. The answer lies in rejecting the traditional "collectivist" form of nation-state and in abandoning the feudalistic "wage system" economic policies of all existing nations. It would be based on a radically new process of nation-building, grounded upon the inherent sovereignty of every individual and the sanctity of the family unit, in which "ownership-sharing" economics would surpass politics in the daily lives of its citizens.

Finding Common Ground

Is it conceivable to create a new country in the Middle East which accommodates Arabs and Israelis? Could a new state be structured to avoid becoming either a Palestinian state or an extension of Israel or any bordering Arab state? Could such a state offer a new form of sovereignty to stir the hearts and dreams of Arabs and Jews in new ways? Could it avoid, on the one hand, the anarchy and violence of Lebanon, and, on the other, the totalitarian regimes and genocidal societies from which Jews escaped to what is now Israel?

In short, could a new country be created that could guarantee peace and justice for all?

The idea for a new country may first seem far-fetched. But with a reexamination of the conflict, it becomes surprisingly workable. And with the added boost of a new economic base—namely, ownership sharing linked to creating new resources rather than quarreling over existing ones—the idea of a new nation becomes downright irresistible.

Let's look at the problem.

The present Arab-Israeli dispute over land—particularly the major impasse over the West Bank occupied by Israeli forces since June 1967—is a classic illustration of a "zero-sum" game. In a zero-sum game, one side can gain only at the other's expense. In other words, a win-or-lose situation.

The two sides have fought over this land for centuries. The land is holy to three major religions. It is the symbolic crossroads of the world community as it is strategically set between the East and the West, as well as the North and the South. Everyone, therefore, has a stake in a peaceful and just resolution of the dispute—not just Arabs and Israelis.

Two important points must be faced before we consider the creation of a new nation. First, present hostilities must not be ignored. This should be obvious. But any new approach would rest on political quicksand unless it recognized existing hatreds and fears of Jews and Arabs, as well as their legitimate hopes and aspirations. To overcome these hostilities to the point where Arabs and Jews can work out their differences, we must look to the past for a common bond.

The Point of Reunification: Abraham

Arabs and Jews have a point of unity both can understand: Abraham, the Old Testament patriarch.

All Arabs trace their ancestry to Abraham through Ishmael, whom he fathered through his wife's servant Hagar. All Jews trace their blood roots to Abraham through his son Isaac and grandson Jacob, who, according to the Bible, God later renamed Israel. The name "Abraham" literally means "father of many nations." Having once separated the descendents of Ishmael from the children of Israel, Abraham, 3,700 years later, could fulfil the biblical prophecy not only of their unification but of the eventual unification and harmony of all nations and peoples.

Symbols of the past often serve as useful symbols for charting new futures. A new federation of the spiritual and blood descendents of Abraham could offer a radically new political framework for taking small steps in a new direction. Thus, rather appropriately, the new nation could be named the "Abraham Federation."

With this philosophical common thread, the question is: Where do we start? The answer is: In the historic region of Judea and Samaria—the West Bank—where Arab and Jewish settlements exist today under Israeli military control.

Although the legitimacy of all Israeli territory would be disputed by some Arabs, the Israeli military has the power to maintain law and order over all areas it now patrols. Despite the intifada and mounting international pressures on Israel, this reality is unlikely to change in the foreseeable future, although easy diffusion of modern military technology among Arab guerrillas and their allies make a military status quo uneasy at best.

The main obstacle to peace, in this author's view, is not the Israeli military or the deep-seated Holocaust fears which justify in the minds of many Jews the continued Israeli military presence. Rather, the deeper issue is whether a more just society can be conceived and created, which will eventually allow the Israeli military presence to "wither away," at least in the occupied territories.

Some occupied territory under Israeli control, is now open to negotiation for a new status—at least as a foothold for a more comprehensive solution later.

The biblical region of Judea and Samaria—the West Bank—could provide that foothold. It includes Bethlehem, Hebron and all the surrounding mountain region west of the Jordan River. It also encompasses Jerusalem, which deserves special handling, perhaps serving in the transition period as the capital of the new nation-state as well as present Israel.

The new beginning would go beyond the demeaning "autonomy" proposals of the Israeli Likud Party. It would be less threatening to

Jewish settlers than the Labor Party's "land-for-peace" proposals. And it would offer a radically more just future for all Palestinians than what they are now demanding.

If a new beginning can be made in Judea and Samaria, plus perhaps the Gaza strip, a more comprehensive regional approach could later be negotiated, based on the new Abraham Federation model.

The New Nation's Unique Economy

As a testing ground for a new nation, today's West Bank would be transformed into a "win-win" situation. Rejecting artificial and unproven assumptions of scarcity, the West Bank residents would work together to create new resources which could be shared more equitably. The primary focus would be on the "open frontier" being created by modern science and technology.

Land, of course, is finite. But as the philosopher-scientist R. Buckminster Fuller has pointed out, creative energy can be channeled into what he calls "ephemeralization," the process of doing-more-with-less. This entails continuing re-design of existing technologies, structures, and social "tools."

By introducing the world's most sophisticated technologies (particularly in energy and food production) and redesigning methods of participatory ownership, Arab and Jewish settlers could transcend their competing exclusive claims to the "Holy Land." They could complement each other's existing strength's and potentials: Jewish settlement experience and advanced energy and agricultural technologies, Arab financing, and Palestinian self-assertion and drive.

Neither Capitalism Nor Socialism

Guidelines for constructing this model for peace in the Middle East involve a radical departure from traditional industrial development. Neither capitalism nor socialism is adequate for building a successful economy for the Abraham Federation. Neither combines maximum justice with maximum efficiency. Both ignore the need for building economic sovereignty into each citizen. Both leave ownership and control of modern technology, natural resources and business enterprises to a ruling few.

To avoid these dangers, the Abraham Federation would neither own property nor permit future monopolies over the ownership of the means of production. This principle alone would make "sovereignty' in the Abraham Federation uniquely distinct from any nation in history.

The Abraham Federation would recognize that sovereignty connotes power and power can only be exercised by human beings, not by a "collective." The major issue to be addressed in a democratic world is which people will exercise what kinds of power, either directly or by delegation.

Escape from the "Wage System"

In a society where all power is supposed to rest with the people, economic sovereignty must start at the individual and family level. Since power follows property, property must be spread broadly. The best antidote to concentrated power and monopolies is to empower all citizens through decentralized ownership of all of society's enterprises. Only then can those who run government and other social institutions be held accountable to the people. Such a society would be comprised of highly autonomous, interdependent people, capable of associating with other "sovereign" individuals for their mutual interests. Genuine economic democratization is thus the ultimate check on the potential abuse of state power, and of the majority against highly vulnerable minority groups and individuals.

What is common to all of today's economies is that the average worker and his family have little or no chance to escape from the feudalistic "wage system." The worker is powerless and defenseless against advancing technology and those who control his jobs and income levels.

The Abraham Federation would offer an economic system structured to give each citizen a status beyond that of a wage earner. In a national ownership sharing program, citizens would own something more than raw land. They would accumulate and receive property incomes from direct ownership in new technologies, agribusinesses, and industries. Moreover, by the systematic spreading and sharing of ownership power, one of the basic conditions for any future Holocausts—large numbers of alienated workers—would gradually disappear.

The Vehicle: A National Ownership Strategy

Why should a national ownership sharing strategy capture the attention of those now residing in Judea and Samaria? The answer lies in the fact that the universal right to own property (Article 17 of the Universal Declaration of Human Rights) is frustrated systematically by every nation today. This is especially the case within modern industrial societies where fewer than 1 percent of their citizens directly own and control most of the industrial capital.

The key to economic justice is widespread individual access to technologically advanced agricultural, industrial, and commercial enterprises and the means to finance them. Fortunately, precedents are now well established for creating new enterprises, with skilled management and advanced technologies, whose ownership is shared by all employees.

In the United States, over 10,000 companies with a total of over 11 million employees have adopted employee stock ownership plans or "ESOPs." Most of these have been adopted since 1972. Employees with no savings or credit have used an ESOP to become owners of their companies—in some cases with up to 100 percent of equity participation.

The credit privileges and special tax advantages which the U.S. government has given to workers who adopt ESOPs, allow workers without savings to purchase shares on credit wholly secured by the future profits of the company. Because employees are directly linked to productivity increases and profits through their ownership rights, studies indicate that firms financed through ESOPs, when combined with participatory management and gain sharing, generally perform better than their competitors.

Twenty laws have already been passed by the U.S. Congress to encourage the expanded use of ESOPs, including the reorganization of the Northeast rail system, pension reform, tax reform, trade policy, foreign economic development policy, as well as other measures designed to greatly accelerate the adoption of ESOPs by major U.S. corporations. Other variations of the expanded capital ownership concepts being developed would build individual equity stakes in capital-intensive industries into the general population. These include consumer stock ownership plans (CSOPs) and community investment corporations (CICs) for resident share ownership of new communities and land renewal projects.

The ESOP is no longer a mystery in the Middle East. In 1989, the $160 million Alexandria Tire Company was launched in Egypt, creating the Middle East's largest radial truck tire plant, in a joint venture with Pirelli Tire of Italy and other investors. Thanks to USAID, 750 worker-shareholders will benefit from this transaction, "earning" their ownership stakes through the most advanced ESOP in the developing world.

Other significant developments indicating a growing worldwide interest in the expanded capital ownership approach, include:

- Endorsement by President Reagan in 1987 of the work of the Presidential Task Force on Project Economic Justice. This Congressionally-mandated task force issued a report, *High Road to Economic Justice*, which offered a bold strategy of expanded capital ownership for economic revitalization in Central America and the Caribbean.
- The translation and publication into Polish in 1989 of *Every Worker An Owner* [published by the Center for Economic

and Social Justice, Arlington, VA], a compendium of writings by leading thinkers in the expanded capital ownership area. 15,000 copies of this Polish translation were distributed throughout Solidarity channels in Poland.

- USAID Administrator Alan Woods' transmittal in May 1988 of this compilation of writings to every USAID mission in the world;
- The development of a "parallel legal system" for Costa Rica to foster system-wide experimentation based on economic democratization;
- ESOPs in the Soviet Union (now the Commonwealth of Independent States); 100% ESOPs in such corporate giants as AVIS and Weirton Steel; China's interest in ESOP; and U.S. aid supporting ESOPs in Poland and Hungary.

The Abraham Federation would have the historic opportunity to become the first nation to be launched with a comprehensive and workable program to provide its citizens the means to share ownership of all its resources.

Highlights of the Abraham Federation

Here are some suggestions for initiating the Abraham Federation:

- First steps should start small, focusing on a relatively small territory over which no existing nation-state has yet declared its sovereignty, namely ancient Judea and Samaria, and possibly the Gaza strip. If it works, the beachhead, with its capital in the Old City of Jerusalem, will expand naturally.
- A revolutionary advance over all existing nation-states would be formed. The new nation would reject collectivist and exclusionary concepts of nationalism and would carry the concept of sovereignty or "self-determination" down to the personal and family level, an ideal implicit in Judaism, Christianity, and Islam.
- It would aim at bringing a higher order of justice than any nation has ever offered its citizens. It would offer acceptable safeguards to Israeli demands for security and guarantee the right of all Jews and Palestinians to visit and settle in "the holy land." It would offer Palestinians "self-determination" and the "democratic secular state" they are seeking. It would be neither a collectivist Zionist state nor a collectivist Palestinian state, but a new form of nation that both groups could build together.

- Politically, it would be a Jeffersonian form of democracy, open to all, with clearly defined and limited functions given to government and all political institutions. In addition to normal democratic checks and balances on the "minimalist" government of the new nation, the major check on future concentrations of power would be outside of government, based on policies that would systematically spread economic power and free enterprise ownership broadly, right down to the individual level.

- The widespread diffusion of property would become the ultimate constitutional safeguard for human rights. Although the new nation would have no "official" state religion, by systematically spreading property and economic power among its citizens, it would insure that freedom of religion, of association, of the press and other fundamental protections of the individuals vis-à-vis the government would be built upon a solid economic foundation.

- Thus the new nation would be built on a foundation of personal (as opposed to collective) political sovereignty, and that foundation would in turn rest on personal economic sovereignty. It would be sovereignty built from the ground up, rather than from the top down. Individual, family, and minority rights would thus be protected from the potential abuses of political majorities or traditional power elites. In this way, religious freedom and cultural pluralism would have stronger economic supports than in such places as war-torn Lebanon.

- During the transition to full self-determination, the Abraham Federation would have bonds to Israel and its Arab neighbors. Primary governmental functions would be shared among all citizens of the Abraham Federation—Arabs, Jews, Christians, and nonbelievers.

- The initial thrust of the new nation would be economic, not political: It would strive to absorb the creative energies of Arabs, Jews, displaced Palestinians, Christians, and others moving to this new nation, and channel them into building a technologically advanced and more just form of free enterprise economy than exists in all other nations.

- The new economy would transcend the collectivist and feudalistic "wage systems" of existing nations by offering an "ownership sharing" system in which all persons could work, accumulate industrial forms of property, and participate as individual co-owners of the new enterprises to be developed upon the land. Free and open markets and respect for private property in the means of production would be basic pillars for further limiting the power of the state. Instead of redistributing existing property, the new role of the state would be to help create new property and new owners at the same time.

- To foster maximum growth opportunities for the citizens of the Abraham Federation, other countries in the Middle East, including Israel, and other major industrial nations such as the U.S. and the U.S.S.R., would treat the Abraham Federation as a global democratic free market zone. Such a special international barrier-free trade status would allow all goods and services produced in the Abraham Federation to be sold in these cooperating countries without duties, quotas, or other trade restrictions. This would attract new technologies and accelerate new investment and job opportunities which could be broadly shared.

- Instead of continuing historic and legalistic disputes over something as finite as "holy land," the primary focus would be on building ever-expanding "new frontiers" upon the land, based on new technologies and new enterprises that could provide the pioneers of the new nation with the economic basis for realizing personal "self-determination" for every one of its citizens.

- The "tools" and fundamental principles for building such a model nation already exist and have been tested. They work. (The Ministry of Planning of Costa Rica is now considering a "parallel legal system" structured along these lines.)

- Start-up industries might include advanced energy projects and integrated, high technology agribusinesses broadly owned by workers and farmers.

- As a compromise to legitimate Israeli fears for their security and freedom to settle in the Holy Land, the Israeli military would be allowed to continue to patrol the Abraham Federation for a reasonable period until the new nation creates stable conditions to remove the need for Israeli military presence.

- As revolutionary as this new framework may appear to some, it is based on virtually universal moral principles. The process of change, however, is inescapably evolutionary and depends largely on conservative, case-tested methods and "tools."

- Because it is grounded on common and traditional principles of economic justice, religious Jews and Muslims, including several PLO representatives, have reacted in an open-minded way to the Abraham Federation concept when it has been explained to them.

- The next step forward is to test whether this new frame-work might serve as a basis of a new dialogue between those with power to speak for all Israelis and those with power to speak for all Palestinians. This framework too may be in-adequate and prove to be unworkable. But it is new and certainly deserves to be more fully understood by all key decision-makers concerned with peace in the Middle East.
- Many nations are offering their "solutions" to end Israeli occupation of the West Bank. None of these initiatives seem to be satisfactory to both sides of the conflict. In that light, the Abraham Federation concept might well offer a new framework for those directly affected to recapture the ini-tiative, not merely for their own survival, but for leading all mankind to a more just and peaceful future.

Conclusion: Transition to the New Nation

No rational dialogue and no genuine steps toward peace among Arabs and Jews in the Middle East is possible within traditional con-ceptual and ideological frameworks. Competing interest groups offer competing frameworks, all of which suffer from faulty assumptions, semantic ambiguities, and poorly defined, often contradictory, objec-tives. A new and more realistic framework is demanded, one which can lead to small steps toward a broader, more comprehensive, and more just solution than is even conceivable under the old frameworks.

There would be many problems in moving from the initial blue-print stage to implementation, especially regarding security and con-trol over the Israeli military, immigration, and land-use matters. But within a less threatening framework, even these problems could be addressed for the mutual self-interest of all citizens of the Abraham Federation.

Just as the offer of 160 acres of land to its propertyless pioneers sparked America's development as an agricultural power, the indus-trial equivalent of that ownership incentive can now be offered to the propertyless Arabs, Jews, and others living in Jerusalem and other places in the Abraham Federation. Truth, justice, and peace can again go forth from Jerusalem.

Building a just and pluralistic new nation is, of course, a complex undertaking. But by focusing on the limitless possibilities of indus-trial growth, rather than on endless confrontation over scarce land resources, Arab and Jewish settlers of the Abraham Federation can take a new look at their common problem. Under the mantle of Abraham, they can step back into the past in order to leap forward into a more just and hopeful future.

— 13 —

The Third Way: America's True Legacy to the New Republics

*by Norman G. Kurland
and
Michael D. Greaney*
(Reprinted from **Social Justice Review**, *November/December 1992,
translated into Russian by the Gorbachev Foundation and
printed in* **Svobodnaya Misl**, *Moscow)*

With the failure of socialism, many western academicians and investment bankers have rushed headlong into the new republics of the former Soviet Union to fill an economic and ideological vacuum with traditional capitalist solutions: more foreign investment, a Wall Street-style stock market, and numerous tax breaks and special privileges to mirror the labyrinthine U.S. tax system.

But the West can surely do better than to sell its own recession-ridden, class-divided model, complete with grossly concentrated ownership of corporate equity, over-dependence on foreign investment to fuel the economy, increasing marginalization of the labor force, and institutionalized gambling on a national stock exchange.

Before their future is decided for them, people in the new republics should ask whether the prescriptions being touted will really build a better society for every citizen. Or will the "Western capitalist model," once again, merely empower a small elite? Is capitalism the *only* logical alternative for building the economy of the Commonwealth of Independent States? Is it possible to conceive of a free enterprise alternative to the wage/welfare systems of capitalism and socialism, one consistent with the vision of America's founding fathers—a truly revolutionary "Third Way"?

Looking Beyond Socialism and Capitalism

Both socialism and capitalism concentrate economic power at the top. It makes little difference that under capitalism the concentration is in private hands and under socialism the concentration is in the hands of the State. Both systems are excessively materialistic in their basic principles and overall vision. Both, in their own ways, degrade the individual worker. Both bring forth economic systems which ignore and hinder intellectual and spiritual development.

Amalgams of the two systems, as in America's so-called "mixed economy" or the Scandinavian Welfare State model, differ only in their degree of social injustice, corruption, economic inefficiency, human insecurity and alienation which permeate each level of class-divided societies. What then would be the true "Third Way" for moving toward a freer, more just and economically classless society?

What the Third Way is Not

Most of the schemes being sold by Western experts do not approach the problem of transforming socialist, State-controlled economies from the logical framework of a Third Way, but keep repeating the mistakes of the past. One such proposal is geared towards pumping billions in foreign money each year into the economy, promoting a public-sector wage system that would ensure every worker a wage packet in return for his labor.

Another plan, coming out of Liberal American Academia, advocates a capitalist brand of State socialism, where confiscatory progressive income taxes would "rob from the rich and give to the poor," thus ensuring a handout for every citizen on the dole, regardless of his efforts or the demands of justice.

The Fatal Omission

Each of these approaches commits a fatal error. The first implicitly limits the ownership of productive assets to a tiny elite. Such a plan ensures that most workers will receive income only from selling their labor, in direct competition with advancing technology and an expanding global work force. This ultimately reduces the worker to an input of production. He can then be purchased cheaply and forced into unemployment if owners decide to relocate where labor rates are lower, or to replace people with machines. This approach also makes the recipient country dependent upon regular infusions of foreign capital to keep the economy going.

Historically, capitalism and socialism violate the rights that owners of productive property have in the fruits of production. Any excess is taken from owners and productive workers and redistributed among nonproductive nonowners. This leaves more economic power in the hands of the State than is healthy for achieving genuine social and economic justice for all.

Ownership Without the Full Rights of Private Property— Socialism With a Different Face

Other schemes also have severe flaws. One seemingly attractive approach, the Scandinavian Plan (erroneously billed as the "Third Way"), relies on forcing companies to issue shares to a *collective* ownership trust set up in the name of the workers. Workers are insulated from direct shareholder rights and are paid retirement or disability wages out of the earnings of the trust. No worker has any access to the power or profits associated with property rights in any of the company shares held by the trust. Payments are determined by labor leaders and company managers who control the shares as trustees for the workers. This perpetuates the dependency of workers on their leaders and invites new forms of corruption.

The Yugoslavian self-management model also falls short of embodying the Third Way. The workers have more say over their workplaces and jobs and have some input into decisions. However, this is joint management, not joint ownership. All ownership is in the hands of the State or in some other form of politicized ownership. The self-management model sometimes deteriorates into "management by committee," a lack of checks and balances in corporate governance, and an inability to make long term investment and operational decisions for meeting global competition.

The Basic Weakness of Any Wage System

What all of these approaches have in common is a reliance on the wage system. Whether the economy is capitalist, socialist, a variety of the welfare State, or some combination thereof, they all depend on the worker receiving his sole income and support in the form of wages for the only thing he has to sell: his labor.

No plan or proposal based on a wage system can truly call itself the Third Way. Whether the bosses are politicians or paid hirelings of a small ownership elite, the worker ends up being a wage-serf. Even a labor union, when it confines itself to obtaining higher wages and greater fixed benefits, does nothing to empower the worker or gain him real liberty and justice. The worker may be well paid, but in the end he is simply a slave who gets more than the other slaves.

What the Third Way Is

Higher wages are not the focus of the real Third Way. The Third Way is a systematic approach, balancing the demands of participative and distributive justice by lifting institutional barriers which have historically separated owners from nonowners.[1] This involves removing the roadblocks preventing people from participating fully in the economic process as both workers and owners. More people can then begin earning incomes from both labor and capital.

The emphasis of the Third Way is not on redistribution of income, but on providing people with social means and a legal system which will encourage them to create their own new wealth and share in profits broadly and equitably.

A major flaw in most wage systems is that wages are obtained through government intervention or collective bargaining pressures rather than by the free choice of people within a system of equal ownership opportunities. If owners are better bargainers, wages are low. If workers can out-argue owners or force them to implement minimum wages supported by the State, wages are high. Neither side considers, except peripherally, real productivity and value of the activity. And since capital is more mobile than labor in the global marketplace—being able to relocate to take advantage of lower wages in other areas—wage system workers remain at a permanent disadvantage.

Four Pillars for Building an Economically Just Society

All wage systems ignore one or more of what can be called the "Four Pillars," the essential principles for building a more just economy. During this dangerous transition period of the Commonwealth of Independent States, leaving out any one of these pillars weakens the entire fabric of the economy and leads to eventual collapse. The four pillars of the Third Way are:

- Limited Economic Power for the State
- The Restoration of Free And Open Markets
- The Restoration of Private Property
- Expanded Ownership of Productive Assets

Limited Economic Power of the State

Limiting the economic power of the State ultimately involves the goal of shifting ownership and control over production and income distribution from the State to the people. To do this, the economic power of the State should be specifically limited to:

- Encouraging growth and policing abuses within the private sector;
- Ending economic monopolies and special privileges;
- Lifting barriers to equal ownership opportunities, especially access to productive or capital credit;

- Protecting property, enforcing contracts and settling disputes;
- Preventing inflation and providing a stable currency;
- Promoting democratic unions to bargain over worker and ownership rights;
- Protecting the environment; and
- Providing social safety nets for human emergencies.

Within these limits the State would promote economic justice for all citizens. Coincident with this objective would be the goal of reducing human conflict and waste and increasing economic efficiency and creation of new wealth. This would increase total revenues for legitimate public sector purposes, reducing the need for income redistribution through confiscatory income taxes and social welfare payments.

Free and Open Markets

Artificial determinations of prices, wages and profits lead to inefficiencies in the uses of resources and scarcity for all but those who control the system. Those in power either have too little information or wisdom to know what is right, or will set wages and prices to suit their own advantage. Just prices, wages, and profits are best set in a free, open and democratic marketplace, where consumer sovereignty reigns. Assuming economic democratization in the future ownership of the means of production, everyone's economic choices or "votes" on prices and wages influence the setting of economic values in the marketplace.

Establishing a free and open market would be accomplished by gradually eliminating all special privileges and monopolies created by the State, reducing all subsidies except for the most needy members of society, lifting barriers to free trade and free labor, ending all non-voluntary, artificial methods of determining prices, wages and profits. This would result in *decentralizing economic choice* and *empowering each person* as a consumer, a worker and an owner.

Private Property

Owners' rights in private property are fundamental to any just economic order. Property secures personal choice, and is the key safeguard of all other human rights. By destroying private property, justice is denied. Private property is the individual's link to the economic process in the same way that the secret ballot is his link to the political process. When either is absent, the individual is disconnected or "alienated" from the process.

Restoring the idea as well as the fact of private property would involve the reform of laws which prohibit or inhibit acquisition and possession of private property. This would include ensuring that all owners, including shareholders, are vested with their full rights to participate in control of their productive property, to hold management accountable through shareholder representatives on the corporate board of directors, and to receive profits commensurate with their ownership stakes. Private property links income distribution to economic participation—not only by owners of existing assets, but also by new owners of future wealth.

The Moral Omission:
Indifference to Concentrated Capital Ownership

One of the most crucial problems that Marx addressed in his economic theories was that ownership of productive assets—"capital"—was limited to the very few. Unfortunately, Marx's solution was to concentrate wealth and power even more by mandating State ownership of all productive assets. This resulted in enormous concentrations of wealth and power in the hands of a new elite. The real problem, however, is not ownership of productive property, but *concentration* of ownership.

The Democratization of Productive Credit:
A New Right of Citizenship

The primary social means to bring about expanded ownership of productive assets involves the *democratization of productive, self-liquidating credit*, which, like the secret ballot in politics, is a uniquely "social good."

Anyone familiar with the overly consumption-oriented economy of the West knows that it is far easier for the average citizen to obtain credit for *nonproductive* purposes than to acquire productive property. Many of the Third World debtor nations have fallen into the same trap, incurring huge burdens of debt and spending the loan proceeds on projects that do not generate revenue to repay the loans. Consumer credit and other nonproductive forms of credit entrap workers and nations into dependency on those who own and control capital.

One way to unshackle workers from the slavery of the worker-for-hire system is to redirect society's uses of credit from nonproductive and consumer purchases to acquisition of ownership shares in productive enterprises. Productive capital assets, under professional management, are expected to pay for themselves out of future profits, and thus are inherently better credit risks.

By making productive credit available on a truly democratic basis, society moves people toward economic self-sufficiency and independence. A broad dispersion of wealth and power serves as the ultimate check against abuse of power by the State or by the majority against minorities or individual citizens.

Practical Applications

In judging the efficacy of any plan of economic reconstruction, certain criteria are clear. First, it must be *practical*, avoiding the concentrations of wealth and power embodied in the capitalist and communist systems. Second, it must be *efficient*, providing the greatest benefit for the lowest cost. Finally, the plan must be *just* for all the people, not only the few at the top, to ensure that the efforts of the former Soviet people accrue to their benefit.

As the U.S. has one of the more successful economies in the world, the temptation is simply to copy the present American model. From the standpoint of democratizing economic power, this would be a mistake. As things stand now, most of the directly held corporate equity in the United States is concentrated in a few hands. Going from the mega-concentration of wealth and power under socialism to the super-concentration of wealth and power under capitalism would result in only a minor lessening of injustice.

The Homestead Act—An Historical Precedent

However, there are experiences in the history of the United States which account for its current relative success in the world. One historical analogy would provide an effective approach for broadening the base of capital ownership in order to avoid the evils of capitalism, and would place ownership and power directly into the hands of the people.

In the 1860's, Abraham Lincoln's Homestead Act turned thousands of people into owners of land, the single most valuable productive asset at the time, by giving them the opportunity to earn ownership of one hundred and sixty acres. The land itself wasn't given away. Each homesteader had to develop the land and work it for five years. He was then granted title.

Today's vast corporate wealth in the United States was largely created after the Homestead Act had turned many Americans into owners of productive property, and consisted of a kind of productive property not addressed by the Act. That most of the corporate wealth in the United States is appallingly concentrated in the hands of a few is due to the monopolistic tendencies of capitalism itself.

But a land-based Homestead Act is not the only method that can be used by the average worker to accumulate income-producing wealth. Since most of the newly-produced wealth in the world today is industrial, limiting everyone to ownership opportunities in the land would merely result in a growing population dividing up a static amount of wealth into ever smaller pieces, ensuring poverty for themselves and their descendants. There are, however, social technologies that can be used to democratize individual ownership of a type of wealth that has no limits save human creativity and ingenuity: the wealth created in the expanding industrial frontier.

A New Social Tool—The Employee Stock Ownership Plan

One modern financial technology to enable the acquisition of companies by their employees is known as the Employee Stock Ownership Plan (ESOP). The ESOP has been enacted into over twenty U.S. laws and being increasingly used in the U.S., the United Kingdom and a growing number of other countries.

The ESOP is a social technology which is totally different from collective ownership or the "Bolshevization of Capital," because it is based on the full restoration of private property in the means of production. The ESOP diffuses economic power by enabling workers who have no savings to purchase shares in the companies in which they are employed.

An initiative to study the ESOP and its related technologies could point the way for a restructuring the economy of the former Soviet Union. In promoting economic and social stability of the emerging republics, the Third Way would ultimately contribute to world peace.

As Marx observed, conflict between owners and workers is built into the capitalist system. But by turning workers into owners of the companies in which they labor, class conflict between labor and capital largely disappears. Professional managers are still needed to make day-to-day decisions, but are subject to a democratic accountability. Conflict is reduced because labor and capital now share a common interest.

With workers as owners, companies would be able to maximize their competitive edge. It would be to the advantage of the workers to keep costs down by keeping their own fixed wages at the lowest possible subsistence level, and then receive most of their money by dividing up—as owners—the greater profits that would result.

The role of the union would change under this scenario. Instead of continually confronting management and owners with higher wage and benefit demands, the union would work with owners and management while serving as a check on the power of capital concentrated in the hands of management. The union would protect the ownership rights of nonmanagement workers.

The Industrial Homestead Act—A Long-Range Plan

The former socialist countries of the world now have the same opportunity with their governmental accumulation of industrial wealth that the United States had with its vast holdings of land. The question is how best to take advantage of this historic, but quickly disappearing opportunity. The U.S. used the Homestead Act to attain widespread capital ownership. It is now up to the people of the Commonwealth of Independent States to choose what method they will use.

What is needed today is an "Industrial Homestead Act" for the transforming economies. This would give the former Soviet people access to the means to earn ownership of the current and future wealth of the nation, rather than having the ownership handed to them or sold out from under them. The Communist Party and the government of the former Soviet Union hold tremendous industrial resources which the citizens of the new Commonwealth of Independent States need to transform into a more just economy and political order.

Essentially, the question is how to make a free enterprise economy work while building a broader political constituency for free enterprise growth. How can we avoid the concentration of wealth in the hands of the few that inevitably accompanies capitalism, and the predictable and even more destructive backlash of socialism?

An Industrial Homestead Act[2] would approach the problem on both the macro- and micro-economic scale. Components of an Industrial Homestead strategy are interdependent, supporting the total program like the legs of a tripod:

- Simplifying the national tax system,
- Conforming national monetary policy to supply-side economic goals, and
- Linking tax and monetary reforms to the goal of expanded capital ownership.

Simplification of the National Tax System

The simplest income tax system for the modern industrial state is one where income from all sources, whether from labor or capital, is taxed at a single rate, while exempting incomes of the very poor. This would eliminate the unfairness of tax systems that exempt income derived in "special" ways or act punitively against income that exceeds a certain amount.

A simplified, flat-rate tax system would give a direct means for balancing the national budget and restraining overall government spending, including spending on social welfare programs. It would also eliminate the traditional double taxation of profits in ways that would maximize greater savings and investments in new plant and equipment, plus removing other features that discourage ownership. This would also force politicians to compete on who can provide the best government at the lowest cost.

Reforming National Monetary Policy to Conform to Supply-Side Economic Goals.

New policies would aim at immediate reduction in interest rates to an *unsubsidized* minimal level for industrial purposes. A two-tiered interest policy would allow substantially higher interest rates for nonproductive purposes. The national banking authority would be restrained from monetization of national deficits or encouraging other forms of nonproductive uses of credit, causing the demand-side credit to seek out already accumulated savings at market rates.

Any increase in the money supply would be linked to actual growth of the economy. This would be achieved by the central bank discounting at low charges (but subject to a 100% reserve requirement) eligible industrial, agricultural and commercial paper financed through the banking system. This would provide the public with an asset-backed currency reflected in more efficient instruments of production.

Linking Tax and Monetary Reforms to the Goal of Expanded Capital Ownership.

It is important to encourage all citizens to accumulate a direct private property ownership stake in the country's growing industrial frontier, and to ensure the broadest possible base of direct beneficiaries (and thus political supporters) of future free market reforms and policies.

This would create for every citizen an "Industrial Homestead Exemption" large enough to provide an income from dividends. This personal estate, or "Industrial Homestead," would be exempt from all taxes, and would be the modern equivalent of the quarter-section of land provided by the original Homestead Act. The Employee Share Ownership Plan (ESOP) and its variations such as the Consumer Share Ownership Plan (CSOP), the Individual Share Ownership Plan (ISOP) and the Community Investment Corporation (CIC), would serve as the basic capital credit vehicles for linking new monetary and tax incentives for productivity growth with the expanding base of owners under an Industrial Homestead Act. Each of these vehicles would help accelerate rates of growth of private sector enterprises by providing their new shareholders easy access to low-cost bank credit for buying growth shares repayable out of future growth profits.

The Goal of the Industrial Homestead Act

As productivity of technology increases, fewer workers are needed to produce the necessities and even the luxuries of life. In the future offered by both capitalism and socialism, the worker will change from being a slave dependent for his subsistence on a wage system to a slave dependent on the politicians and bureaucrats of a social welfare system.

The crucial element for avoiding this bleak future is *expanded capital ownership.* In transforming State-owned enterprises and farms into effective competitors in the global marketplace and in building the new enterprises of a successful growth economy, today's unemployed and underemployed can be absorbed into a more dynamic productive sector. Connecting the worker through ownership to an expanding pool of wealth created by more and more efficient technology will ensure that each citizen can participate directly in that wealth.

In its initial stages, a program of expanded capital ownership will primarily affect the workers—the people who will have to turn failing or unproductive companies and industries into successes. The ultimate goal of the Industrial Homestead Act, however, is for every citizen to have access to sufficient credit to become an owner of productive assets. Each citizen's "industrial homestead" would ensure that he could attain a living income without having to rely on wages from his labor alone. Such a system would greatly reduce society's burden of supporting the unemployed and permanently incapacitated. By producing a living income, ownership of productive assets could liberate human beings to enrich their lives materially, intellectually and spiritually.

A New Vision of the Future— The Transformation of Human Work

An Industrial Homestead Act represents one concrete proposal for moving toward the long-range vision of the Third Way. The Third Way itself embodies a moral philosophy and evolutionary process for transforming the institutional environment—legal, financial, cultural and moral systems—to improve the quality of life for everyone.

In striving to "make every worker an owner," the Third Way recognizes that by nature *every* person is a worker. Under the wage system framework, the concept of "work" has been stripped of much of its dignity, consigned only to that portion of human endeavor dealing with "making a living." In its larger context, however, work involves physical, mental and spiritual forms of human activity, from manual labor to meditation.

Within the paradigm of the Third Way, the highest form of work is not economic labor, but unpaid "leisure work"—the work of building a civilization which no machine can perform. Throughout history, creative work has mainly been engaged in by individuals with independent incomes, those who were supported by a patron or by someone else's labor. The Third Way provides a means whereby more people can engage in "leisure work" and be supported by an independent capital income produced by their own "technology slaves."

Pursuing Economic Justice, Not Utopia

Mankind will probably never achieve the "perfect" economic system where all drudgery is eliminated and people are free to do the work they prefer, the work of building a better civilization, creative work which no machine can perform. However, before the opportunity passes, it becomes imperative for all economies of the world to implement effective programs of expanded ownership of productive assets. The alternative is a pendulum swing between capitalism and socialism, where any period of stability merely serves as preparation for the next violent overthrow.

Many aspects of the Third Way will be determined by tax and banking laws that affect the process of democratizing productive credit. How this democratization is brought about—the timing, priorities and procedures—are social issues best discussed in an open and democratic fashion by people aspiring to build a free and just future for themselves.

For years the West has guarded against the importation of the communist revolution. In this rare moment in history, America has a chance to rediscover and export our own revolution of ideas, born out of the vision of our Founding Fathers. As they search for a better life, the citizens of the new Commonwealth of Independent Republics need something better than the outmoded and dehumanizing systems of socialism and capitalism. America can offer them a true third way forward.

Notes:

[1]The moral framework of the Third Way is discussed in greater detail in Chapter V of Louis Kelso and Mortimer Adler's profound book with the misleading title, *The Capitalist Manifesto* (New York: Random House, 1958). A further refinement of the specific principles can be found in *Toward Economic and Social Justice* (Center for Economic and Social Justice, P.O. Box 40849, Washington, D.C. 20016).

[2]For details, see pages 123-147 of *Every Worker an Owner* (published by the Center for Economic and Social Justice) and "Beyond ESOP: Steps Toward Tax Justice," *The Tax Executive*, April/July 1977 (published by Tax Executive Institute, Inc., 1001 Pennsylvania Avenue, NW, Washington, D.C. 20004) and included in this volume.

Epilogue

Where do we go from here? In this book, the problem of widespread poverty has been redefined within the context of the maldistribution of ownership opportunities. Basic principles for determining a cure have been set forth. Tools have been developed, and the soundness of the entire approach has been both clinically examined and tested under actual field conditions in essentially hostile political and economic environments.

Fortunately, a single monolithic World Economic Health Organization does not exist that would attempt to control the spread of poverty through universal application of failed methods. Agencies such as the United Nations, World Bank, International Monetary Fund or the United States Agency for International Development have agenda of their own which can conflict with the teachings, goals and aims of the Catholic Church, other religions, or, indeed, anyone committed to universal principles of morality. Additionally, programs by these and other agencies have generally been abortive and ineffectual, or tend toward maintenance of the status quo and current concentrations of power. Even if people were willing to surrender their sovereignty for the guarantee of sufficient food, fiber and fuel, only failure could result under any proposed solutions based on the usual models. This is particularly true of those programs billed as "New Age" or a "New World Order," which, in most cases, are only socialism and capitalism in new guises, and with new catch-phrases. The only change would be increased concentrations of power.

The economies of many countries of the world are terminally ill and need drastic and effective medicine. They are unlikely to achieve anything other than a short term placebo effect if accepted cures are relied upon, based, as they are, on unsound principles and unworkable premises. This has been demonstrated time and again. Something new is needed. This book provides that something new.

While addressed primarily to a Catholic audience, the message in this book is truly universal, applying to believers of all faiths as well as nonbelievers. In accordance with Pius XI's instructions on social justice, it is essential that people work together to reorganize the social order for their common good. How can concerned individuals and organizations begin to act?

(1) **Read.** A good place to start is with an investigation of writings on the subject, many of which are listed in the selected bibliography that closes this book. In addition, there a number of organizations which disseminate information on expanded ownership concepts and applications.

(2) **Critique.** The sharper the understanding, the more effective the action. As people begin to discuss and distinguish the underlying logic and morality of expanded capital ownership from the traditional economic systems, they will be better equipped to act in a consistent and purposeful way.

(3) **Organize.** Work with others to restructure defective institutions according to the principles of economic and social justice. As Pius XI reminded us, an individual acting alone cannot correct an unjust institution. Some of the specific methodologies discussed in this book may offer solutions to previously unsolvable problems.

Can widespread world poverty be cured? Yes. Will the cure be effected? If this book is taken merely as another proposal of vested academic or governmental interests and ignored, no, there will be no cure. If the initiatives in this book are put into practice by companies and governments unshackled from traditional and unworkable solutions, then yes, there is every hope that the devastating disease of widespread poverty will indeed disappear.

Additional Sources of Information

For further information concerning free enterprise approaches to worker ownership and other forms of expanded capital ownership, the reader may want to make contact with the following organizations.

Center for Economic and Social Justice (CESJ)
P. O. Box 40849
Washington, DC 20016
Telephone: (703) 243-5155
Fax: (703) 243-5935

The ESOP Association
1726 M Street, NW
Suite 501
Washington, DC 20036
Telephone: (202) 293-2971
Fax: (202) 293-7568

National Center for Employee Ownership (NCEO)
426 17th Street
Suite 650
Oakland, California 94612
Telephone: (510) 272-9461
Fax: (510) 272-9510

Foundation for Enterprise Development (FED)
8301 Greensboro Drive
Suite 1201
McLean, Virginia 22102
Telephone: (703) 749-9080
Fax: (703) 749-9082

UNIAPAC (International Christian Union of Business Executives)
Place des Barricades, 2
B - 1000 Brussels (Belgium)
Telephone: 32-2-219.31.14
Fax: 32-2-219.70.37

Author Profiles

Robert H. A. Ashford ("The Binary Economics of Louis Kelso") Robert H. A. Ashford is Professor of Law at Syracuse University College of Law, where he teaches Corporations, Securities Regulation, Business Planning, Professional Responsibility and Binary Economics. After graduating with honors from Harvard Law School in 1969, he practiced law for six years in San Francisco, specializing in tax, securities regulation and ESOP financing. Before beginning teaching in 1978, he served as General Counsel and then Chief Operating Officer for Kelso & Company. He has authored or co-authored articles related on various subjects including securities regulation, implied liability, evidence, workers compensation, public utilities regulation, and binary economics. He is author of "The Securities Regulation of Banks" (Volume 5, of *Banking Law*, published by Matthew Bender).

Dawn K. Brohawn ("Value-Based Management;" "Beyond Privatization: An Egyptian Model for Democratizing Capital Credit for Workers"—co-author) Dawn Kurland Brohawn is a board member and corporate officer of Equity Expansion International, Inc., an ESOP investment banking and consulting firm. As Director of Communications, she designs and facilitates Value-Based Management systems and ownership education and communications programs for ESOP clients. She was the editor of *Every Worker an Owner*, a compilation of writings on the philosophical and strategic aspects of the ESOP, which served as the orientation book for the Presidential Task Force on Project Economic Justice, spearheaded by the Center for Economic and Social Justice. Since 1989 Ms. Brohawn has served on the Employee Communications and Participation Committee of the ESOP Association, a national trade association of ESOP companies and professionals. She is also volunteer Director of Communications for the Center for Economic and Social Justice (CESJ), and serves on the Board of Directors and Executive Committee.

Kathy V. Friedman ("Capital Credit: The Ultimate Right of Citizenship") Kathy Vallone Friedman, a Political Sociologist, received her B.A. from Cornell University, and her M.A. and Ph.D. from the University of North Carolina at Chapel Hill. She authored *Legitimation of Social Rights and the Western Welfare State: A Weberian Perspective* (1981) published by the University of North Carolina Press. She is currently working on a volume that treats economic rights in capital credit as a potential fourth right of citizenship. Her career highlights include a teaching position on the Sociology faculty at Tulane University (New Orleans), several years of legislative work on Capitol Hill, and, at present, a position at the Center for Economic Studies at the U.S. Census Bureau. Her interest in the work conducted at the Center for Economic and Social Justice stems from her continuing concern with the social institutions of society that connect the citizen to the sovereign. All groups entail authority structures, and the nature of the connections between the rulers and the ruled—and the quality of life resulting therefrom—absorbs the attention of the Political Sociologist in general, and Dr. Friedman in particular.

Michael D. Greaney ("Charity or Justice: Where is the Hope of the Poor?;" "The Third Way: America's True Legacy to the New Republics"—coauthor) A CPA who works in ESOP administration, Mr. Greaney has written numerous articles on economic and social justice, and is the author of the *ESOP Administration and Accounting Manual* for the Alexandria Tire Company, the first ESOP in a developing country. Mr. Greaney received his BBA in Accounting from the University of Notre Dame in 1977 and his MBA from the University of Evansville in 1979. Currently in private practice and an associate with the ESOP investment banking and consulting firm of Equity Expansion International, Inc., he has audited worldwide with the American Red Cross, Georgetown University Medical Center, and the United States Federal Election Commission.

Peter S. Grosscup ("How to Save the Corporation") Peter Stenger Grosscup is known to historians of the labor movement as the judge who issued the injunction against Eugene Debs during the Chicago Railway Strike of 1894, making a call for federal troops when the injunction was ignored. Judge Grosscup's apparent sympathy with big business was further evidenced when his court unanimously reversed Judge K. M. Landis's decision in the Standard Oil of Indiana case which fined Standard Oil $29,240,000 for accepting rebates. Yet as federal judge he also enjoined the Beef Trust from combinations or conspiracies in restraint of trade. He refused offers by the railroads—effectively bribes—to become their attorney at several times his judicial salary. Clearly Judge Grosscup was not for either labor or business, but for justice. Peter S. Grosscup was born February 15, 1852, in Ashland, Ohio. He attended Wittenberg College and Boston Law School. He first practised in Ashland, and then moved to Chicago in 1883. He was appointed United States District Judge of the northern district of Illinois in 1892, and Judge of the United States Circuit Court of Appeals in 1899, becoming presiding judge in 1905. He resigned from the bench in 1911. Peter Grosscup died at sea on October 1, 1921.

Matthew Habiger ("Papal Tradition on Distribution of Ownership") Fr. Matthew Habiger, O.S.B., is a Benedictine monk at St. Benedict's Abbey in Atchison, Kansas. He was ordained to the priesthood on June 14, 1968. He earned a doctorate in moral theology at the Catholic University of America in 1986, working under Dr. William E. May. The topic of his dissertation was *Papal Teaching on Private Property 1891-1981*. He has been an associate pastor, pastor (1968-72), Newman chaplain at the University of Kansas (1972-76), professor and chaplain at Benedictine College (1977-80, 1986-90), and teaches moral theology at Benedictine College. Following a November 29, 1990, guest appearance on the Eternal Word Television Network show "Mother Angelica Live!," to discuss Catholic Social Teaching, Mother Angelica asked him to develop a series on Catholic Social Teaching for EWTN. He has taught courses in Chicago to Catholic laity, under the auspices of the Institute for Religious Life. Other courses taught included: Christolology, Moral Theology, Catholic Apologetics, *Christifidelis Laici*, and Population Myths and Planned Parenthood. He belongs to the Fellowship of Catholic Scholars, and delivered a paper, "The Retrieval of the Sacred in the Socio-Economic Order" at the 12th annual convention of the Fellowship in 1988 at Atlanta. Since January 1, 1991, he has been working as a pro-life missionary with Fr. Paul Marx, O.S.B., and Human Life International.

Stephen F. Hardiman ("Value-Based Management"—contributing) Stephen F. Hardiman, a member of the Value-Based Management project team of Equity Expansion International, is an Information Technology Consultant with CSX Corporation, specializing in strategic information systems. He is completing his Master's degree at Johns Hopkins University, in strategic marketing and information technology management.

Louis O. Kelso ("Uprooting World Poverty: A Job for Business"— coauthor) Louis O. Kelso originated the species of capital acquisition financing techniques of which the Employee Stock Ownership Plan (ESOP) is the best known. In 1958 his theory of free-market, private-property economics was published in *The Capitalist Manifesto*, coauthored with philosopher Mortimer J. Adler. In 1967 he and Patricia Hetter Kelso published *Two-Factor Theory: The Economics of Reality*. From 1970 the Kelsos devoted virtually all of their time and efforts to establishing Kelso & Company as an investment banking firm specializing in ESOP financing. Later they concentrated on advancing the adoption of the seven other capital financing methods, changing the national economic policy, and introducing two-factor economic policies and investment banking methods into other developed and developing economies. Kelso held the degrees of B.S. in finance, *cum laude*, and J.D. from the University of Colorado, where he was editor-in-chief of *The Rocky Mountain Law Review* and later taught constitutional law and municipal finance as an associate professor. A corporate and financial lawyer, he headed his own law firm in San Francisco from

1958 to 1975. In 1963 he was awarded the degree of honorary Doctor of Science in economics from Araneta University, Manila, The Philippines. Mr. Kelso died in 1991.

Patricia Hetter Kelso ("Uprooting World Poverty: A Job for Business"—coauthor) Patricia Hetter Kelso is a vice president of Kelso & Company and also vice president of the Institute for the Study of Economic Systems. For many years she worked in Stockholm as an international marketing specialist. She has co-authored with Louis Kelso *Two-Factor Theory: The Economics of Reality* and *Democracy and Economic Power: Extending the ESOP Revolution* as well as many articles, monographs, occasional papers, and congressional submissions. She holds a B.A. degree in government and philosophy from the University of Texas at Austin.

Norman G. Kurland ("Economic Justice in the Age of the Robot;" "Beyond ESOP: Steps Towards Tax Justice;" "The Abraham Federation: A New Framework for Peace in the Middle East;" "The Third Way: America's True Legacy to the New Republics"—coauthor; "Beyond Privatization: An Egyptian Model for Democratizing Capital Credit for Workers"—coauthor) Norman G. Kurland, a lawyer-economist with a Doctor of Laws degree from the University of Chicago, is President and Managing Director of Equity Expansion International, Inc. (EEI). Mr. Kurland was appointed by President Reagan and served as Deputy Chairman of the Presidential Task Force on Project Economic Justice. This group recommended ways to encourage privatization by expanding capital ownership among workers in Central America and the Caribbean. He serves as volunteer President of the Center for Economic and Social Justice (CESJ), an ecumenical nonprofit think tank headquartered in Arlington, Virginia. Closely associated from 1965 to 1976 with Louis Kelso, the ESOP's inventor, Kurland over 28 years authored and orchestrated several major U.S. ESOP legislative initiatives, including the Project Economic Justice task force. In 1975, while working for Kelso & Company, he was project manager in creating the world's first 100% leveraged buyout by 500 workers at South Bend Lathe, which served as the prototype for such ESOPs as Weirton Steel and AVIS. As USAID's senior ESOP consultant, Mr. Kurland headed the team which implemented the landmark ESOP at the $160 million Alexandria Tire Company in Egypt. At the request of the Minister of Planning in Costa Rica, he served as senior consultant to the team which designed a "parallel legal system" for facilitating widescale use of ESOPs. In 1992 he served on a team funded by the Inter-American Development Bank at the request of the Mexican Ministry of Finance, to develop Plan APOYE, a legislative project to reform Mexican laws to encourage ESOPs.

Lorenzo Servitje Sendra ("Reevaluating Private Enterprise") Lorenzo Servitje Sendra, respected throughout the world as one of Mexico's leading business statesmen, was born in Mexico on November 20, 1918. He studied accountancy and administration. He is currently the Chairman of the Grupo Industrial BIMBO, S.A. de C.V., a 45,000 employee enterprise. After having served as the Vice-Chairman of the Center for Social Studies of the Coordinating Council of Mexican Entrepreneurs from 1982 to 1985, he is currently its Chairman. From 1965 to 1973 Señor Servitje was the Chairman of Unión Social de Empresarios Mexicanos, the Mexican association of Uniapac, the International Christian Union of Business Executives. He is also a founding member of the Mexican Foundation for Rural Development, and was its Chairman from 1969 to 1973. In addition, he was the Chairman of the National Advertising Council from 1986 to 1987. After having sat for a number of years on the Executive Committee of Uniapac International, he was Second Vice-President from 1985 to 1987, and assumed the office of First Vice-President from 1987 to 1989. He is a Professor at IPADE and the author of a number of books, including *Contemporary Society and the Entrepreneur* and *Thoughts and Comments of a Business Leader*.

Thomas J. Simon ("Value-Based Management"—contributing) Thomas J. Simon, a member of Equity Expansion International's Value-Based Management project team, has spent over twenty years in financial and administrative management in both the public and private sector. As a senior administrator in the U. S. Office of Personnel Management, he was a principal designer of FED-COOP, the U. S. Government's strategy to use the ESOP to transfer government activities to the private sector. From 1988 to 1989, he served under appointment from President Reagan as Chairman of the U. S. Railroad Retirement Board.

Jack Stack ("The Great Game of Business") John P. (Jack) Stack is the president and CEO of the Springfield Remanufacturing Corporation (SRC), a rebuilder of engines and engine components. Born in 1948, he grew up in Elmhurst, Illinois, a suburb of Chicago. His father worked as a welding manager at the International Harvester plant in Melrose Park, Illinois, where Stack himself got a job as a mailboy at the age of twenty. During the next ten years, he held ten different posts at the plant, rising to superintendent of engine assembly. In 1979 he was appointed plant manager of Harvester's remanufacturing facility in Springfield, Missouri. Four years later, he joined with twelve other managers and supervisors to buy the factory from Harvester, which was selling off assets in an attempt to stave off bankruptcy. Despite an enormous debt load, the new company prospered. Mr. Stack is the author of *The Great Game of Business: The Only Sensible Way to Run a Business*.

Selected Bibliography

Adler, Mortimer J. and Gorman, William. *The American Testament.* New York: Praeger Press, 1975.

Bailey, Norman A. "The American Economy: Power and Paradox," *The Yale Review.* New Haven: Yale University Press, 1966.

Bailey, Norman A. "Fed Should Share the Wealth," *The Journal of Commerce*, May 15, 1989.

Belloc, Hilaire. *The Crisis of Civilization, Being the Matter of a Course of Lectures Delivered at Fordham University, 1937.* Rockford, Illinois: TAN Books and Publishers, Inc., 1991.

Blasi, Joseph R. and Kruse, Douglas L. *The New Owners: The Mass Emergence of Employee Ownership in Public Companies and What It Means to American Business.* New York: Harper Business, 1991.

Blasi, Joseph R. *Employee Ownership: Revolution or Ripoff?* Cambridge, Massachusetts: Ballinger Publishing Company, 1988.

Brohawn, Dawn K., ed. *Every Worker an Owner: A Revolutionary Free Enterprise Challenge to Marxism.* Arlington, Virginia: Center for Economic and Social Justice, 1987.

Brohawn Dawn K., ed. *The Role of Property in Building Economic and Social Justice: Questions and Answers for Participants, CESJ Seminar, De La Salle Conference Center (Rome).* Arlington, Virginia: Center for Economic and Social Justice, 1991.

DePree, Max. *Leadership is an Art.* East Lansing: Michigan State University Press, 1987.

Ferree, William. *Introduction to Social Justice.* New York: Paulist Press, 1948.

Ferree, William. *The Act of Social Justice.* Washington D.C.: Catholic University, 1944.

Friedman, Kathy. *Legitimation of Social Rights and the Western Welfare State.* Chapel Hill: University of North Carolina Press, 1981.

Fuller, R. Buckminster. *Utopia or Oblivion: The Prospects for Humanity.* New York: Bantam Books, 1969.

Gorga, Carmine. *The Economic Process.* Gloucester, Massachusetts: The Somist Institute Press, 1978.

Greider, William. *Secrets of the Temple: How the Federal Reserve Runs the Country.* New York: Simon and Schuster, 1988.

Habiger, Matthew. *Papal Teaching on Private Property 1891-1981.* Lanham, Maryland: University Press of America, 1990.

Hanke, Steve H., ed. *The Political Economy of Privatization.* New York: The Academy of Political Science, 1986.

Joint Economic Committee, U.S. Congress, *Broadening the Ownership of New Capital: ESOPs and Other Alternatives*, Staff Study, June 17, 1976.

Joint Economic Committee, U.S. Congress, *Employee Stock Ownership*

Plans (ESOPs), Hearings (2 volumes), December 12, 1975.

Kelso, Louis O. and Adler, Mortimer J. *The Capitalist Manifesto*. New York: Random House, 1958. [Currently being reprinted by Greenwood Press, Inc., 10 Bay Street, Suite 110, Westport, CT 06880, Tel. (203) 226-3571.]

Kelso, Louis O. and Adler, Mortimer J. *The New Capitalists*. New York: Random House, 1961. [Currently being reprinted by Greenwood Press, Inc., 10 Bay Street, Suite 110, Westport, CT 06880, Tel. (203) 226-3571.]

Kelso, Louis O. and Hetter, Patricia. *Two-Factor Theory: The Economics of Reality*. New York: Random House, 1967.

Kelso, Louis O. and Kelso, Patricia Hetter. *Democracy and Economic Power: Extending the ESOP Revolution*. Cambridge: Ballinger, 1986. (Paperback) Lanham, Maryland: University Press of America, 1991.

Kuhn, Thomas S. *The Structure of Scientific Revolutions*. Second Edition, London, U.K.: The University of Chicago Press, 1970.

Kurland, Norman. *An Illustrated Guide for Statesmen: A Two-Pronged Strategy for Implementing ESOP Privatizations in a Developing or Transforming Economy*. Arlington, Virginia: Center for Economic and Social Justice, 1991.

Kurland, Norman. "Future of the Multinational Corporation: Who Will Own It?", Occasional Paper. Arlington, Virginia: Center for Economic and Social Justice, 1988.

Kurland, Norman. *The Community Investment Corporation (CIC): A Vehicle for Economic and Political Empowerment of Individual Citizens at the Community Level*. Arlington, Virginia: Center for Economic and Social Justice, 1992.

Kurland, Norman. "The Industrial Homestead Act: National Infrastructural Reforms to Make Every Citizen a Shareholder" Occasional Paper. Arlington, Virginia: Center for Economic and Social Justice, 1990.

Kurland, Norman. "Who Will Liberate the Worker, Karl Marx or Leo XIII," *Social Justice Review* (Saint Louis, Missouri), September/October 1991.

Levering, Robert; Moskowitz, Milton, and Katz, Michael. *The 100 Best Companies to Work for in America*. New York: Plume, 1984.

Meade, J.E. *Efficiency, Equality and the Ownership of Property*. London: Geo. Allen & Unwin Ltd., 1964.

Metzger, Burt L. *Increasing Productivity through Profit Sharing*. Evanston, Ill.: Profit Sharing Research Foundation, 1980.

Moulton, Harold G. *The Formation of Capital*. Washington, D.C.: The Brookings Institution, 1935.

New York Stock Exchange, Office of Economic Research. *People and Productivity: A Challenge to Corporate America*. November 1982.

Novak, Michael. *The Spirit of Democratic Capitalism*. Washington: American Enterprise Institute/Simon and Schuster, 1982.

Peters, Thomas J. and Austin, Nancy. *A Passion for Excellence*. New York: Random House, 1985.

Peters, Thomas J. and Waterman, Robert H. Jr. *In Search of Excellence.* New York: Harper & Row, 1982.

Presidential Task Force on Project Economic Justice, *High Road to Economic Justice: U.S. Encouragement of Employee Stock Ownership Plans in Central America and the Caribbean..* Arlington, Virginia: Center for Economic and Social Justice, 1986.

Quarrey, Michael; Blasi, Joseph; and Rosen, Corey. *Taking Stock: Employee Ownership at Work.* Cambridge, Massachusetts: Ballinger Publishing Company, 1986.

Ragland, Robert A. *Employee Stock Ownership Plans: An Assessment of the Contribution of ESOPs to Private Wealth, Business Productivity and Economic Growth.* Washington, D.C.: National Chamber Foundation, 1989.

Rockefeller III, John D. *The Second American Revolution: Some Personal Observations.* New York, Harper and Row, 1973.

Rosen, Corey; Klein, Katherine J. and Young, Karen. *Employee Ownership in America: The Equity Solution.* Lexington, Massachusetts: Lexington Books, 1985.

Sabre Foundation. *Expanded Ownership.* Fond du Lac, Wisconsin, 1972.

Schirra, William A. "The Moral Basis for Broadening Ownership of Productive Property: From a Catholic Perspective," Occasional Paper. Arlington, Virginia: Center for Economic and Social Justice, 1987.

Simmons, John and Mares, William. *Working Together.* New York: Knopf, 1983.

Sithole, Ndabaningi. *The Secret of American Success: Africa's Great Hope.* Washington, D.C.: Gazaland Publishers, 1988.

Smiley, Robert W. Jr. and Gilbert, Ronald J., eds. *Employee Stock Ownership Plans: Business Planning, Implementation, Law & Taxation.* Larchmont, New York: Maxwell Macmillan/Rosenfeld Launer, 1989.

Stack, Jack. *The Great Game of Business: The Only Sensible Way to Run a Business.* New York: Currency Books, 1992.

Weitzman, Martin L. *The Share Economy.* Cambridge, Massachusetts: Harvard University Press, 1984.

Papal Encyclicals:

Leo XIII, *Rerum Novarum* (On the Condition of Workers), 1891.

Pius XI, *Quadragesimo Anno* (On Restructuring the Social Order), 1931.

John XXIII, *Mater et Magistra* (On Christianity and Social Progress), 1961.

Paul VI, *Popularum Progressio* (On the Development of Peoples), 1967.

John Paul II, *Laborem Exercens* (On Human Work), 1981.

John Paul II, *Sollicitudo Rei Socialis* (On Social Concerns) 1987.

John Paul II, *Centesimus Annus* (The Hundredth Year), 1991.

John Paul II, *Veritatis Splendor* (The Splendor of Truth), 1993.

Index